001-92002
669

72950

DATE DUB			
GAYLORD M-2			PRINTED IN U.S.A.

STUDIES IN MEDIEVAL AND RENAISSANCE HISTORY

Volume VII

STUDIES IN
Medieval and Renaissance
History

Volume VII

Edited by
WILLIAM M. BOWSKY
University of California, Davis

UNIVERSITY OF NEBRASKA PRESS · LINCOLN
1970

Copyright © 1970 by the University of Nebraska Press

International Standard Book Number 0–8032–0657–7
Library of Congress Catalog Card Number 63–22098

Manufactured in the United States of America

CONTENTS

INTRODUCTION

Studies in Medieval and Renaissance History is a series of annual volumes designed for original major articles and short monographs in all fields of medieval and renaissance history.

The first impetus for the creation of this series came from a belief that there is a need for a scholarly publication to accommodate the longer study whose compass is too large for it to be included regularly in existing media but too small for it to appear in book form. The editors will consider articles in all areas of history from approximately the fourth through the sixteenth centuries—economic, social and demographic, political, intellectual and cultural, and studies that do not fit neatly into a single traditional category of historical investigation.

The editorial board hopes that the *Studies* creates another link between the work of medieval and renaissance scholarship; for many articles pertinent to both disciplines appear in publications consulted almost exclusively by either medieval or renaissance scholars.

While this series is devoted primarily to the publication of major studies it contains occasional bibliographic essays and briefer articles dealing with unpublished archival or manuscript resources. The *Studies* also makes available in translation original articles by scholars who do not write in English.

Studies in Medieval and Renaissance History is not the official organ of any association or institution. Publication in the series is open to all historians whose research falls within its scope and fields of interest.

TWO FIFTH-CENTURY
CONCEPTIONS
OF PAPAL PRIMACY

Arthur Stephen McGrade

University of Connecticut

ACKNOWLEDGMENTS

The author is indebted to Professor Walter Ullmann, whose generous encouragement and advice have made this study possible. Research for the study was carried out while the author held a Cross-Disciplinary Fellowship from the Society for Religion in Higher Education, whose support is gratefully acknowledged.

TWO FIFTH-CENTURY CONCEPTIONS
OF PAPAL PRIMACY

The importance of Leo the Great for the idea of papal primacy has recently been emphasized by Walter Ullmann, in whose judgment Leo's conception of his office was to prove nothing less than the permanent *Rechtsidee* of Christianity.[1] The present study offers further evidence that the end of the classical world—the period of Leo and his successors, Simplicius, Felix III, and Gelasius I—was indeed a crucial time for the idea of papal primacy. I shall argue, however, that two different views of religious authority are at work in the papal writings of this period: an inclusive or ecumenical view, found in Leo, most clearly in the early years of his pontificate; and an exclusive or papalist view, attributable chiefly to Gelasius. Although each can be understood as a form of Petrinology,[2] the two positions differ markedly in their attitudes toward other ecclesiastical authority and toward secular power. After indicating these differences, I shall try to account for the shift from one position to the other.

The papal writings of this period present difficulties to historians interested in systematic thought about religious and political authority. Although the popes clearly intended many of their statements to have universal import, they themselves did not aim at precise, systematic formulations. Accordingly, although it seems appropriate to seek fundamental ideas and principles in this literature, no uniquely authentic basis for interpretation immediately presents itself. Some aspects of this problem are discussed in the first part of the essay. The second section, presenting the sources and my conclusions from them, can be read separately, but the essay as a whole is intended as an approach to a single subject.

1. W. Ullmann, "Leo I and the Theme of Papal Primacy," *Journal of Theological Studies*, N.S., XI (1960), 25–51. For other estimates of Leo, see below, notes 3, 4, and 6.
2. "Leo I's juristic theology contained what for want of a better name may be called Petrinology, the essence of which is the Christ-determined idea of right and law, applicable to the government of the whole Christian *corpus*: within the precincts and the scope of the Christian framework this idea presents itself as the permanent *Rechtsidee*." W. Ullmann, "Leo I and the Theme of Papal Primacy," p. 51. And see below, note 7 and pp. 21–23.

I

An older Protestant view of the religious history of the fifth century is that there was none,[3] yet from the standpoint of other historians, Catholic by profession or sympathy, doctrinal and institutional developments here are of capital importance.[4] To some historians, fifth-century Christianity has seemed radically unintelligible,[5] while others find in it a clear presentation

3. At least not in the centers of civilization. Thus, John Foxe's *Acts and Monuments*, 1st ed. (London, 1562–63); 4th ed. (London, 1877), after an account of the persecutions of the primitive church, gives an exciting religious and political history of Anglo-Saxon England, but says little about the popes, emperors, and doctrinal controversies of the Graeco-Roman world. Only in succeeding centuries does the papacy become an interesting, sinister subject for Foxe.

Some later historians have also had difficulty in making religious sense of the fifth-century papacy. According to A. C. Flick, in *The Rise of the Medieval Church* (New York, 1909), p. 154, other churches did to an extent bestow their affection, confidence, and obedience upon the Church of Rome in the early centuries "as a reward of her fight for the simple gospel-truth." Flick apparently saw Leo's considerable importance in the rise of papal power as due to extraordinary personal ability (*ibid.*, pp. 180–185) and considered that after him "no important Pope filled the Chair of St. Peter until the time of Gregory I." *Ibid.*, p. 185. J. Haller, in *Das Papsttum*, Vol. I: *Die Grundlagen* (Stuttgart and Berlin, 1934), p. 143, saw Leo as "der erste Fall in der Geschichte der römischen Kirche" and devotes some attention to his immediate successors as well. Nevertheless, Haller, convinced (*ibid.*, p. 4) of the inauthenticity of the central gospel text on which papal claims to primacy have always been founded, fails to find here a religiously compelling subject.

4. L. Duchesne, *Early History of the Christian Church*, Vol. III: *The Fifth Century*, trans. C. Jenkins (London, 1924). *Idem, L'Église au VIe Siècle* (Paris, 1925). H. Grisar, *History of Rome and the Popes in the Middle Ages*, trans. L. Cappadelta, Vol. II (London, 1912). P. de Labriolle, G. Bardy, L. Brehier, and G. de Plinval, *Histoire de L'Église*, ed. A. Fliche and V. Martin, Vol. IV: *De la mort de Théodose à l'élection de Gregoire le Grand* (Paris, 1937). T. Jalland, *St. Leo the Great* (London, 1941). *Idem, The Church and the Papacy* (London, 1944). J. Gaudemet, *L'Église dans l'Empire Romain, IVe–Ve Siècles, Histoire du Droit et des Institutions de l'Église en Occident*, Vol. III (Paris, 1958). P. Stockmeier, *Leo I. des Grossen Beurteilung der kaiserlichen Religionspolitik* (Munich, 1959).

5. E. Gibbon, *The Decline and Fall of the Roman Empire*, 2 vols. (London, 1936), an excellent example of what could be called the bedlam view of ecclesiastical history. Introducing his "Theological History of the Doctrine of the Incarnation," Gibbon remarks (*ibid.*, II, 459): "After the extinction of paganism, the Christians in peace and piety might have enjoyed their solitary triumph. But the principle of discord was alive in their bosom, and they were more solicitous to explore the nature, than to practise the laws, of their founder . . . [The] disputes of the TRINITY were succeeded by those of the INCARNATION, alike scandalous to the church, alike pernicious to the state, still more minute in their origin, still more durable in their effects."

A naturalism more refined than Gibbon's is found in W. H. McNeill's *The Rise of the West—A History of the Human Community* (Chicago, 1963). McNeill's specific aim, and his motto (title page), is "to understand, and if I can / to justify the ways of man to man." In

of the main ideological theme of medieval history—the development of papal government.[6] The differences among these accounts are determined not so much by variation in the source materials available to their authors as by variation in point of view or principles of interpretation.

To be sure, a historian is not entitled to *have* a point of view if that means making assumptions about historical fact which no change in the sources could alter. It does not follow, however, that historians should approach their sources with empty minds. For example, Ullmann's work on the medieval papacy depends on a key idea, that of treating the papacy precisely as a juristic subject. The resulting interpretation, which has applications in medieval secular as well as ecclesiastical government,[7] is

pursuing this aim, he finds that religion is sometimes important in human affairs, but it seems to have no inherently positive significance. He notes (pp. 390–391) that "the rise of religion to a central place in personal and public affairs gave a radically new character to the high cultural traditions of both Rome and Persia," and suggests (p. 412) that "unusual instability, arising out of violent oscillation from one extreme [in this case, the naturalism and rationalism of Hellenism] to the other [the transcendentalism and mysticism of the fifth and sixth centuries], may in fact be the most distinctive and fateful characteristic of the European style of civilization." McNeill shows more sympathy than Gibbon for the theological dimension of human activity, when (p. 406) he depicts the fourth- and fifth-century disputes among Christians as having many dimensions, which, however, "should not obscure the basic and authentic theological anxiety which lay behind the urge to compel all heretics to cease and desist from spreading false doctrine, lest God himself should take the matter in hand and revenge himself both upon the false prophets and upon those who allowed them to preach."

6. In addition to the article cited in n. 1, see W. Ullmann, *The Growth of Papal Government in the Middle Ages*, 2nd ed. (London, 1962); *idem*, "The Papacy as an Institution of Government in the Middle Ages," in *Studies in Church History*, II (1965), 78–101; and *idem*, *Principles of Government and Politics in the Middle Ages*, 2nd ed. (London, 1966). Also see E. Caspar, *Geschichte des Papsttums*, 2 vols. (Tübingen, 1930 and 1933). The approach is clear from the beginning (I, vii): "Eine Geschichte des Papsttums soll und will mehr sein als Geschichte der einzelnen Päpste, nämlich Geschichte einer Idee." Leo and Gelasius are given credit for expounding important aspects of the one papal idea.

7. In Ullmann, *Principles of Government and Politics in the Middle Ages*, papal government is presented as the most logical and historically most effective application of the "descending thesis" of law and government, in accordance with which governmental authority and law-creating competency are distributed "downwards," ultimately from God himself (pp. 20–21). This conception was also central, however, in the development of ideologies of theocratic kingship (*ibid.*, pp. 117–211). For the transformation of Germanic kingship by the Christian descending theme, see E. Ewig, "Zum christlichen Königsgedanken im Frühmittelalter," in *Das Königtum: seine geistigen und rechtlichen Grundlagen*, ed. T. H. Mayer (Darmstadt, 1965), pp. 7 ff. Also see, in the same volume, W. Schlesinger, "Über germanisches Heerkönigtum," pp. 105 ff.; O. Höfler, "Der Sakralcharakter des germanischen Königtums," pp. 75 ff.; and R. Buchner, "Das merowingische Königtum," pp. 143 ff.

certainly founded in the sources, but it depends equally on an awareness of the possibilities for juristically coherent schemes of government. In general, it may be suggested, the historian's view of the possibilities of his subject, or of human possibilities as a whole, is seldom or never uniquely determined by his sources; rather, the meaning to be ascribed to the sources will be determined in the light of those possibilities.[8] Depending upon our philosophical preference, we can think of the historian's scheme of possibilities either as a range of possible descriptions or interpretations which he is prepared to draw upon in giving an account of his subject, or as a vision of the potentialities inherent in the subject he has set out to describe. In either case, the problem is not to avoid having a view of the possibilities, but to find one which improves historical understanding rather than diminishing it.

Among the many questions that can be raised here, I should like to discuss two which seem especially relevant to ecclesiastical history. I want to ask, first, whether we should in general seek historical understanding by means of broad or narrow conceptions of human possibilities, and second, whether contemporary ideas of man should be deliberately employed in historical research.

On the first question, my proposal is that we should be deliberately generous, that the concept of man which should be preferred for historical purposes is one which maximizes the range and value of human possibilities rather than reducing them. In contrast with attempts to explain historical agents and events by identifying man with—to put it crudely— economic man, or political man, or a dogmatically determined idea of religious man, this proposal aims directly at discovering the richness and complexity of human experience.

It is this aim, indeed, which provides the most concrete justification for generosity. As William James argued in "The Will to Believe,"[9] we can get to know some things only by having faith in their existence in advance. James developed his argument with regard to faith in God and relations with our living acquaintances, but does it not also apply to history? To put the matter in a somewhat edifying way, is it not reasonable to suppose that we will get to know the heroes and saints of the past only if our own

8. For contrasts in interpretation due to different views of possibilities, compare Gibbon with, e.g. Grisar, *History of Rome and the Popes in the Middle Ages*. For the latter, there are possibilities of religious insight which are simply out of the question for Gibbon. A still richer scheme of interpretation is implicit in Duchesne's work, which shows an appreciation of a possible eastern point of view which is rare in western historians. See, for example, his *Early History of the Christian Church*, III, 312–315, 340–341, and 357–358.

9. W. James, *The Will to Believe, and Other Essays in Popular Philosophy* (London, 1897).

range of human responsiveness encompasses sanctity and heroism? In general, the greater the possibilities we are independently aware of, the greater is the historical understanding available to us.

It was suggested earlier that human possibilities could be thought of either as potentialities grounded in historical realities or as descriptions available to the historian. The James-like argument for generosity just given takes the first approach. Another argument can be based on the second.

The cognitive significance of any description a person actually offers is a direct function of the range of descriptions he could have given but in fact did not give. This is intuitively plausible if we compare what we learn from some simple statement like, "it's raining," made by a small child who has not learned to discriminate among rain, hail, snow, etc., with what we learn from the same remark made by a meteorologically sophisticated adult. In the same way, historical descriptions will have greater cognitive significance the greater the range of qualities available to the historian for purposes of description.[10] Assuming, then, that we wish our historical accounts to be as significant as possible, we should strive for command of the greatest possible range of terms and relations which might coherently be employed in the description of human beings, their relationships and their institutions. We should aim at having a generous conception of man.

It should be clear that in advocating a rich conception of human possibilities, I am not proposing whitewash as the medium of history. The availability of a description to a historian by no means entails that he must apply that description to any particular subject. Generosity in constructing the concept of man does not entail sentimentality in describing men. Indeed, with a more adequate conception of humanity we might be more rather than less strict in our judgment of historical human beings. For example, if we resist the temptation to think of politics as a symptom of economics, or religion as a device of politics, we may become more rather than less critical of historical personages whose religious action or political behavior *was* just a function of other sorts of circumstances. For all we can tell to the contrary on an a priori basis, reductive historical accounts may be damningly plausible for some or all historical subjects. The principle of generosity only prevents our dismissing *non*reductive accounts a priori.

The second broad issue I should like to discuss is the relevance of contemporary views of human possibilities to historical research. Should

10. For discussions of information theory, the source of this point, see C. E. Shannon and W. Weaver, *The Mathematical Theory of Communication* (Urbana, Ill., 1949), and E. C. Cherry, *On Human Communication* (New York, 1957).

we in general assume that our own way of looking at things provides an adequate conceptual structure for understanding the past, or should we work on the assumption that historical subjects must be understood in terms other than our own? I resurrect this question in order to defend the unpopular alternative. It is my contention that in dealing with the past we should start from where we are. We should approach the inhabitants of the past as contemporaries, in the sense that we should try to regard our own basic problems and values as making claims upon all men.

The principle of generosity provides some justification for such an approach. According to that principle, we should think of the past in terms of the broadest and richest conception of human possibilities available to us. But everyone thinks of his own problems and values in such terms. Hence, everyone should approach the past in the terms with which he deals with his own situation. If, in other words, we should be ready to discover that the inhabitants of the past were fully human, we must be ready to apply to them the same ideas of humanity that we would wish applied to ourselves.

A second argument can be based on a rough historical guess as to how the people of the past would *want* us to regard them. It is hard to think of a single historical period whose inhabitants would wish to be thought of solely in terms of their own beliefs and values, with no question at all being raised of whether those beliefs and values were correct. To the extent that this guess is accurate, historical positivism is self-stultifying, for if we start out to deal with the past in its own terms, we shall soon hear the past reply that it is interested in being understood in accordance with the best terms or the highest standards, whatever those may be. But we ought to be employing just such standards ourselves, and so again, the best ideas for trying to understand the past are those which it is reasonable for us to apply to the present.

Just as generosity does not mean flattery, so approaching the past in our own terms does not entail distortion by overlooking important historical differences. For looking at two subjects in the same terms does not at all mean that we must judge the subjects to be identical, or even similar, with respect to those terms. If, for example, I decide to look at automobiles in terms of their color, there is no necessity that I should judge all automobiles to be of the same color, or even that I should judge red and purple ones to be more similar in color than they really are.

The objection may be pushed a step or two further. It may be argued that, although using a set of terms will not lead us to overlook differences with respect to *those* terms, we may yet be led to ignore important differences with respect to *other* terms. Thus, a person who spends his energy classifying automobiles by color may tend to overlook differences in engine power or safety features, which are generally more important than color. But this last clause is crucial. Granted that emphasis on some terms will lead to a blurring of distinctions with respect to other terms, the question is, "Are the blurred distinctions important ones?" But this question only gets us back to where we started, for to ask whether a particular distinction is important for understanding a subject is equivalent to asking what terms we ought to employ in dealing with that subject, and *this* is the question which the arguments above were meant to answer.

A last form of the objection would be that looking at the past in our own terms may lead us to overlook *relevant* differences between historical subjects. For vast areas of "the past" may be monotonously similar to one another by our standards, although a great deal could be said about them if we were willing to use terms other than our own. Now, the objection continues, our terms may be better for us than the others, or better in some absolute sense, but the fact that they are less discriminating with regard to certain historical subjects—i.e., fail in relevance to those subjects—makes them worse for historical purposes than terms which *do* discriminate. In this form, the objection deserves a good deal of respect, but should be turned aside to a more appropriate target. It does not tell against the use of current ideas in dealing with the past, but the use of *narrow* current ideas. If the past is *worth* understanding in a discriminating way, and if current modes of thought do not facilitate such understanding, then there is something wrong with the current modes of thought. But that accusation needs to be argued out in the present. On the other hand, if there are *trivial* historical subjects which are not illuminated by current ways of thinking, the difficulty is with the past, not the present.

But if it is granted that we should start from a contemporary view of human possibilities, what is that view? It is precisely the fact that there is no single, universally accepted response to such a question which suggests how we should proceed. For the prevailing pluralism[11] suggests its own conception of human possibilities. It suggests, for example, that

11. The ecumenical movement in the church and the ideology of peaceful coexistence in the world may be cited as broad-scale examples. For constructive pluralism in contemporary philosophy, see the writings of R. P. McKeon, e.g., *Freedom and History* (New York, 1952), and P. Weiss, *Modes of Being* (Carbondale, Ill., 1958) and *idem*, *History: Written and Lived* (Carbondale, Ill., 1962).

the vigorous defense of one view of man and the universe need not be based on intolerance of the defenders of alternative views. Although there is the obvious danger that tolerance can degenerate into indifference or a random eclecticism, there are also today genuine possibilities of communication, possibilities for a constructive pluralism in which common truths and values can be recognized in distinctively different formulations and programs.

This aspect of contemporary values could be expected to have a two-fold effect upon our historical outlook. In general, instead of expecting the past to disclose itself as a play of mutually irrelevant blind forces or as the clear working out of a single, comprehensive idea, we should expect to find encounters between the holders of positions—religious, social, intellectual, and so on—which offer basically different but not *necessarily* incompatible viewpoints. Historical explanation would consist primarily of showing where, and how, cooperation and enmity have resulted from success or failure in achieving communication between persons and positions that in principle can communicate and coexist with one another. A more specific effect upon our outlook is that we may find ourselves especially alert for examples of such a pluralistic outlook *in* history. In ecclesiastical history, for example, we should not expect to find viewpoints exactly similar to those held today, but ecumenism is not a religious novelty, and it is not implausible to suppose that those aspects of the human situation which make it a necessity have been seen with clarity by some before us.

II

The chief conclusion of the preceding discussion was that historians should attempt to understand the past in relation to problems and values they are prepared to take seriously for themselves. It was further argued that today, although basically different views of human possibilities are accepted in different quarters, there is a significant readiness on all sides to take other positions seriously. Accordingly, this study tries deliberately to remain open to the values stressed by a variety of historical viewpoints. There is no thought of suggesting a synthesis of Protestant liberty of conscience, Catholic dogma, healthy secularism, and juristic effectiveness, but the general picture of the world which both underlies and emerges from the following survey is of a place in which such values can sometimes coexist—and a place in which we often fail to realize this possibility.

The present study is concerned with the religio-political ideas of the fifth-century papacy. I want to ask, most particularly, whether the transition from Leo I to Gelasius I on questions of authority within the church and in the political community was a process of natural development. Do we find in Gelasius only a normal working out of the consequences of essentially Leonine ideas on such matters as papal primacy and the religious position of emperors, or do we find that there are basic qualitative differences on such matters? If there are important differences between Leo and Gelasius, how did the shift from one to the other come about? These are the questions with which we shall be immediately concerned. The attempt to answer them will carry us some way into the broader issues sketched above.

Let us begin at the end. By noticing some characteristics which are at least more prominent in Gelasian thought than they are in the sermons and correspondence of Leo, we shall be able to form a picture of what can be called an exclusive or papalist conception of religious authority. With this Gelasian position in mind, we shall be better able to determine whether the ideas of his great predecessor should be understood primarily as the seeds of Gelasius's position or as forming a coherent alternative.

Forms of address in ordinary life are sometimes so casual as to lack any specific meaning. In papal letters, where nothing is casual, they may express the most important attitudes. The term *filius* is first applied by the papacy to a Roman emperor, in our period at least, by Simplicius, the pontiff next but one after Leo. On first occurrence[12] the word is hedged about with more reverential epithets in the phrase, "*gloriosissime ac clementissime fili imperator Auguste.*" Later, under Felix III, respect is still present, but the emperor's sonship is sometimes equally prominent.[13] Under Gelasius we can see clearly that this way of referring to an emperor is meant to imply, not affection for the emperor, but an opinion of his

12. Simplicius, *Epistola* 3, in A. Thiel, *Epistolae Romanorum Pontificum Genuinae* (Braunschweig, 1867), p. 180; hereafter cited as Thiel, *Epistolae*. For all of the papal writings used in this study, references will also be given to the most readily available collection, J. P. Migne (ed.), *Patrologia cursus completus. Series latina*, to be cited as *PL*, followed by volume and column numbers. In this case, the reference is to *PL*, LVIII, 38. In discussing Gelasius's application of the expression *filius ecclesiae* to an emperor, Caspar (*Geschichte des Papsttums*, II, 64) identifies it as an Ambrosian formula and gives a passage from *Epistola* 21, sec. 36 (*PL*, XVI, 1018): "Quid enim honorificentius quam ut imperator filius ecclesiae esse dicatur?"

13. "Domnum filium nostrum religiosum principem." E. Schwartz, "Publizistische Sammlungen zum Acacianischen Schisma," in *Abhandlungen der Bayerischen Akademie der Wissenschaften, Philosophisch-historische Abteilung*, N.S. X (1934), 72; *PL*, LVIII, 897. (This collection of documents will be cited hereafter as Schwartz, "Acacian. Schisma.") "Domni filii nostri Christianissimi principis." Schwartz, "Acacian. Schisma," p. 79; *PL*, LVIII, 975. "Domnus filius noster uenerabilis imperator." Schwartz, "Acacian.

subordination to ecclesiastical authority: *"filius est, non praesul ecclesiae."* [14] We shall consider later the import of Pope Leo's rather different way of designating the holders of imperial power. Suffice it to say now that the parent-child relation does not characteristically enter into it.

The attitude of superiority conveyed in the Gelasian *"filius non praesul"* is expressed more directly in other ways. The two most celebrated passages are those in which Gelasius asserts that the function of the emperors at Constantinople is to learn, not teach (*discere*, not *docere*) what is Christian and what is not, and that the pontifical *auctoritas* and royal *potestas* (on which together the world depends) are so related that the former is accountable for, hence, by implication, should have some control over, the actions of the latter. It is unnecessary to cite these passages at length. [15] There are, however, less well known themes in the

---

Schisma," p. 80; *PL*, LVIII, 976. "Domnum filium nostrum." Schwartz, "Acacian. Schisma," p. 80; *PL*, LVIII, 977. The sequence of these expressions, in one letter, is interesting. Even when affection is involved, the weight of paternal authority is by no means absent: "Haec, ego reuerentissime princeps, beati Petri qualiscumque uicarius non auctoritate uelut apostolicae potestatis extorqueo, sed tamquam sollicitus pater salutem prosperitatemque clementissimi filii manere cupiens diuturnam fidenter imploro." Schwartz, "Acacian. Schisma," p. 84; *PL*, LVIII, 970.

14. Schwartz, "Acacian. Schisma," p. 35; *PL*, LVIII, 950. Gelasius may also have been responsible for some of the expressions referred to in the previous note, for he was very active in the service of his predecessors. See H. Koch, "Gelasius im kirchenpolitischen Dienste seiner Vorgänger, der Päpste Simplicius, 468–483, und Felix III, 483–492," in *Sitzungsberichte der Bayerischen Akademie der Wissenschaften, Philosophisch-historische Abteilung,* No. 6 (1935).

15. For *discere-docere* see Schwartz, "Acacian. Schisma," p. 35; *PL*, LVIII, 950. The opposition to Caesaro-papism offered here is noteworthy considering that the Emperor Zeno's stand was by all accounts inspired by the patriarch of Constantinople, Acacius, and in view also of the long history of imperial initiatives in religious affairs. For Leo's pontificate, see below, pp. 29–32. As late as 477, an emperor is congratulated by a pope because "in omnibus doceas causam tibi cum deo esse communem." Simplicius to Zeno, in Thiel, *Epistolae,* p. 187; *PL*, LVIII, 45.

The authority and power of pontiffs and secular rulers are discussed in a letter of Gelasius to the Emperor Anastasius, in Schwartz, "Acacian. Schisma," p. 20; *PL*, LIX, 42. There is evidence of how seriously Gelasius took the idea that a strict account would be required of him by God. See the eulogy by Dionysius Exiguus, in Thiel, *Epistolae,* p. 287: "Honorem summae dignitatis gravissimum pondus existimans, parvamque negligentiam pontificis ingens animarum discrimen esse contestans...." J. Gaudemet argues (*L'Église dans l'Empire Romain,* pp. 414–415) that the contrast between *auctoritas pontificum* and *regalis potestas* in this letter is not of great importance. His discussion of the point gains force, however, from the assumption that Gelasius held basically the same position as Leo. For Leo see below, n. 74. For Gelasius also see *Tomus de Anathematis Vinculo,* in Schwartz, "Acacian. Schisma," pp. 7 ff.; *PL*, LIX, 102 ff. For a generally appreciative discussion of Gelasius as a defender of the primacy of the spiritual, see Jalland, *The Church and the Papacy,* pp. 319–329.

Gelasian assertion of the primacy of the spiritual which deserve fuller illustration.

One is the very forcefully presented argument that religious orthodoxy ought to be coercively enforced in the Roman Empire because (1) secular laws are coercively enforced, and (2) the will of God ought more to be obeyed than the will of man. In order to distinguish it from another argument for the same conclusion which we shall consider later, we may call this the higher values argument for religious coercion:

> Etenim, imperator auguste, si contra leges publicas aliquis... quippiam fortasse temptaret, nulla id pati ratione potuisses; ad diuinitatis puram sinceramque deuotionem ut tibi plebs subdi redigatur, conscientiae tuae non putas interesse? postremo si unius populi ciuitatis animus non putatur offendi, ne diuina, ut res postulat, corrigantur, quanto magis, ne diuina offendantur, catholici nominis uniuersi piam fidem nec laedere debemus omnino nec possumus?[16]

A still more penetrating expression of essentially the same argument is to be found in the *De Vitanda Communione Acacii*. The question of who is entitled to be bishop of Alexandria is under discussion, a matter on which the will of man might be thought to have some bearing. Even on such a matter, however, the Gelasian line is unhesitatingly in favor of the enforcement of orthodoxy from above. It should be noted that Gelasius does not here indulge in the assumption that the people really want what is good for them. He envisages clearly a conflict between what the people want and what the holders of imperial power are able to enforce upon them:

> Sed populus, inquit, Alexandrinus hoc magnis desideriis postulauit nec Petrum sibi patitur ulla ratione subduci. quid si peteret populus Alexandrinus idololatriam debere parari? quid enim interest utrum haereticus an profanus ecclesiae catholicae permittatur imponi? quid si alterius haeresis cuiuslibet hominem sibi praesulem poscat adhiberi? qui enim fecit hoc de aliqua haeresi, potest et de alia, si id delectat,

16. "For if anyone should attempt something against the public laws..., august emperor, you could by no means allow it; do you not think it is your concern that a populace subject to you should be brought back to pure and sound devotion to the divinity? Finally, if it is thought that there is no harm to the soul of the people of one city if divine matters are not corrected as they require to be, yet how true it is that, lest there be harm to divine things, we neither ought nor can wound the world's pious faith in the name of catholic." Gelasius to Anastasius, in Schwartz, "Acacian. Schisma," pp. 23–24; *PL*, LIX, 46.

expetere. si inter hominum mores aliquid perpetrari temptaretur contra leges publicas, nullatenus id bonus imperator annueret: contra deum poscentibus acquiescit? si praua cupientibus annuendum est, ubi est imperialis auctoritas? ubi moderatio? ubi legum gubernatio? si contra catholicam fidem et ecclesiasticam regulam petentibus concedendum est quod petatur, quomodo catholicus imperator ** ac per hoc ne fiat contra hominum uoluntatem, fiat contra deum? ne corripiantur uiliter inproba, immo letalia corripientes, ne corrigantur insana molientes, pereant in aeternum? nec boni imperatoris est nec catholici principis sibimet poscentibus inimica concedere, immo et ipsis de quibus agitur, et omni rei publicae et saluti eius et regno quae contra deum sunt, non cessisse salutare est.[17]

In the course of time, such passages must undoubtedly have provided inspiration for uses of coercive power which would at present be generally rejected as morally inappropriate and spiritually ineffective.[18] It would be a serious mistake, however, to depict Gelasius as a fanatic, indifferent to such values as peace, sincerity, and brotherly love. He is not indifferent to these values, but he is convinced that they can be present only as a consequence of religious orthodoxy and only in a setting of religious uni-

17. "But, he says, the people of Alexandria have asked for this with the greatest eagerness, nor will they by any means allow Peter [Mongus] to be removed. What if the people of Alexandria asked to be provided for the practice of idolatry? For what difference is there whether it is permitted to impose a heretic or a profane person on the catholic church? What if they should demand that a man of some other heresy be set over them? For those who have done this with one heresy can affect another if it pleases them. If there were an attempt to establish among men some practice which was against the public laws, a good emperor would surely not assent to it: does he accede to demands against God? Where is the imperial authority, if perversion is to be allowed for those who desire it? Where is moderation? Where is the rule of law? If those seeking things contrary to the catholic faith and to ecclesiastical rule are to be granted what they seek, how [will there be] a catholic emperor** and lest anything be done against the will of man, shall it be done against God instead? Lest wicked things be usefully [reading *utiliter* with the MS] taken in hand, [shall we have] people taking hold of things that are fatal? Lest those struggling for insane things be corrected, let them perish eternally? It is not for a good emperor or a catholic ruler to give in to those demanding things which are harmful to him. Indeed, both for those concerned and for the whole political order and its safety and control, not to have ceased from things which are against God is to show them respect." Schwartz, "Acacian. Schisma," p. 37; *PL*, LVIII, 952. At ** Thiel (*Epistolae*, p. 295) supplies *fuerit* or *dicatur*. Schwartz notes that many words have been lost.

18. For one example across many centuries, Duns Scotus blames the princes of his time, "quia magis ad commodum temporale quam ad honorem Dei et per hoc plus puniunt et reprimere volunt peccata in proximum quam in Deum." *Opus Oxoniense*, IV, d. 15, q. 3, quoted in G. de Lagarde, *La Naissance de l'Esprit Laïque au Déclin du Moyen Age*, Vol. II (Paris, 1958), p. 259 n.

formity. In the letter to Anastasius quoted earlier, he expresses this conviction with his usual vigor:

> Sed, precor te, cuiusmodi debeat esse pax ipsa [ecclesiarum], non utcumque, sed ueraciter Christiana mente libremus. quomodo enim potest esse pax uera, cui caritas intemerata defuerit? caritas autem qualiter esse debeat, nobis euidenter per apostolum praedicatur, qui ait: et caritas de corde puro et conscientia bona et fide non ficta. quomodo, quaeso te, de corde erit puro, si contagio inficiatur externo? quomodo de conscientia bona, si prauis fuerit malisque commixta? quemammmodum fide non ficta, si maneat sociata cum perfidis? quae cum a nobis saepe iam dicta sint, necesse est tamen incessabiliter iterari et tamdiu non taceri quamdiu nomen pacis obtenditur, ut nostrum non sit, ut inuidiose iactatur, facere pacem, sed talem uelle doceamus qualis et sola pax esse et praeter quam pax nulla esse monstratur.[19]

It would be misleading, therefore, to interpret Gelasius as intending to reject moral values which can plausibly be regarded as at least partially independent of religious values in their realization. It may be true that Gelasian policies will *in fact* tend to endanger such values, but the tragedy of the Gelasian position is not that it intentionally sacrifices moral values in order to realize other values, but that its policies are partly animated by a concern for precisely those values which their implementation may destroy.

19. "But, I beseech you, let us weigh what sort of peace there ought to be [in the churches], not in any way, but with a truly Christian mind. For how can there be true peace when undefiled charity is lacking? But how there should be charity is put clearly before us by the apostle, who says: and charity of a pure heart and good conscience and a sincere faith. How, I ask you, will it be from a pure heart if it is corrupted by contact with what is polluted? How from a good conscience if it is thrown together with the perverse and evil? In what way with a sincere faith if it remains in association with faithlessness? Although we have often said these things before, it is yet necessary to repeat them unceasingly and not to keep silent as long as the name of peace is alleged, so that, as men spitefully cry out, it is not for us to make peace, but let us teach men to wish for such as is the only peace and besides which there is shown to be no peace." Schwartz, "Acacian. Schisma," pp. 21–22; *PL*, LIX, 44. A similar line is taken, though with less moral detail, in the *De Vitanda Communione Acacii*, in Schwartz, "Acacian. Schisma," p. 42; *PL*, LVIII, 958: "Sed nunc, inquis, utilitatis interest rei publicae. sed sacerdos allegare debuit utilitatis interesse potius publicae ut diuina communio et fides integra seruaretur. utile est rei publicae religionis euersio et utilis non erit rei publicae religionis integritas? nescio si sunt eiusdem religionis qui ista praetendunt, aut si eiusdem religionis debeant homines ista praetendere."

A second relatively distinctive element in the papal correspondence of the late fifth century also deserves our attention, for it would seem to be the conscious or unconscious basis for much of the support given to the church by Christian rulers throughout the middle ages. It may be described as the theme of religious propitiation in politics, or propitiationism. Like the higher values argument for coercion, propitiationism is at least more prominent in Leo's successors than in Leo himself. So far as I have been able to determine, the following passage from a letter of Simplicius to the Emperor Zeno is the first strongly marked occurrence of this theme in the papal literature. Very roughly, the argument is that (1) God has given the empire to the emperor; (2) in return, God expects the emperor to do everything in his power to ensure that proper religious worship is offered to Him in propitiation; (3) if this propitiation is not forthcoming, God will take the empire away from the emperor. Perhaps significantly, this letter was written in the year which saw the deposition of Romulus Augustulus, the last Roman emperor in the West:

> Respicite, quaeso, ad diuina beneficia, et quae sint uobis collata perpendite, atque ut haec prospera ualeant permanere, propitiandum esse censete auctorem muneris, non laedendum. inter quaslibet enim occupationes publicas a religioso principe magnopere procurandum est, quod eius protegit principatum, et praeferenda cunctis rebus est coelestis obseruantiae rectitudo, sine qua recte nulla consistunt.[20]

The importance of this passage does not lie in its basic ideas, which are well precedented, but in the decisively practical turn it gives these ideas. For example, there is nothing novel in the idea that the earthly prosperity of the human race is dependent upon God, or even in the idea that God rewards human communities in accordance with their piety. There are also long-standing precedents for the idea that divine rewards and punishments stand in a more or less *readily apparent* relationship to a society's observable behavior, although this idea had been greatly reinforced by the recent historical writings of Augustine and Orosius. In the present passage, however, such ideas are translated from the realm of speculative history to that of practical politics. In the manner of a prophet,

20. "Have regard, I beg you, to the divine benefits, and weigh what has been given you. And reckon that in order for this prosperity to continue, the source of the favor must be propitiated, not offended. For among all public occupations, that must be greatly attended to by a religious prince, which shields his government from danger, and uprightness in divine observance must be preferred to everything else—without it nothing rightly endures." Thiel, *Epistolae*, p. 181; *PL*, LVIII, 39.

Simplicius here makes use of an imminent threat to back up an appeal for the enforcement of religious conformity. The suggestion is made, in other words, that divine wrath or mercy is a factor that can be counted on in the political equation. God, in this way of thinking, which is remarkably lacking in earlier papal argumentation, is a foreign power of infinite might who must be placated by all possible means. The implication is, furthermore, that outward conformity, such as can be obtained by the use of imperial force, is a sufficient appeasement. It might be thought that this argument merely counsels the emperor to do what he reasonably can on behalf of orthodoxy, but does not logically constrain him to use coercion. For Gelasius, however, permitting error is equivalent to endorsing it.[21] On this reasoning, an emperor would seem to have no option but to use every resource at his disposal for enforcing orthodoxy upon his subjects.[22].

21. "Cum auctoritas diuina [Rom. 1:32] dicat non solum qui faciunt praua reos esse, sed et qui consentiunt facientibus," in Schwartz, "Acacian. Schisma," p. 17; *PL*, LIX, 28.

22. The move from propitiation to coercion in Gelasian politics is in some contrast with both Augustinian and Leonine attitudes. On the former, see P. F. L. Brown, "St. Augustine's Attitude to Religious Coercion," *Journal of Roman Studies*, LIV (1964), 107–116; *idem, Augustine of Hippo* (London, 1967), pp. 235–238. Augustine's final position, though far from liberal, seems at least to be based on the possibility of an eventual free inner conversion of the coerced, rather than on the presumed self-interest of the agents of coercion. For Leo, see below, pp. 30, 38–41. Other passages linking the enforcement of orthodoxy with the emperor's need to propitiate God are the following, from the letters of Simplicius, Felix, and Gelasius.

". . . exsultantes, uobis inesse animum fidelissimi sacerdotis et principis, ut imperialis auctoritas et iuncta Christianae deuotioni acceptabilior deo fieret . . . . in quo et quieti ecclesiasticae et uestro consuletis imperio: quia uindicata dei contumelia ulciscentis est gratia, et conciliatur his diuini fauoris auxilium, quorum cura sacrilegium non reliquerit impunitum." Simplicius to Zeno, in Thiel, *Epistolae*, p. 203; *PL*, LVIII, 51–52.

"Per hanc igitur uelut cominus honorificentiae functus alloquiis precor ut supplicationem meam benignis auribus sicut princeps Christianus accipias. nec aestimet pietas tua quod quisquam magis sincera mente te diligat quam qui te pacem cum deo uult habere perpetuam, quando fideli mente non ambigas et temporalis culminis potestatem et aeternae uitae consortia de superna propitiatione pendere." Felix to Zeno, in Schwartz, "Acacian. Schisma," p. 63; *PL*, LVIII, 899. Is there not a slightly menacing note in the discreet suggestion that having peace with God may be a problem for the emperor?

"[Deus] depulit ille uestrae regiae uastatorem, uos ab eius ecclesiae ceruicibus inruptionem deturbate praedonum; pacauit ille rem publicam, sicut uester quoque sermo testatur, a tyrannide haeretica liberatam, uos ab ipsius haereseos praeceptoribus populos exuite Christianos; restituit ille uos aulae legitimo imperii iure suffultos, reddite uos magistro discipulum et sedem beati euangelistae Marci ad communionem sacratissimi Petri. . . ." Felix to Zeno, in Schwartz, "Acacian. Schisma," p. 69; *PL*, LVIII, 904.

"Cum sibi redditam pacem compressis per uos haereticis qui se nitebantur attollere, universalis gauderet ecclesia et uestrae pietatis imperio etiam de inimicis suis uictoriam

It can readily be seen that the two points just examined reinforce one another, forming together a coercive doctrine of religious authority. The higher values argument, that religious laws should be enforced because they are religious, gains a tremendous sanction from the belief that God will temporally reward or punish the holders of power in accordance with their effectiveness in seeing that they are enforced, while the frightening doctrine that God rewards and punishes holders of power on *some* basis becomes much more effective in practice when the appropriate basis is specified. This begins to be accomplished when we can point to a definite set of religious observances (including, most importantly, subscription to certain doctrines) as the crucial ones. Before considering the Felician-Gelasian position on this further problem, we may note an important contemporary example of propitiationism outside the papacy.

Discussion of the Emperor Zeno's *Henoticon* usually turns on a single phrase from one of its concluding sections. There, after the sufficiency of Nicaea, Constantinople, and Ephesus has been asserted, all contrary doctrines are anathematized, "whether taught at Chalcedon or any other synod." A disquieting indifference to theological principle may seem to be expressed here, an attempt to paper over the genuine difficulties of the Christological controversy, motivated by an understandable but hardly admirable desire for ecclesiastical tranquillity at any cost.[23] If we consider the whole document, however, it provides no reason to question Zeno's religious sincerity. Zeno fervently concedes that his power comes from God and that God demands proper worship. Accordingly, we must suppose that he was eager to render unto God a true confession of faith, *whatever that might be.*[24] This is not indifference to theological truth, but an *instru-*

---

reportasset, per uniuersum orbem pro salute uestrae serenitatis oratio cunctorum erat ad dominum sacerdotum ut uestra pietas fidei custos et defensor orthodoxae sub aeterni regis propitiatione regnaret. . . ." Felix to Zeno, in Schwartz, "Acacian. Schisma," p. 74; *PL,* LVIII, 978.

"Dignas referre deo nostro gratias, fateor, mens humana non sufficit, quod tantam religionis curam in uestrae pietatis sensibus inspiratio diuina constituit, ut eam et uniuersis negotiis anteponi et soliditate rei publicae contineri quam ueraciter Christiano, tam augusto iudicio censeretis, quia re uera propitiatione caelesti rerum subsistit uniuersitas." Felix to Zeno, in Schwartz, "Acacian. Schisma," pp. 82–83; *PL,* LVIII, 969.

23. Jalland, *The Church and the Papacy,* p. 317.

24. The *Henoticon* has been edited by E. Schwartz, "Codex Vaticanus gr. 1431, eine antichalkedonische Sammlung aus der Zeit Kaiser Zenos," in *Abhandlungen der Bayerischen Akademie der Wissenschaften, Philosophisch-philologisch und historische Klasse,* XXII (1927), *Abh.* 6, pp. 52–56. An English translation is in H. Bettenson, *Documents of the Christian Church* (London, 1963), pp. 123–126. The literal orthodoxy of the document has usually been conceded, sometimes reluctantly: "cette formule paraît à peu près orthodoxe." Labriolle *et al., Histoire de l'Église,* IV, 292.

mental concern with it. The truth is not something to be lived with, or lived in. It is something to be professed in order to obtain some other goal. The profession of orthodoxy is a *quid pro quo* to even accounts with God for his bestowal of temporal power. It is not, however, a matter of indifference to Zeno whether the *truth* is professed, for it is entirely granted that God demands true rather than false professions of faith. The basis for criticizing Zeno is not the intensity of his concern for truth, but the reason for it. To a considerable extent, this instrumental orientation in political theology was accepted and reinforced by Zeno's papal contemporaries.

But let us resume our main line of argument. Propitiationism instructs us to profess the truth, whatever it may be. But how does one determine the content of that truth which it is so necessary to profess? At this stage, the Felician-Gelasian papacy presents itself as final arbiter. It is true that emperors are instructed to learn what things are divine from pontiffs, but this advice recommends deference "especially to the vicar of blessed Peter," [25] and this is not an isolated instance. We find Felix asking, in a letter to Zeno, "nonne mea fides est, quam solam esse ueram et nulla aduersitate superandam dominus ipse monstrauit, qui ecclesiae suae in mea confessione fundandae portas inferi numquam praeualituras esse promisit?" [26] This is but the strongest of a number of passages. [27] As we shall see, there are also passages in the sermons of Leo which can be cited

25. Gelasius, in Schwartz, "Acacian. Schisma," p. 19; *PL*, LIX, 30.

26. Schwartz, "Acacian. Schisma," p. 64; *PL*, LVIII, 900.

27. "Sed ait dilectio tua tantum circa me sese caritatis habuisse, ut solo ad scribendum fueris contentus affectus auditu. legeras sententiam fides ex auditu, auditus autem per uerbum dei, illud scilicet uerbum quod confessione beati apostoli Petri portas inferni numquam praeualituras esse promisit, atque ideo rationabiliter aestimasti quia fidelis dominus in uerbis suis non, nisi aliquid tale promisisset, instituit unde sponsionis suae promissionem impleret.

"Agit denique magnas diuinae prouidentiae gratias tua dilectio quod inde monstrauerit sanctarum ecclesiarum se non deserere caritatem, quia me in pontificali sede locauerit non indigentem, sicut ais, doceri, sed circumspicientem omnia necessaria ad ecclesiastici corporis unitatem. ego quidem sum omnium minimus hominum, satis immeritus tantae sedis officio, nisi quod superna gratia semper operatur magna de paruis. quid enim de me sentiam, cum hoc ipsud de se magister gentium ille testatur, qui se ultimum et non uocari dignum apostolum profitetur? uerumtamen, ut ad dilectionis tuae uerba redeamus, si ueraciter executus es haec diuinitus mihi fuisse collata, quia et profecto quaecumque sunt bona, dona sunt dei, sequere ergo hortamenta non indigentis doceri et secundum supernam dispositionem uniuersa circumspicientis quae ad ecclesiarum pertinent unitatem, et aduersus diabolum conturbatorem uerae pacis atque compagis, ut asseris, fortiter resistentis, si ergo de me ista pronuntias, aut sectanda tibi sunt quae a Christo perhibes constituta, aut palam te, quod absit, Christi dispositionibus obuiare depromis aut, da ueniam, lusorie de me cognosceris ista iactare." Gelasius to Euphemius, in Schwartz, "Acacian. Schisma," p. 50; *PL*, LIX, 14–15. For other primacy passages see the following note.

in support of a strong view of papal primacy, but these Leonine ideas are
first brought into use in the political sphere, or misused there, by Felix
and Gelasius. These pontiffs are quite willing to match the spiritual might
of the apostolic see against that of any adversary.[28] In this regard, the
papacy's response to the charges of pride and arrogance which were an
inevitable result of its intervention in the affairs of the eastern churches
is noteworthy. There is no question of conciliating the opposition or of
recognizing an independent standard of truth to which both sides could in
principle legitimately appeal. "Nonne mea fides est, quam *solam* esse
ueram et nulla aduersitate superandam dominus ipse monstrauit?" The
relation of the papacy to those who disagree with it is not that of parties
contending before a neutral judge, but the relation of a doctor to a very
sick patient:

> Sed adhuc apostolicam sedem sibi medicinalia suggerentem superbam
> uocare arrogantemque contendunt. habet hoc qualitas saepe lan-
> guentum ut accusent medicos congruis obseruationibus ad salubria
> reuocantes quam ut ipsi suos noxios adpetitus deponere uel reprobare
> consentiant. si nos superbi sumus, qui animarum remedia con-
> uenientia ministramus, quid uocandi sunt qui resultant? si nos superbi
> sumus, qui oboediendum paternis dicimus constitutis, qui refragantur
> quo appellandi sunt nomine? si nos elati sumus, qui diuinum cultum

28. And ready to cast the papacy by itself in a role of leadership over and against
the *universalis ecclesia*: "In Calchedonesi itaque synodo, quae de Nicaeni concilii tenore
procedens ⟨pro⟩ Christianae confessionis integritate seruanda tam auctoritate sedis
apostolicae quam uniuersalis ecclesiae est celebrata consensu. . . ." Felix, in Schwartz,
"Acacian. Schisma," p. 79; *PL*, LVIII, 975.

Texts from Gelasius would seem to provide the first clear examples of the interpretation of Matt. 16:18 in the sense of a totality of power. "In quibus ⟨quae⟩ cumque
omnia sunt quantacumque sint et qualiacumque sint." Schwartz, "Acacian. Schisma,"
p. 10; *PL*, LIX, 105. "His uerbis nihil constat exceptum . . . et totum possit generaliter
alligari, et totum consequenter absolui." Thiel, *Epistolae*, p. 445; *PL*, LIX, 189.

"Quod sedes apostolica non consensit nec imperator imposuit nec Anatolius usurpauit
totumque dictum est in sedis apostolicae positum potestate. ita quod firmauit in synodo
sedes apostolica, hoc robur obtinuit; quod refutauit, habere non potuit firmitatem et sola
rescindit quod praeter ordinem congregatio synodica putauerat usurpandum, non
promulgatrix iteratae sententiae, sed cum apostolica sede ueteris executrix. . . ."
Gelasius, in Schwartz, "Acacian. Schisma," p. 12; *PL*, LIX, 107.

For the *principatus* of the Roman church in Gelasius, see Ullmann, *The Growth of
Papal Government*, pp. 14 ff. Primacy texts in Felix and Gelasius are also treated in
Gaudemet, *L'Église dans l'Empire Romain*, pp. 435 and 444. Grisar notes (*History of Rome
and the Popes in the Middle Ages*, II, 214) that some passages from Gelasius were incorporated
by the (first) Vatican Council in the constitution *De ecclesia Christi*, particularly in those
portions relating to the primacy of the Holy See.

puro atque inlibato cupimus tenore seruari, qui contra diuinitatem quoque sentiunt, dicant qualiter nuncupentur.[29]

In this context, the next sentence, just to the extent that it claims divine support for the papal position, seems to deny even the possibility of such support for the papacy's opponents: "sic et nos ceteri qui in errore sunt, aestimant, quod eorum non consentiamus insaniae; ubi tamen spiritus superbiae ueraciter consistat et pugnet, ueritas ipsa iudicat."[30] Confrontation with the papacy is an ultimate confrontation.

There is not in Gelasius's writings a fully worked out doctrine either of the relation of spiritual to temporal authority or of the rightful power of the pope within the church. It is clear, however, that Gelasius held both an extremely strong view of papal primacy and an extremely strong view of the right of the church to demand the imposition of religious orthodoxy. A chief function of secular rulers is to enforce without question and with all the power at their disposal an orthodoxy determined by specifically religious authorities, among whom ultimate authority rests exclusively with the apostolic see. This, very briefly, is the picture of an exclusive or papalist position with which we must now compare the religio-political ideas of Leo the Great.

As our chief question with regard to Leo is whether he should be understood as a forerunner of Gelasius or as presenting a coherent alternative position, it will be well to begin by examining certain passages in his writings which seem to offer compelling support for the most extreme papalism imaginable. These are the passages expressing the Leonine claim

29. "But moreover, they exert themselves in citing the Apostolic See for pride and arrogance when it suggests medicines. This condition often possesses the feeble, that they would rather [supplying *magis* with *PL*] accuse the doctors who with accurate observations recall [them] to health than agree to give up or condemn their own harmful appetites. If we who provide suitable remedies for souls are proud, what should those who refuse them be called? If we who say that the ordinances of our forefathers must be obeyed are proud, by what name should those who withstand them be called? If we who desire divine worship to be maintained pure and unimpaired are exalted, let them say what name to call those who also declare against the divinity." Gelasius to Anastasius, in Schwartz, "Acacian. Schisma," p. 24; *PL*, LIX, 46. The emperor, though not classified as a patient, is also on a distinctly lower level. "[Imperator] habet priuilegia potestatis suae, quae amministrandis publicis rebus diuinitus consecutus est; at eius beneficiis non ingratus contra dispositionem caelestis ordinis nil usurpet. ... imperatores Christiani subdere debent exsecutiones suas ecclesiasticis praesulibus, non praeferre. ..." Gelasius, in Schwartz, "Acacian. Schisma," pp. 35–36; *PL*, LVIII, 950.

30. "Let the rest, who are in error, value us from this, that we do not consent in their madness; but where the spirit of pride truly abides and contends, truth itself judges." Gelasius to Anastasius, in Schwartz, "Acacian. Schisma," p. 24; *PL*, LIX, 46–47.

that the pope acts as the "heir," albeit unworthy, of St. Peter. This relation to St. Peter is stated by Leo in two sermons given on anniversaries of his elevation to the papacy:

> Si quid itaque a nobis recte agitur, recteque discernitur . . . *illius* est *operum atque meritorum*, cuius in sede sua uiuit potestas, et excellit auctoritas. . . . his itaque modis, dilectissimi, rationabili obsequio celebretur hodierna festiuitas, ut in *persona humilitatis meae ille intelligatur*, ille honoretur, in quo et omnium pastorum sollicitudo . . . perseuerat, et cuius dignitas etiam *in indigno haerede* non deficit. . . . quem non solum huius sedis praesulem, sed et omnium episcoporum nouerunt esse primatem. . . . ipsum uobis, *cuius* uice fungimur, loqui credite. . . .[31]

> . . . gratias agentes sempiterno regi redemptori nostro Domino Iesu Christo, quod *tantam potentiam* dedit ei quem totius ecclesiae principem fecit, ut si quid etiam nostris temporibus recte per nos agitur, recteque disponitur, *illius* operibus, *illius* sit *gubernaculis* deputandum, cui dictum est: et tu conuersus confirma fratres tuos. . . .[32]

When these passages are interpreted in accordance with the classical Roman law sense of heirship as complete juristic continuance of the deceased, and when Christ's charge to Peter is remembered ("Whatsoever you shall bind . . . whatsoever you shall loose . . ."), it becomes evident that Leo has here laid down a unique primatial claim on behalf of himself and later popes. This, indeed, is Ullmann's key discovery. It is as the originator of "juristic theology"[33] that Leo must be credited with the fixation of papal primacy. "From the purely intellectual standpoint it can be said without fear of gainsaying that the medieval papacy was built on

31. "And so, if anything is done rightly and determined rightly by us . . . it is *of his work and merits* whose power lives and whose authority prevails in his see. . . . And so, most beloved, today's festival is celebrated with a reasonable obedience, that *in my humble person he may be understood* and honored in whom abides the care of all the shepherds . . . , and whose dignity does not cease even *in his unworthy heir*. . . . [Peter] whom they recognize as not only the patron of this see but as the primate of all bishops. . . . Believe him to be speaking to you in whose place we act." *Sermo* 3; *PL*, LIV, 146–147. Italics added.

32. ". . . giving thanks to the everlasting king, our redeemer, the Lord Jesus Christ, that he gave *such power* to him whom he made ruler of the whole church that, even today, if anything is done rightly or disposed rightly by us, it should be counted as *his work and government* to whom it was said: 'and when you are converted, confirm your brothers.'" *Sermo* 4; *PL*, LIV, 152. Italics added. Also see *Sermo* 5; *PL*, LIV, 155.

33. Ullmann, "Leo I and the Theme of Papal Primacy," [cited above n. 1], p. 33.

the juristic foundations laid by Leo." [34] In the light of such judgments, it at first is difficult to see how any degree of papalism in Gelasius, no matter how extreme, could be anything but a natural development from the Petrinology of Leo.

Although this case seems to me to be quite compelling as far as it goes, I wonder whether it does not leave untouched at least some questions which are of importance for an adequate historical understanding of Petrinology itself. Is it not relevant to raise questions here about the relations of one aspect of human life, namely the juristic aspect, to the full reality of what men say and do? My own suggestion, which will be elaborated in the next few pages, is that the whole conception of juristic theology needs to be understood in terms of a broader political and religious context. When so interpreted, this theology, or Petrinology, remains indispensable, yet ceases to be the *exclusive* source of legitimate principles for Christian political theory.

In order to suggest the broader perspective from which I would like to consider Leo's thought, I should like briefly to direct attention to three problems which are *logically* inescapable in any attempt to base a "totalitarian" conception of papal government on a combination of the Matthean commission to Peter and a juristically literal conception of heirship.

First, the Matthean commission is only one passage among many in the Bible from which a Christian person or society might seek practical guidance. If it has no greater weight than other passages (the Beatitudes, for example), cases of apparent conflict cannot *automatically* be settled in favor of obedience to Petrine commands. Judgment is called for. The logical possibility—which need not be a real possibility—of a heretical pope must be taken into account. If it should be said that the Matthean commission *does* have greater weight than other passages in the Bible, since it provides a means of achieving in practice a consistent interpretation of the others, by instructing us to interpret them as Peter would have us interpret them, the difficulty remains of showing why *that* sort of practical consistency is to be preferred religiously to some other sort. For example, we could also achieve consistency by stipulating that we would deny that Peter had commanded anything contrary, say, to the Beatitudes, even if we were confronted with anti-Beatitudes with otherwise impeccably Petrine credentials. If such a stipulation is objected to on the basis that each person would then need to be his own judge of what was and what was not consonant with the Beatitudes, and that what one wants is

34. *Ibid.*, p. 46.

precisely a workable procedure for avoiding the conflicts which would result from such an arrangement, we come to a second problem.[35]

The relation of jurisprudence to politics, our second problem, may be seen as part of a yet broader problem, that of determining the proper place of legal systems in the world in general. Evidently, Camus's man in revolt will have a different position on this matter than, say, Thomas Hobbes. Or again, an Alexandrian schismatic of the fifth century, mindful that Christ came to bring not peace, but a sword, cannot plausibly be expected to rate the Matthean commission as having a high claim to his obedience *simply because it offers juristic peace and consistency*. Since he must judge for himself anyway what the Matthean commission means (whether this task is hard or easy does not matter to the argument here), the fact that "private" judgment will be required in support of, say, his Christological convictions, poses no logically compelling impediment to his defending those convictions to the death. The general problem raised here is whether any juristic system at all can claim to be an adequate embodiment of absolute values unless it has a basis in moral or religious principles that are not themselves juristic.

A third problem is posed by the fact that the normal use of the concept of heirship is as *part* of a system of juristic and political ideas which includes more basic ideas. Now if inheritance laws by their very nature presuppose a broader juristic and political context, it could be argued that any use of the concept of heirship in justifying absolute political (or more than political) power must be metaphorical.

However inescapable these problems may be logically, they have sometimes been ignored in the course of history, and it may seem inappropriate to bring them up in a discussion of the fifth century. It seems to me that this objection is not convincing. The fifth century precedes the middle ages; it succeeds, and to some extent continues the ideas of, a civilization in which the latter two problems could not fail to have occurred to many people. Furthermore, if only because the papal literature was just beginning, most Christians interpreted most passages in the Bible without at all referring them to the passages traditionally used in support of papal primacy. It is reasonable to assume, then, if only as an initial hypothesis, that Pope Leo did not intend to put forth a view of his office which took no account at all of problems such as those we have raised.

To put the hypothesis in different terms, let us distinguish two possible

---

35. Avoiding such conflicts is the paramount aim of some theories of law and the state. Cf. Hobbes's *Leviathan* and, for a position in most respects very different from Hobbes's, the writings of Hans Kelsen, for example, *What is Justice?* (Berkeley, 1957.)

senses of Petrinology. The term can be taken in one sense as both affirming the juristic primacy of the papacy within the precincts of the Christian faith and denying the validity of any principle of action disapproved of by the papacy.[36] This could be called the papalist or exclusive sense of Petrinology. The term might also be used, on the other hand, in asserting a juristic primacy for the pope—a unique status among bishops with respect to the government of the church—which would *not*, however, rule out any other principle of action simply because it might lead to conflict with the papacy. This could be characterized as the ecumenical sense of Petrinology. Gelasius, it can be said, was a proponent of Petrinology in the first sense. He was a papalist, either claiming or coming very close to claiming that papal precepts ought to be automatically obeyed and coercively enforced *just because* of their papal origin. The hypothesis I propose to follow out in the next few pages is that Leo originated Petrinology in the second, or ecumenical, sense. This hypothesis can claim some support from a close reading of the passages already quoted from Leo's anniversary sermons. It derives additional confirmation from his other statements and actions.

As to the sermons, is it not significant in the first place that the *haeres* passages are from sermons? The considerable body of Leo's sermons is almost entirely free of politics, either secular or ecclesiastical. If Leo's characteristic stance in preaching is not one of laying down the law, perhaps that is not his intention here. Should we not seek a nonpolitical, or at least nontotalitarian, interpretation of the passages in question? A possible interpretation would be that Leo is here being *modest*. Conscious of the great respect and reverence which he has inspired in his people, he offers a humble, literally "self-effacing" explanation of anything outstanding he may have accomplished: "Not I, but Peter working through me." [37] If one comes to these passages from reading the Leonine epistles, it is hard to take this interpretation seriously. In his correspondence with the rulers of church and empire, Leo's style is not patronizing or paternalistic, but it is assuredly majestic, not at all retiring. His letters do not lead one to suspect him of unusual personal humility. On the other hand,

36. For the development of the "derivational principle," the idea that the totality of papal power excludes the possession of autogenous or inherent rights by other Christians, see Ullmann, *Principles of Government and Politics in the Middle Ages*, p. 48 and *passim*.

37. Reference to 1 Cor. 15:10 ("non ego autem, sed gratia Dei mecum") seems clear in *Sermo* 5; *PL*, LIV, 154, where the qualifier, *recte*, is again found: "quandoquide pie et veraciter confitemur, quod opus ministerii nostri in omnibus quae recte agimus, Christus exsequitur; et non in nobis, qui sine illo nihil possumus, sed in ipso, qui possibilitas nostra est, gloriamur."

a reading of the same pope's sermons produces a different impression. The characteristic tone of these is reverence and awe. The preacher does not set himself apart from his hearers or exalt himself above them. He and they are parts of the same human race, they share the same human nature which Christ redeems.[38] As preacher, Leo might be capable of using his succession from Peter as a way of reducing, rather than accentuating, the gap between himself and others.

Even if the reader does not dismiss the considerations offered in the last paragraph as moral or literary speculations, he will still ask for something more solid on which to base the supposition that Leo's Petrinology leaves room for values or practical principles independent of papal derivation. There is something more: the important word *recte*. This term is present in both of the anniversary sermons. It is stressed by repetition in each of the passages linking Peter's power and authority with the pope's own performance: "quid a nobis *recte* agitur *recteque* discernitur," "quid *recte* per nos agitur *recteque* disponitur"—*that* is owing to the work, merit, and government of Peter. Can we avoid supplying the antithesis: whatever I do *wrongly* is due to my own shortcomings? To be sure, the implication that papal acts may be wrong is not followed up by Leo, yet precisely that implication is present in these passages; one does not use "rightly" in this way except by contrast with a relevant "wrongly." Leo is far too careful a stylist to employ with literary emphasis a term which has no logical force. And it should be noted that official acts, judgments and dispositions are involved here, not just the personal behavior of the pope. Hence, although this is no doubt far from his primary intention, it is hard to avoid the conclusion that Pope Leo, even in stressing the continuity of his office with St. Peter, has left what could be called logical space in his Petrinology for those problems which a papalist Petrinology tends to ignore.[39]

38. The strong sense of human solidarity in Leo stands in some contrast with the idea that in becoming Christian we cease to be human. The bearing of this latter idea on hierocratic thought is noted in Ullmann, *Principles of Government and Politics in the Middle Ages*, pp. 33, 144, and 245 ff.

39. Some further questions may be raised about these very suggestive passages. Is it clear that *indignus* in the first passage is meant simply to contrast the pope's personal unworthiness with the juristic possession of authority expressed through *haeres*? After all, Leo's statement is that, just as Peter's universal *sollicitudo* perseveres in him, so also, Peter's *dignitas* is in some way *not* lacking to him. Compare this with the passage cited from *Sermo* 4, where Christ is said to have given Peter so much power that it is felt "etiam nostris temporibus." Even accepting fully the juristic interpretation of *indignus haeres*, may we not find, as it were, a loophole? As Ullmann points out, in Roman law the *indignus haeres* was one who "for mainly moral reasons, *was incapable of functioning* as an heir: a notion which

Our examination of the sermon passages in which Leo lays the basis for juristic theology has suggested that he *could* have acted on an inclusive or ecumenical conception of his office without being inconsistent with the idea of Petrinology. What remains to be shown is the extent to which he did so act.

It must be said at once that Leo's frequent calls for religious peace and freedom[40] were not primarily intended to encourage tranquil accommodation of opposed theological viewpoints. He was as zealous for the establishment of dogmatic unity as Gelasius.[41] Nevertheless, his idea of this goal seems to differ at least in emphasis from the Gelasian notion that orthodoxy is to be formally accepted in order to avoid divine retribution. Much greater contrasts with Gelasius are to be found in the attitude of cooperation with which he pursues his goal.

Leo's aim is to promote the peace of God and, hence, the freedom of— or freedom for—Christian faith. He tells us that "tunc est uera pax homini et uera libertas, quando et caro animo iudice regitur, et animus

---

included offences against the deceased, or the disregard of his wishes ... and the like." "Leo I and the Theme of Papal Primacy," [cited above n. 1], p. 34; italics added. It would seem that, within the precincts of this sort of juristic theology, proceedings against the pope are not necessarily inadmissible. A judgment of *indignus haeres pronuntiatus* is not inconceivable, although, to be sure, it is not easy to suggest an appropriate due process by which such a judgment might be obtained. This difficulty bears, of course, on the third preliminary reflection offered on p. 24, that the concept of heirship is normally employed in a juristic and political context which includes other bases of authority.

40. He writes to one emperor after another to ask or acknowledge help in promoting the peace of the Catholic church and *libertatem fidei*. He tells Marcian that "inter ... dissensiones ... euangelii erat defendenda libertas." E. Schwartz, *Acta Conciliorum Oecumenicorum, Concilium Universale Chalcedonense*, II, iv (Berlin, 1932), p. 55; *PL*, LIV, 991. Schwartz's text will be used wherever possible and will be cited as Schwartz, *Chalcedon*. Leo sends legates to the Emperor Leo of Thrace so that "pro quiete uobis doctrinae euangelicae supplicarent et libertatem fidei ... optinerent." Schwartz, *Chalcedon.*, p. 110; *PL*, LIV, 1148. And see Schwartz, *Chalcedon.*, pp. 19–21, 41, 81–82, 102–103; *PL*, LIV, 815–816, 827–831, 1069–1070, and 1128 and 1130.

41. Within what has been described as his own patriarchate, the West, Leo acted with considerable administrative vigor, as, for example, in the dispute about the episcopal jurisdiction of Hilary of Arles (see Caspar, *Geschichte des Papsttums*, I, 440–445). He dealt especially severely with Manichaeism in Rome (*ibid.*, pp. 432–435; Jalland, *St. Leo the Great*, pp. 43–50) and showed a similarly stern attitude toward Priscillianism (Caspar, *op. cit.*, pp. 436–437; Jalland, *op. cit.*, pp. 152–156), even furnishing a text which Gelasius must often have called to mind (see n. 21 above) and which was incorporated in the canon law on heresy (A. Friedberg (ed.), *Corpus Iuris Canonici*, [Leipzig, 1879], II, col. 778): "qui alios ab errore non reuocat, seipsum errare demonstrat." *PL*, LIV, 688.

deo praeside gubernatur." [42] The contrast implied here between ordinary peace and freedom and true peace and freedom has been drawn at greater length in an earlier sermon:

> . . . *pacem meam do uobis, pacem meam relinquo uobis.* et ne sub nomine generali pacis suae qualitas lateret, adiecit: *non quemadmodum mundus dat ego do uobis.* habet, inquit, mundus amicitias suas, et multos facit peruerso amore concordes. sunt etiam in uitiis pares animi, et similitudo desideriorum aequalitatem gignit affectuum. et si quidam forsitan reperiantur quibus praua et inhonesta non placeant, quique illicitas consensiones a foedere suae charitatis excludant, tamen etiam tales, si uel Iudaei sint, uel haeretici, uel pagani, non de amicitia dei, sed de pace sunt mundi. [43]

It may be noted that no incompatibility is asserted here between the attainment of the last mentioned form of "this world's peace" and the attainment of the peace of God. [44] There is no necessity that good morals and legitimate human associations should lead to a decline in faith, much less that widespread orthodoxy should lead to civil unrest. It is rather the case that concern with the higher, true peace sets up problems and goals for politics which are distinctively *different* from the problems and goals central to a concern for this world's peace. Thus, for example, the Leonine claim that "inter . . . dissensiones . . . euangelii erat defendenda libertas," [45] is paradoxical if we take freedom as freedom *to* dissent. For Leo, on the contrary, dissent is a sign that at least one of the parties involved is not free—in the highest sense of freedom. [46] Nevertheless, deeply contrast-

42. ". . . then there is true peace and true freedom for man when the flesh is ruled by the judgment of the mind, and the mind is governed by God over it." *Sermo* 39; *PL,* LIV, 264.

43. "'I give you my peace, I leave you my peace.' And in case the character of his peace should be hidden under the general term, he added: 'I do not give to you as the world gives.' The world has its friendships, he says, and it brings many together in perverse love. There are also companions in viciousness, and a similarity of desires produces a likeness of feelings. And if any should happen to be found who are not pleased with what is crooked and dishonorable, and who exclude illicit agreements from the terms of their love, even these, if they are either Jews or heretics or pagans, belong not to God's friendship, but to the peace of the world." *Sermo* 26; *PL,* LIV, 215–216.

44. But cf. the exposition of "Blessed are the peacemakers," in *Sermo* 95 (*PL,* LIV, 465–466), where there is no mention of the imperfect but still legitimate peace of those non-Catholics who are not pleased with *praua et inhonesta.*

45. "Among dissensions . . . the freedom of the gospel had to be defended." Schwartz, *Chalcedon.,* p. 55; *PL,* LIV, 991.

46. Other passages relevant to the idea of religious freedom as freedom for the truth: Schwartz, *Chalcedon.,* pp. 12, 21, 57, 67, 90, 105–107 (esp. 107); *PL,* LIV, 789–790, 831, 997–998, 1031, 1098, 1143–1146 (esp. 1146). In these terms, the problem of determining who is the peaceful party in a doctrinal controversy resembles the modern problem of determining who is the true aggressor in a war of liberation.

ing conceptions of what freedom is do not necessarily entail radical oppositions in practice. There is no contradiction in supposing that freedom in Leo's sense can best be defended in circumstances which are also free in the worldly, political sense, just as there is no contradiction in supposing that concern for Leo's true freedom will normally characterize any community which is viably free in its political and social institutions.

Leo would seem to have had a more positive and less monolithic conception of the goal of his activity than Gelasius. Still, the crucial question for distinguishing him from Gelasius is not whether religious orthodoxy is to be promoted, but how. For Gelasius, an important part of this task consisted of inducing others to acknowledge the unique authority of the papacy and to act accordingly. An alternative approach would treat the promotion of orthodoxy as a cooperative effort to recognize and accept religious truth on some basis other than the fact that it was prescribed from above. There need be no denial here of the pope's superior powers of insight, but acknowledgment of this superiority by others may cease to be an essential target.

In dealing with the highest worldly authorities of his day, Leo implicitly acknowledges the autonomy of secular values, while at the same time treating his imperial correspondents as if he and they were acting, in religious matters, on the basis of mutual understanding and in pursuit of common values. Thus, the principle on which he rejects the elevation of Constantinople to the rank of an apostolic see, "alia tamen ratio est rerum saecularium, alia diuinarum," [47] is not brought forth merely as a tactical weapon for putting down a rival patriarch. It expresses in abstract form a contrast which is drawn over and over again in Leo's letters, more concretely, as between the political community and the religious. Not empire as church, nor church as empire, but empire *and* church: "ad utilitatem Romanae rei publicae *et* ad catholicae ecclesiae pacem," "non solum ecclesiae status, sed *etiam* uestri robur . . . imperii," "Romanae rei publicae *et* catholicae ecclesiae in omni prosperitate," and so on.[48]

47. Schwartz, *Chalcedon.*, p. 56; *PL*, LIV, 995.

48. Schwartz, *Chalcedon.*, pp. 42, 57, 67, 68, 81, 82–83, and 96; *PL*, LIV, 919, 997, 1031, 1035, 1070, 1071, 1073, and 1115. Herod was blindly wicked to fear Christ as a successor, for the Lord of the world, who offers an eternal kingdom, seeks not a temporal one ("Dominus mundi temporale non quaerit regnum, qui praestat aeternum."), *Sermo* 31; *PL*, LIV, 236. A similar lack of hierocratic ambitions is shown in Leo's interpretation of the beatitude "the meek shall inherit the earth," in which the earth meant is the spiritual body of the resurrection, which will be perfectly subordinate, in the blessed, to the spirit or inner man. *Sermo* 95; *PL*, LIV, 463–464. P. Stockmeier has noted (*Leo I. des Grossen Beurteilung der kaiserlichen Religionspolitik*, p. 217) the contrast between Leo's *Romanitas* and the less hopeful attitude toward classical civilization shown by Augustine. Possible Manichaean sources for Augustine's dualism of the heavenly and earthly cities

If Leo avoids even the appearance of bringing spiritual pressure to bear on the imperial authorities,[49] it is not from any lack of appreciation of the divine basis or religious uses of temporal power.[50] It is not this, but

are given by Gaudemet (*L'Église dans l'Empire Romain*, p. 490). In his opposition to Manichaeism (see n. 41), Leo expresses an intense moral indignation not completely dependent on dogmatic considerations.

49. The theme of propitiation is not entirely absent from Leo's thought. Indeed, it develops during his pontificate in a Gelasian direction. At first it is introduced after expressions of joy at what the Emperor Theodosius has already done for the church. The mood is thus rhetorical, not imperative, when he asks, "quid enim rebus humanis ad exorandam misericordiam dei efficacius suffragetur quam si una gratiarum actio et unius confessionis sacrificium maiestati eius ab omnibus offeratur?" Schwartz, *Chalcedon.*, p. 17; *PL*, LIV, 811. A few years later, the tone is still positive, but instead of thanksgiving we find propitiation, when Leo extolls the value of religious unity in a letter to Marcian, "ut propitiato per unam confessionem deo simul et haeretica falsitas et barbara destruatur hostilitas." Schwartz, *Chalcedon.*, p. 41; *PL*, LIV, 917. Note, however, that propitiation is not demanded of the emperor alone. Finally, in a letter to Leo of Thrace written with regard to the continuing turmoil in the Alexandrian church, the pope speaks rather of averting God's wrath than of incurring his blessings. The emperor is urged to take action, "ut correctionibus tuis dei iracundia mitigata religiosae antea ciuitati non retribuat quae ammissa sunt, sed remittat." Schwartz, *Chalcedon.*, p. 103; *PL*, LIV, 1130. All of this undoubtedly offers raw material for the development of an institutional propitiationism, but there must remain the question of whether such a position is a development of the whole Leonine position or an overdevelopment of one part of it.

50. It is clear from a number of passages that Leo regards God as the *auctor, custos*, and *rector* of an empire which is ruled only on the basis of his *munis, gratia*, and *protectio*. Schwartz, *Chalcedon.*, pp. 10, 20, and 48; *PL*, LIV, 785–787, 829, and 933. Also see *Sermo* 82; *PL*, LIV, 423, where Leo employs the Augustinian-Orosian idea that God used the *pax Romana* to spread the gospel. Similarly, it is God, he tells the Emperor Marcian, "qui in uirtutibus prouidentiae uestrae . . . ad catholicae ecclesiae pacem gloriosissimum praesidium collocauit." Schwartz, *Chalcedon.*, p. 81; *PL*, LIV, 1070. There is no doubt that Leo conceives of Christian emperors ruling in some sense *as* Christian. This is expressed briefly but well in a letter to the saintly Pulcheria in which he refers to the faith of her brother, the Emperor Theodosius, as "fidem in qua renatus per dei gratiam regnat." Schwartz, *Chalcedon.*, p. 24; *PL*, LIV, 835. The position of *per dei gratiam* between *renatus* and *regnat* suggests with subtle efficiency that, for a Christian, religious rebirth and political rule are dependent on the same divine grace. Furthermore, the way a ruler behaves toward the church will have an effect on the success of his temporal reign. "Defendite contra haereticos inconcussum ecclesiae statum," Leo exhorts Theodosius, "ut uestrum Christi dextera defendatur imperium." Schwartz, *Chalcedon.*, p. 21; *PL*, LIV, 831. "Res humanae," he writes Pulcheria, "aliter tutae esse non possunt, nisi quae ad diuinam confessionem pertinent, et regia et sacerdotalis defendat auctoritas." Schwartz, *Chalcedon.*, p. 29; *PL*, LIV, 873–874. One basis for requesting assistance from Marcian is, "ut regnum uestrum Christo regente tranquillum Christo defendente sit ualidum." Schwartz, *Chalcedon.*, p. 91; *PL*, LIV, 1099. More than a third of the letters published by Schwartz are either to request or to acknowledge the benefit of imperial protection for the catholic faith.

the cooperative attitude with which he approaches the authorities, which distinguishes him from Gelasius. Leo always deals with Catholic emperors and empresses as if the care of religion were a task to be carried out cooperatively, and he goes out of his way to attribute to them the same kind of concern and status as he would claim for himself. He speaks, for example, of their *auctoritas* in religion, both in general and in specific terms.[51] He frequently refers to them as having priestly minds, or even, on occasion, priestly *doctrina* or *sanctitas*,[52] and he presents his own lengthy doctrinal instruction of Leo of Thrace as almost a work of supererogation.[53]

51. "Res humanae aliter tutae esse non possunt, nisi quae ad diuinam confessionem pertinent, et regia et sacerdotalis defendat auctoritas." Schwartz, *Chalcedon.*, p. 29; *PL*, LIV, 873–874. More impressive than this somewhat incidental and indefinite remark is the claim, just after Chalcedon, that "definitarum rerum quas tantae synodi uel Christianissimi principis sanxit autoritas et apostolicae sedis confirmauit assensus, nihil oportet discuti, ne contra fas aliquid uideretur infringi." Schwartz, *Chalcedon.*, p. 108; *PL*, LIV, 1142. A most important way in which imperial religious authority could be exercised was in the calling of ecumenical councils. Although Leo repeatedly urged the inutility of a council in 450, there is no suggestion in his letters that the emperor lacked the authority to call such a council. When a council was indeed held at Ephesus, the result justified his fears. He accordingly came to feel that another synod *was* needed. It is worth noting that he nowhere contests the exclusive authority of the emperor to call the new synod. Even when he expresses doubts about having it in the East, he says nothing to suggest that he has authority to dictate in these matters. Finally, he feels an evident obligation to respond to the imperial invitation to attend this synod, which was eventually held at Chalcedon. Although *nulla ratio* permits him to attend, he sends two fellow bishops (he refers to them elsewhere as "my brothers") to represent him ("qui uicem meam implere"). Considering all the circumstances, including the fact that Italy was being ravaged by barbarians at just that time, we can hardly conclude that he was on principle above participating in such an assembly. See Schwartz, *Chalcedon.*, pp. 17–18, 47–48, 48, 50–51, and 107–108; *PL*, LIV, 811–812, 930–931, 932–934, 942–944, and 970–972.

52. ". . . et non solum regiam, sed et sacerdotalem ipsius mentem. . . ." Schwartz, *Chalcedon.*, p. 101; *PL*, LIV, 1126. The emperor's priestly mind is also referred to in Schwartz, *Chalcedon.*, p. 105; *PL*, LIV, 1143. And see Schwartz, *Chalcedon.*, p. 68; *PL*, LIV, 1036: "quoniam principibus temporis nostri non solum regiam potentiam, sed etiam sacerdotalem cognoscimus inesse doctrinam"; and Schwartz, *Chalcedon.*, p. 1; *PL*, LIV, 735: "ut uobis non solum regium sed etiam sacerdotalem inesse animum gaudeamus. . . ." In Schwartz, *Chalcedon.*, p. 69; *PL*, LIV, 1038, Marcian and Pulcheria are said to have "omnem excellentiam ipsorum non solum regii culminis, sed etiam sacerdotalis . . . sanctitatis."

53. "Oficii tamen mei est et patefacere quod intellegis, et praedicare quod credis." Schwartz, *Chalcedon.*, p. 113; *PL*, LIV, 1155. Grisar perhaps had this phrase in mind when he referred to the epistle's "clever introduction" (*History of Rome and the Popes in the Middle Ages*, II, 60). It is possible to go too far in estimating the religious inspiration attributed by Leo to Christian rulers. Although they may be possessors of priestly doctrine, their special virtues would seem to be *industria* (Schwartz, *Chalcedon.*, p. 67; *PL*, LIV, 1033),

In general, the tone of superiority, whether paternal or magistral, which is so prominent in the imperial correspondence of his successors, is entirely missing from Leo's letters. He requests assistance for the church, he does not demand it. Very fittingly, therefore, he addresses his various emperors, not as "your majesty," not as "my son," but as "your clemency." [54]

---

studium, and *fervor* (Schwartz, *Chalcedon.*, p. 69; *PL*, LIV, 1037–1038). The function assigned to them by providence is that of protecting the faith, not defining it. "Quantum praesidii dominus ecclesiae suae in fide uestrae clementiae praeparauit. . . ." Schwartz, *Chalcedon.*, p. 1; *PL*, LIV, 735. This phrase, from a letter to Theodosius, is virtually repeated in Schwartz, *Chalcedon.*, p. 12; *PL*, LIV, 789, to Pulcheria. "necesse est ut ad uestrae pietatis recurratur auxilium, quod ad custodiam catholicae ueritatis diuina prouidentia praeparauit. . . ." To Marcian, Schwartz, *Chalcedon.*, p. 63; *PL*, LIV, 1020. (This letter is regarded as of doubtful authenticity by C. Sylva-Tarouca, "Nuovi studi sulle antiche lettere dei Papi," *Gregorianum* XII [1931], 547.) ". . . imperatoris . . . pietate . . . ad uniuersalis ecclesiae firmamentum a domino praeparatam. . . ." To Julian of Cos, in reference to Marcian, Schwartz, *Chalcedon.*, p. 69; *PL*, LIV, 1037. "Cum enim clementiam tuam dominus tanta sacramenti sui inluminatione ditauerit, debes incunctanter aduertere regiam potestatem tibi non ad solum mundi regimen, sed maxime ad ecclesiae praesidium esse collatam. . . ." To Leo of Thrace, Schwartz, *Chalcedon.*, pp. 102–103; *PL*, LIV, 1130. But also see Schwartz, *Chalcedon.*, p. 67; *PL*, LIV, 1031–1033, to Marcian: "unde ineffabiliter deo gratias ago, qui eo tempore quo oboritura haereticorum scandala praesciebat, uos in imperii fastigio conlocauit, in quibus ad totius mundi salutem et regia potentia est sacerdotalis uigeret industria." We should probably not be surprised if a sharp structure of dogmatic authority fails to emerge from these passages. A hard and fast distinction between *docere* and *discere* is precisely what we do not have in Leonine political theology. In Christ's gospel, "doctrina ueritatis *sua luce* manifestata est." Schwartz, *Chalcedon.*, p. 111; *PL*, LIV, 1150; italics added.

54. See Schwartz, *Chalcedon.*, Index VIIII, *Dignitates Imperii*, p. 189. *Gloriosissimus princeps* and the like are common enough, but *uestra clementia* and similar phrases are clearly predominant. These forms of address, like the very different ones employed by Leo's successors (nn. 12–14 above), epitomize important attitudes. It is not that Leo regards emperors as generally infallible in religious matters (but see P. Stockmeier, *Leo I. des Grossen Beurteilung der kaiserlichen Religionspolitik*, p. 146); rather, he approaches them as if they may be *generous* to the church. This is nowhere better illustrated than in the parallel construction based on the idea of generosity at the beginning of a letter to Pulcheria: "Quantum praesidii dominus ecclesiae suae in uestra clementia praeparauit, multis probauimus saepe documentis, et quidquid nostris temporibus contra impugnatores catholicae ueritatis industria sacerdotalis optinuit, ad uestram maxime gloriam redundauit, dum sicut spiritu sancto docente didicistis, illi per omnia potestatem uestram subicitis, cuius munere et protectione regnatis." Schwartz, *Chalcedon.*, p. 12; *PL*, LIV, 789–790. The imperial authority is here placed "over" the church, not in the sense of presiding in its affairs, but rather as generously protecting it. Similarly, God is placed over the imperial reign as generously protecting it, not as subjecting it to direction and instruction from pontificial superiors.

Cooperative also seems a fair word to describe Leo's attitude toward at least some church councils. He says nothing to suggest that he regards his own authority as derived from any council, but neither does he suggest that councils owe their authority to the papacy or are normally subordinate to it. We have already seen him referring to the *auctoritas* of "so great a synod" as Chalcedon, along with the authority of a most Christian ruler, as "sanctioning" the definitions of certain things.[55] To be sure, the assent of the Apostolic See is mentioned as confirming the council's definitions. Could one argue that Leo considered this assent *necessary?* Fortunately, there need be no doubt on this question. As it happens, there was a brief period during which the canons of the Council of Chalcedon were in circulation without papal confirmation. If Leo was indeed a papalist, we would expect to find evidence that he objected to this state of affairs, or at least that he regarded the canons as seriously lacking in authority in these circumstances. We find, on the contrary, that he would *rebuke* those who express such reservations. Indeed, he issues a confirming judgment, not because he himself regards it as needed, but because the emperor believed it necessary in order to quiet those who refused to accept the council's decisions without papal approval.[56] It seems clear from this that Leo regarded ecumenical councils as having, at least in some cases, authority which was both important and independent of the papacy. This point is of some interest, in view of the attention currently being given to the idea of collegiality in the Roman church.

55. Schwartz, *Chalcedon.*, p. 108; *PL*, LIV, 1142.

56. "Quod ergo necessarium credidit clementissimus imperator, libenter impleui, ut ad omnes fratres qui Calchedonensi synodo interfuerunt, scripta dirigerem quibus placuisse mihi quae a sanctis fratribus nostris de regula fidei confirmata sunt, demonstrarem, propter eos scilicet qui ad occasionem uelandae perfidiae suae infirma uel dubia uideri uolunt statuta concilii quae nulla sint consensus mei sententia roborata...." To Julian of Cos, Schwartz, *Chalcedon.*, p. 69; *PL*, LIV, 1037. The Leonine "synodi uel Christianissimi principis sanxit auctoritas" and "apostolicae sedis confirmauit assensus" (Schwartz, *Chalcedon.*, p. 108; *PL*, LIV, 1142), partly reiterated here, receive a striking modification in the Gelasian reference to the canons of Chalcedon as "tam auctoritate sedis apostolicae quam uniuersalis ecclesiae ... celebrata consensu." Schwartz, "Acacian. Schisma," p. 79; *PL*, LVIII, 975. Leo's ascription of divine inspiration to the Council of Nicaea is noted with sympathy by H. Küng, *Structures of the Church*, trans. S. Attanasio (New York, 1964), p. 55. For the view that, according to Leo, the authority of councils depends in the last analysis on Rome, see Gaudemet, *L'Église dans l'Empire Romain*, p. 465. My contention that Leo had an inclusive or ecumenical conception of religious authority is also in some contrast with Jalland's estimate: "We have now laid bare the guiding principle which underlies the whole of St. Leo's work, namely the safeguarding and upholding of the supposed privileges of the Roman See." *St. Leo the Great*, p. 73.

The significance of Leo's cooperative approach both to secular authority and to other spiritual authority may become clearer if we go on to consider a more fundamental issue which this approach brings into prominence. The question of which part, or parts, of a legal or political order has, or have, supreme authority is important, but there is a prior question: Does *any* part always have supreme authority? We may conclude our consideration of Leo by discussing this more fundamental issue in two forms.

First, let us pose the question in terms of the perennial comparison between government by men and the government of law. The ideal of government by laws, rather than men, is both attractive and fraught with difficulties. It has been convincingly argued that men can have genuine authority only to the extent that they embody or are subordinate to principles, laws, objective norms. It has also been convincingly argued that laws can have real effectiveness only to the extent that they emanate from persons with the will and the power to enforce them. Although these claims are by no means mutually contradictory, a political philosophy based on one of them will be very different, in its subsidiary concepts, its location of problems, and so on, from a theory based on the other.[57] It may be illuminating to ask, therefore, where the ideology of papal government stands on this basic question. In regard to the papacy of the late fifth century, a few remarks may be offered here. In the first place, the papacy at this time certainly did not regard the decisions of contemporary ecclesiastical authorities as having a higher status than the established canons of the church. Thus, in sharp contrast with his acceptance of the Chalcedonian definition of the Incarnation, Leo's reaction to the same council's attempt to secure patriarchal status for the see of Constantinople is totally negative. The basis he gives for this reaction is that the decision here is repugnant to the canons of Nicaea.[58] Leo evidently regards himself as having the duty to defend these canons to the end.

57. Compare, for example, the political theories of Thomas Aquinas and Thomas Hobbes. I do not mean to suggest that their philosophies are consistent with one another, but only that their difference on the point in question is not a matter of direct contradiction.

58. To be sure, the Chalcedonian definition of the Incarnation is, as to content, Leo's own. Still, it is the lack of a Nicene rather than a Petrine basis which calls forth Leo's most emphatic exercise of his general apostolic authority, when he annuls Canon 28: "consensiones uero episcoporum sanctorum canonum apud Nicaeam conditorum regulis repugnantes unita nobiscum uestrae fidei pietate in irritum mittimus et per auctoritatem beati Petri apostoli generali prorsus definitione cassamus. . . ." Schwartz, *Chalcedon.*, p. 58; *PL*, LIV, 1000. It is a sign of the lack of theological communication between East and

But if law is to be regarded as superior to those persons who are in positions of authority, what is the basis of law itself? How is one to determine what is lawful, if not, finally, by human decision? One answer which immediately presents itself these days is that valid norms are those which seem good after full, free, and rational discussion. Leo in fact does express a qualified confidence in free discussion as part of the process of determining religious truth. The unbending tone of his successors is in sharp contrast with his own quite gracious endorsement of the discussion of the faith at Chalcedon, even though—or rather, *even because*—some of the bishops temporarily disagreed with the papacy's own position. He states no fewer than four grounds for satisfaction with this aspect of the councils proceedings:

Dulcius siquidem munera gratiae diuinae proueniunt quotiens non sine magnis sudoribus acquiruntur et minus bonum uideri solet pax continuata per otium quam reddita per laborem; ipsa quoque ueritas et clarius renitescit et fortius retinetur, dum quae fides prius docuerit, haec postea examinatio confirmauit. multum denique sacerdotalis officii meritum splendescit ubi sic summorum seruator auctoritas, ut in nullo inferiorum putetur imminuta libertas, et ad maiorem dei gloriam proficit finis examinis, quando ad hoc se accipit exerendi fiduciam, ut uincatur áduersitas, ne quod per se probatur reprobum, silentii praeiudicio uideatur oppressum.[59]

West at this time that both Monophysites and Chalcedonians could insist on the authority of Nicaea, but with no effect on one another. The custom of reciting the Nicene Creed at the mass goes back to Peter the Fuller, a Monophysite bishop of Antioch, who thought of it as a protest against Chalcedon. Duchesne, *Early History of the Christian Church*, III, 352.

59. "For the gifts of divine grace are sweeter when they are gained with mighty efforts, and continued peace with leisure often seems a lesser good than peace restored by labors. Moreover, the truth itself shines more brightly and is retained with greater strength when what faith had already taught is afterwards confirmed by further inquiry. And then, the good name of the priestly office gains much in luster where the authority of the highest is so preserved that it is not thought that the liberty of the lower ranks has been at all infringed. And the result of a discussion contributes to the greater glory of God when the debaters exert themselves with confidence in overcoming the opposition, so that what proves to be wrong in itself may not seem to have been persecuted by the prejudice of silence." To Theodoret, bishop of Cyprus, in Schwartz, *Chalcedon.*, pp. 78–79; *PL*, LIV, 1048–1049. This letter is of doubtful authenticity according to Sylva-Tarouca, "Nuovi studi sulle antiche lettere dei Papi," (cited above n. 53), p. 547.

For Roman Catholic theologians, the significance of Leo's willingness to accept at least temporary disagreement with his own position at Chalcedon (assuming that the passage just cited is authentic) is tied up with the question of whether the document under discussion at the council, Leo's Tome, was a definition ex cathedra. P. Batiffol concludes ("Léon 1er," in *Dictionnaire de Theologie Catholique*, IX [Paris, 1926], col. 251 f.), with

Impressive as this endorsement of free discussion is, it should not lead us to overlook Leo's emphatic reservations about uninspired human wisdom. It was the tenets of philosophy and rhetoric which needed to be crushed in Nero's Rome,[60] and we find Leo pursuing this traditional theme with great vigor when he reminds a Roman emperor that Christ in his wisdom "omnes nationes ad inluminationem fidei uocaturus non de philosophis aut de oratoribus qui praedicando euangelio famularentur, elegit, sed de humilibus et piscatoribus per quos sancta manifestaret, adsumpsit, ne doctrina caelestis, quae erat plena uirtutum, auxilio uideretur indigere uerborum."[61] Even in cases when discussion is useful, it does not itself provide a criterion of truth. The function of the inquiry at Chalcedon was to confirm what faith had already taught, and Leo's account of a discussion in a Roman synod concludes in the same vein: "eadem ergo, quae in sensum nostrum diuina inspiratione uenerunt, frequens etiam fratrum firmauit assensio."[62] A last difference between Leo's position on theological discussion and that of a thoroughgoing religious liberal is that for Leo such discussions can and ought to be

Bellarmine and against Bossuet, that it was not. Rather, Leo here "fait abstraction évidente de l'infallibilité." Even if it is appropriate to speak of such an act of abstraction being made in the fifth century, it remains the case that Leo has here approved of critical discussion of something which he himself had previously laid down as quite certain.

Also see the account of the proceedings of a Roman synod given in *PL*, LIV, 1193: "in synodali, ut diximus, coetu formam huiuscemodi consultationis accepimus, quam diligentius discutientes, pro uniuscuiusque sensu sollicita uoluimus ratione tractari, quo ad ueritatem, adhibita cognitione multorum, certius peruenire possemus."

60. "Hic conculcandae philosophiae opiniones, hic dissoluendae erant terrenae sapientiae uanitates." *Sermo* 82; *PL*, LIV, 424.

61. "... did not choose that all nations should be called to the illumination of faith by philosophers or by orators, who might serve for preaching the gospel, but he took up lowly fishermen, by whom he might show forth holy things, lest his heavenly teaching, which had every excellence, should seem to need help from language." To Leo of Thrace, Schwartz, *Chalcedon.*, p. 111; *PL*, LIV, 1149. In contrast with those who wish to bring it about that "quod maiore facundia defenditur uerius aestimetur," the pope insists that in Christ's gospel, "doctrina ueritatis sua luce manifestata est, nec quaeritur quid auribus placeat, ubi uerae fidei sufficit scire quis doceat." Schwartz, *Chalcedon.*, p. 111; *PL*, LIV, 1150. Pope Leo is fond of contrasting God's grace with both the wisdom and the merits of man. The spread of the faith was planned in such a way that "sola Dei gratia reuelaret quod comprehendere humana intelligentia non ualeret." *Sermo* 25; *PL*, LIV, 211. Also see *Sermones* 22 and 26; *PL*, LIV, 194 and 213; and *Sermo* 67, *PL*, LIV, 370: "ut mirabilior fieret gratia Dei, non secundum merita hominum, sed secundum multitudinem diutiarum sapientiae et scientiae dei misericorditer praeparata."

62. *PL*, LIV, 1193. An interesting variant reading is noted in *PL*: "eadem ergo, quae in somnis mihi diuina inspiratione...."

concluded. The invective against philosophy and rhetoric cited above is directed against those who wish to revive *extincta certamina:*

> nam si humanis persuasionibus semper disceptare sit liberum, numquam deesse poterunt qui ueritati audeant resultare et de mundanae sapientiae loquacitate confidere, cum hanc nocentissimam uanitatem quantum debeat fides et sapientia Christiana uitare, ex ipsa domini Iesu Christi institutione cognoscat, qui omnes nationes ad inluminationem fidei uocaturus non de philosophis aut de oratoribus . . . .[63]

In perfect accordance with the conception of religious peace and liberty referred to previously, Leo insists that "post legitimas et diuinitus inspiratas constitutiones uelle confligere non pacifici est animi, sed rebellis."[64]

Clearly, then, the determination of law—"true law," we may be tempted to say, falling in with the distinction between worldly peace and true peace, worldly freedom and true freedom—does not depend for Leo on human decision or on the results of deliberations guided solely by human wisdom. Not human approval but divine inspiration is the primary criterion for valid law. Leo's claim that, for the true belief in Christ's gospel, it suffices to know who teaches appears to mean that authority in the church belongs to those who speak under the inspiration of the Holy Spirit.[65] Christian rulers may so speak, church councils may so speak, the

63. ". . . for if it were always free to dispute among human opinions, there could never fail to be some who would dare to resist the truth and confide in the chattering of human wisdom, even though we know from the decision of the Lord Jesus Christ himself how much faith and Christian wisdom ought to avoid such noxious vanity, for he [did not choose] that all nations should be called to the illumination of faith by philosophers or by orators . . . ." Schwartz, *Chalcedon.*, pp. 110–111; *PL*, LIV, 1149.

64. "To want contention after legitimate and divinely inspired constitutions is not for a peaceful soul but a rebellious one." Schwartz, *Chalcedon.*, p. 110; *PL*, LIV, 1149. When we remember that Chalcedon was only a few years before this letter, and that many Christians had consistently refused to acknowledge the divine inspiration of its canons, *extincta certamina* must seem a premature phrase. It should be noted, however, that Leo was less dogmatically "Leonine" than his successors in responding to the Alexandrian resistance to Chalcedon. His "second tome," a letter to the new emperor, Leo of Thrace (Schwartz, *Chalcedon.*, pp. 113–119; *PL*, LIV, 1155–1190), makes no use of the offensive phrase, "*in* two natures," and, as noted in Labriolle *et al.*, *Histoire de l'Église*, IV, 282–283, condemns the Cyrillian formula, "one nature of the Incarnate word," only in a special sense. An especially marked place is also given to Alexandrian authorities in the collection of supporting texts that went with the letter.

65. E. Caspar (*Geschichte des Papsttums*, I, 554) regards "sufficit scire quis doceat" as equivalent to "Roma locuta, causa finita," an interpretation which Gelasius, too, may have accepted. It seems difficult to square this interpretation with the preceding phrase

papacy may so speak. But, in contrast with his successors, Leo does not insist that the judgments of any single power on earth be regarded as necessarily always coinciding with the Spirit's teaching. To an important extent, then, Leo's position is that there is no supreme authority in the church, if by supreme one means an authority whose determinations must be accepted as necessarily valid, to the complete exclusion of validity from all contrary determinations—if one holds, in other words, to a totalitarian conception of supreme authority. Given this estimate of his position, Leo's cooperative approach to others in authority appears as a matter of principle, not as a tactic of diplomatic style.[66] Leo was a powerful exponent of the authority, even the primacy, of his office, but there are good grounds for attributing to him an ecumenical rather than a papalist conception of that primacy.

In the last few pages we have been considering the problem of supreme religious authority as it arises within the juristic context of law and government. A further problem is posed by the relation of the juristic context itself to the rest of human existence. Is our life to be regarded as a process to be regulated by external standards or as a project to be carried out in view of values inherent in, or inherently attractive to, each man? The alternatives, again, are not mutually contradictory, but they lead to sharply contrasting moral philosophies. Let us ask, then, what significance

---

(see above, n. 61): "doctrina ueritatis [in Christ's gospel] sua luce manifestata est." It is true that Leo had special confidence in the doctrinal authority of the papacy. At one point, after referring to the Matthean commission, he asks (Schwartz, *Chalcedon.*, p. 102), "quis est nisi aut antichristus aut diabolus, qui pulsare audeat inexpugnabilem firmitatem." But compare this with Schwartz, *Chalcedon.*, p. 70; *PL*, LIV, 1038, where he is willing to take the line that if those opposed to the Chalcedonian definition would not accept his teaching, they should acknowledge the doctrine of Athanasius, Theophilus, and Cyril "cum quibus ita fidei nostrae forma concordat, ut in nullo a nobis discrepet, qui se illis consentire profitetur."

66. The opposite view is suggested by Grisar, *History of Rome and the Popes in the Middle Ages*, II, 59–60: "The Popes and their chancery rarely forgot, when writing to the sovereigns, to express their deep respect for the position, and their devotion to the persons, of the rulers. Such language was required by the laws of diplomatic intercourse and by the curial style, no less than by the dictates of Christianity and prudence.

"In cases where the Popes were forced to protest against the despotism or wrong committed by the Emperor, we may therefore expect to find stress laid on such good qualities as the ruler possessed. Pope Leo's admonitory letter to his Imperial namesake is an instance in point, particularly the clever introduction."

In marked contrast with this "political" interpretation, Stockmeier finds that Leo regards the emperor as having extremely important functions for and in the church. *Leo I. des Grossen Beurteilung der kaiserlichen Religionspolitik*, pp. 75–152. Stockmeier's "theological" interpretation seems much nearer the mark than Grisar's account.

Leo attached to the juristic aspect of human life. What would he have said, for example, to someone who insisted that there is a basic contrast between the "law" of Judaism (or of the Roman law courts) and the freedom of the Spirit found in the New Testament? What place would he give juristic theology in the context of theology *tout court?*

Little in Leo's writings bears on such questions directly. Contrasts between Mosaic law and Christian grace and truth are indeed frequently drawn in his sermons,[67] sometimes as involving a shift from harshness to leniency,[68] but more often as a difference between veiled foretelling and clear fulfillment (*revelata luce*).[69] In general, Leo does not regard the gospel as providing a warrant for laxness,[70] but it does seem to call for a shift from law to voluntarily observed discipline,[71] and Leo ascribes to the individual Christian both the responsibility and the power to weigh the actions of his life according to the standards of God's commandments.[72] Perhaps more important than these fragmentary passages, bearing on questions of law and liberty directly, are the theme and tone of the sermons in general. Leo's central subject is the supernatural restoration of man's fallen nature. On the one hand, human nature is fundamentally good, and its normal life is not marked by constraint. On the other hand, human nature is redeemed in the mystery of the Incarnation, not by the application of external sanctions. Leo has seldom been praised as a creative or subtle theologian,[73] but the vigorous spiritual tone of his

67. *Sermones* 51, 63, 69; *PL*, LIV, 311, 356, and 376–377. John 1:17 is also quoted in Epistle 16; *PL*, LIV, 701–702.

68. Christ's words reached the ears of his auditors quietly and freely when he preached the Sermon on the Mount, "ut per gratiae lenitatem remoueretur legis asperitas, et spiritus adoptionis auferret formidinem seruitutis." *Sermo* 95; *PL*, LIV, 461. Also see *Sermo* 63. *PL*, LIV, 356.

69. *Sermones* 20, 60, 63, 66, 75; *PL*, LIV, 188–189, 342–343, 356, 365–366, and 400–401.

70. "Euangelium gratiae uelamen legis tolleret, non instituta destrueret." *Sermo* 20; *PL*, LIV, 188. If it was right that there should be conformity to laws concerning the marriage of priests "etiam in ueteri Testamento . . . quanto magis sub reuelata iam gratia constituti, apostolicis debemus inseruiae preceptis." Epistle 12; *PL*, LIV, 659. Also see *Sermones* 15 and 63; *PL*, LIV, 175 and 356.

71. "Sicut ergo nemo est credentium . . . cui dona neganda sint gratiae, ita nemo est qui non sit Christianae debitor disciplinae: quia etsi remota est mysticae legis asperitas, voluntariae tamen obseruantiae creuit utilitas, dicente euangelista Joanne: 'Quia lex per Mosen data est, gratia autem et ueritas per Iesum Christum facta est.'" *Sermo* 63; *PL*, LIV, 356.

72. *Sermo* 49; *PL*, LIV, 303–304.

73. As has frequently been noted (for example in Labriolle *et al.*, *Histoire de l'Église*, IV, 220 n.), the Tome is not subtle or refined in doctrine. Its greatness lies in the effective

sermons and their nonpolitical content do not suggest that he regarded effective political power for the church as the one thing needful for humanity or Christianity.[74]

Did Leo have a distinctive position on the basic problems of religious authority, or should he be regarded as essentially a precursor of Gelasian papalism? There is no disputing that some of his statements can readily be developed in a Gelasian direction. However, others clearly invite development in different directions. Whether these various statements are all expressions of a single, coherent position is another question. An affirmative answer to this question has been defended in the last several pages. If it is substantially correct, the Leonine position may be characterized in the following terms. Instead of regarding the promotion of Christian orthodoxy as an essentially technical problem of gaining formal acceptance for papally determined doctrines, Leo recognized an important moral dimension to the task of establishing religious truth. He recognized the need for communication and mutual respect as well as dogmatic enlightenment. As was indicated earlier, he set no positive value on an indefinite tolerance of religious diversity. Furthermore, although he did not regard himself as having a right to demand obedience from the imperial authorities, he does not seem to have questioned *their* right to

---

manner in which doctrine is presented. "Man mag sie vom gelehrt-theologischen Standpunkt aus trivial nennen. . . . Aber man wird ihre Überzeugungskraft und ihre Lebensnähe nicht verkennen durfen. Das blies wie ein frischer Wind in die Nebelschwaden und stiess wider zu den evangelischen Urkunden vor, welche dem Blicke der in Wolken wandelnden philosophierenden Theologen des Ostens zu entschwinden drohten." Caspar, *Geschichte des Papsttums*, I, 481. Cf. A. Flick's remark on the papacy as a defender of the simple gospel-truth (n. 3 above).

74. "Dans les lettres des grands évêques de notre période, il est souvent difficile de distinguer le précepte du conseil, le législateur du docteur." Gaudemet, *L'Église dans l'Empire Romain*, p. 214. This seems markedly more true of Leo than of Gelasius. As Gaudemet points out (p. 415), the notion of universal *sollicitudo* is uppermost in Leo's conception of his office. "Plus que le pouvoir du chef, elle évoque les obligations du pasteur. Le juridisme romain cède devant les préceptes évangéliques et, au delà, les souvenirs bibliques." The whole difficulty is, however, that juristic supremacy and pastoral solicitude are not simple contraries. If the central contention of this essay is correct, then Leo's solicitude was quite compatible with his putting forth the idea of a juristic theology —but that idea need not be specified as an exclusive or papalist Petrinology, and in Leo it was not so specified. On the other hand, even if a papalist position is adopted, lack of pastoral care is not a direct consequence. Gelasius, for example, was renowned for his charitable activities among the poor ("Omnes fere pauperes ditans inops ipse moreretur," according to Dionysius Exiguus, in Thiel, *Epistolae*, p. 287; and see the life in L. Duchesne [ed.], *Liber Pontificalis*, Vol. I ([Paris, 1955], 256 n. 6). Neither law nor care is a simple idea.

enforce orthodoxy upon their subjects.[75] Nevertheless, even when these things are taken into account, Leo comes much closer than Gelasius to regarding the political community as a framework within which orthodoxy has the right to flourish in accordance with its own principles, rather than as an instrument which ought to be at the sole disposal of truth in its struggle against error.

It may be of interest to note here that neither papalism nor the propitiationism of the Emperor Zeno was a success in this period. This is evident in the case of Zeno's policy, for later emperors and their patriarchs felt constrained to make peace with Rome, while the Monophysites and Nestorians of Egypt and the East were never really reconciled with the empire, either religiously or politically. But it can also be argued that the Gelasian policy was not notably successful. In the West it was unnecessary, in the East futile. Its victory in the center of the empire, after a schism of eighteen years, has perhaps seemed more impressive to western churchmen and historians than in fact it was.[76] On balance, assuming even that the formulations of the truths of the Christian faith endorsed by the papacy were uniquely correct, and accepting as valid the papal aim of obtaining the widest possible acceptance for those truths, it is difficult to avoid the judgment that the end of the fifth century was a time of profound ecumenical failure.

75. The distinction may be of slight practical importance when the emperor is eager to enforce orthodoxy, as Pulcheria and Marcian in fact were. It would seem to be of great theoretical importance nevertheless.

76. It is not easy to recount this as a truimph of truth over error. The *Henoticon* was not literally heretical (see above, n. 24). Whether the disciplinary grounds actually given for Acacius's excommunication (Felix to Acacius, in Schwartz, "Acacian. Schisma," pp. 6–7; *PL*, LVIII, 921–923) justified the act and the policy following from it, is another question. Even in Rome, Gelasius found those who doubted whether separation from half the church was necessary over a dead man who had not been convicted, or even accused, of heresy (see Labriolle *et al.*, *Histoire de l'Église*, IV, 306–307).

Discussions of the schism with Constantinople generally assume that the theological opposition between Rome and *Alexandria*, at least, was ultimate. Gibbon (n. 5 above) is not the only one to doubt this. Duchesne remarks, a-propos the definition reached at Chalcedon, that Leo's "was not the only possible formulation of orthodoxy: there was another, Cyril's to which people were accustomed. . . . [In the Chalcedonian definition,] Cyril, the true Cyril, had been sacrificed to Leo." *Early History of the Christian Church*, III, 317. As to the situation later on, W. H. C. Frend has given a convincingly orthodox exposition of the leading Monophysite theologian, Severus of Antioch, in his Birkbeck lectures for 1968, to be published in the near future.

It would be strange if there were not deep differences between the Roman and Monophysite theologies, but it has not yet been shown that the two viewpoints were necessarily incompatible.

Would Leo's approach have succeeded any better in the circumstances? One would like to think so, yet the possibility must be recognized that the "hard line" taken by Felix and Gelasius, extreme as it was, offered the best hope of saving what proved to be an impossible situation. There is certainly no a priori guarantee that the holders of any two alternative creeds or ideologies will find it possible to exist together. The question of whether the religious differences within and among the churches of Rome, Alexandria, and Constantinople *had* to eventuate in bitter denunciation and loss of communion is at least grossly similar to the question of whether the theological and other differences among Christians now *must* make Christian unity impossible today. Perhaps the success of the churches in their present quest for unity will shed light on the possibilities of the fifth century situation, just as an understanding of the struggles of that period might prove of value now.

How did the shift from Leo to Gelasius come about? If the line taken in this essay is correct, we are not confronted here with a process of natural development. Although the positions of Leo and Gelasius are by no means contradictory, we have found reason to regard them as qualitatively very different. How, then, is the change from one to the other to be accounted for? To an extent, differences of persons and circumstances may be called on for explanation. To an extent, the persistence of un-resolved conflicts accounts for the change of papal approach. After giving these causes a hearing, I should like to suggest, however, that a sufficient account of the development of Gelasian papalism requires appeal to a distinctively religious causal factor.

Leo, a Roman through and through (although apparently he was born in Tuscany),[77] dealing for the most part with emperors who were de-scendants of Theodosius the Great and were themselves orthodox, saintly, or strong-willed, may have had little need or inclination to espouse an exclusive doctrine of papal primacy. Gelasius, an African,[78] had to deal with secular authorities whose religious policies showed a somewhat desperate responsiveness to the demands made upon them by others. The political turmoil in the West between the pontificates of Leo and Gelasius, turmoil which was in sharp contrast with the stability of the papacy in the same period, must also have had an influence. The Roman pontiffs,

---

77. Duchesne (ed.), *Liber Pontificalis*, I, 238.

78. *Ibid.*, pp. 255–256. Duchesne's assessment is often quoted: "Il a de Tertullien et le goût de la controverse et les talents du controversiste: le raisonnement rigoureux, impitoyable, la verve, la vigueur, et aussi l'âpreté. Intraitable par devoir, il l'était aussi par nature." *L'Église au VIe Siècle*, pp. 12–13.

fortified by Leo's personal example,[79] could plausibly regard themselves as rightful or promising leaders of Christian civilization; nor would it be unnatural for a papal ideology to emerge magnifying the authority of the see of Peter, demanding that doctrines sanctioned by it be universally promulgated, and ready to condemn strenuously any willingness to consider alternative doctrinal formulations. Such a position might also be thought of as a natural reaction to the eastern churches' persistent failure to accept doctrines wholeheartedly endorsed by the papacy. We have seen that even Leo regarded the Christological struggles over Nestorius and Eutyches as definitively ended by the Council of Chalcedon. All the more, then, must his successors have felt that further contention could only arise from rebellious intentions. Having identified its opponents as aggressors against the peace of the church, the papacy took a militant line against them.

It would be rash to deny the influence of such factors, but are they enough? After all, it was Leo, not Gelasius, who was forced to intercede with barbarian invaders for the safety of his city. And Leo's emperors, though Theodosian, were weak, while his own prestige was consistently high. Surely, he *could* have advanced a more exclusive doctrine of papal authority than he in fact did—if he had wished to do so. On the other hand, the history of the *Eastern* Empire to the end of the century was not such as to diminish respect for it. Granting that there was a power vacuum in the West, why did the papacy attempt to fill it, instead of seeking help from traditional sources? As to the frustrating persistence of doctrinal differences, did it not also become increasingly obvious that the Monophysites were intensely and sincerely attempting to follow the teaching of Alexandrian theologians—chiefly Cyril—whom the papacy itself regarded as orthodox? In these circumstances, was it not easy for the papacy to see that assertions of its own authority were much likelier to produce resentment than religious peace? What basis was there for expecting or demanding a better result?

If the Gelasian conception of authority is as striking a departure as I have suggested, may it not be necessary to appeal to a deeper *sort* of cause in order to account for it? It seems possible to me that papalism depends for much of its strength on a state of religious consciousness expressed by Leo the Great, not in his religio-political thought, but in the chief theological concern of his pontificate, the dogma of the Incarnation.

My suggestion is that someone who comes to accept a conjunction of completely human and completely divine natures in Christ will be more

79. Caspar notes (*Geschichte des Papsttums*, I, 463) the use made of Leo after his death.

ready than before to take seriously the possibility that in other cases, also, divinity is in some way authoritatively present in the decisions of a single, completely human being. Now precisely this conjunction of natures was proclaimed in the Leonine definition of the Incarnation. One would expect, therefore, that those who were most influenced by this formulation would be most inclined to conceive of the structure of church government in terms of implementing absolutely correct, divinely given doctrinal and moral teachings emanating from a single human source. Such an inclination, I submit, may have been the deepest source of Gelasian papalism.

In order to bring this hypothesis into focus, we may imagine alternative views of spiritual authority which would appear related to alternative theologies of the Incarnation. Suppose one held that in Christ humanity was taken up into divinity in such a way that the result was a single, unique nature. Would it not be natural, given this Christological base, to look for absolute authority in exceptional persons, rather than in ordinary mortals? On the other hand, suppose that one believed in such a sharp distinction between the humanity and divinity of Christ that it was difficult to think of dealing with both the divine and the human *at once*. Would it not be natural, given this Christological base, to be skeptical about the absolute authority of any merely human being at any one time —would it not be difficult, in other words, to regard a man with whom one was now confronted as divinely correct in what he taught and commanded? I do not know to what extent the Monophysite and Nestorian Christologies have actually been associated with these attitudes toward spiritual authority. Certainly other factors would enter into one's views on such matters. Nevertheless, it seems plausible to suppose, if only on the testimony of the blood shed in them, that the doctrinal struggles of the fourth and fifth centuries involved oppositions between extremely different views of reality.[80] If this was indeed the case, it would not be at all surprising to find that the acceptance of a certain doctrinal position had consequences for the believer's approach to many other problems, including those of political and spiritual authority.[81]

80. Duchesne mentions, cautiously, an estimate that as many as ten thousand deaths were involved in the expulsion of a Monophysite bishop from the see of Alexandria by imperial forces near the end of Leo's pontificate. *Early History of the Christian Church*, III, 336.

81. There is no need to posit a religious principle favoring social and political discord, but it is a peculiar sort of propitiationism to insist that religious outlooks ought to be socially and politically concordant. McNeill is more enlightened here than Gibbon, when he refers to the "authentic theological anxiety" of the fifth century (n. 5 above), but it is not clear from his account what criteria our anxiety must meet in order to qualify as authentically religious.

I do not suggest that there is a simple logical connection between acceptance of the dogma of the Incarnation and acceptance of a particular human being as the perfect embodiment of divine authority. It could be argued that the acceptance of Jesus as divine and human precludes, rather than encourages, the ascription of absolute authority to anyone else. At the very least, one would need particular reasons, in addition to the dogma itself, for attributing such authority to any specific person. But it is at this point, of course, that a defender of papal authority can refer to the " *Tu es Petrus* " passage in Matthew. The Petrine commission would thus be analogous in function to the personal union of the two natures in Christ. The next step is the establishment of a connection between Peter and later popes. Both in the interpretation of the gospel passage and in establishing · a connection between Peter and his successors, there is a use for juristic concepts, although nonjuristic respect for the papacy must also enter in. What I have meant to propose is the possible importance of a specifically religious development as a *precondition for* the development of papalist ideology in even its juristic aspect. The proposal could be stated this way, as a variation on Ullmann's descending thesis: the dogma of the Incarnation may be taken to imply that absolute authority *has* descended from above, that it subsists in conjunction with an entirely human being, that, consequently, decisive relations of authority may obtain on a *horizontal* level, so that the holder of authority need not be regarded as ontologically above us in order for him to merit all possible respect.[82] On this view, Christian political thought is decisively marked off from every other kind of politics by the possibility of encountering a person who is merely human and yet embodies divine authority, and this line of demarcation becomes explicit with the promulgation of the Leonine-Chalcedonian doctrine of the Incarnation.

82. On this interpretation of the religious basis of papal claims to absolute authority, it was unnecessary for Innocent III to claim to be "minor Deo, sed maior homine" (*Sermo* 2; *PL*, CCXVII, 658), although even expressions of this sort need not be taken as denials of the ordinary humanity of the pope. See W. Ullmann, *Principles of Government and Politics in the Middle Ages*, p. 51.

CHARLES MARTEL, MOUNTED SHOCK COMBAT, THE STIRRUP, AND FEUDALISM

Bernard S. Bachrach

University of Minnesota

CHARLES MARTEL, MOUNTED SHOCK COMBAT, THE STIRRUP, AND FEUDALISM

The classic theory of feudal beginnings is that put forth by Heinrich Brunner in' 1887. Though Brunner's conclusions have been modified both by the arguments of his critics and by the insights of his defenders, the broad outlines of his theory are still widely accepted. Brunner argued that the overwhelming number of warriors in the Merovingian armies were half-naked Frankish infantrymen who served because of the primal teutonic duty of all free men to bear arms. Charles Martel, however, is alleged to have needed large numbers of horsemen to stem the Muslim advance in Gaul; therefore, he is said to have confiscated vast amounts of church land and granted these estates to his warriors so that they would have the means to support themselves as cavalrymen. The grants were to be held by these retainers as long as the stipulated service was performed. To quote a recent scholar: "The ancient custom of swearing allegiance to a leader (vassalage) was fused with the granting of an estate (benefice), and the result was feudalism."[1]

1. Heinrich Brunner, "Der Reiterdienst und die Anfänge des Lehnwesens," in *Zeitschrift der Savigny-Stiftung für Rechtsgeschichte, Germanistische Abtheilung*, VIII (1887), 1–38; reprinted in Brunner, *Forschungen zur Geschichte des deutschen und französischen Rechts* (Stuttgart, 1894), pp. 39–74. All references to Brunner's article are to the former edition. There have been many modifications of Brunner's arguments. For example, where he saw the rapid development of horsemen under the early Carolingians leading to numerical preponderance, his defenders have been willing to admit that horsemen were not numerically preponderant but merely the tactically decisive arm of his forces. On this see Lynn T. White, Jr., *Medieval Technology and Social Change* (Oxford, 1962), p. 5, and the works he cites on pp. 137–138. For the quotation see *ibid.*, p. 5.

The wide acceptance of Brunner's thesis is illustrated by Carl Stephenson, "The Origin and Significance of Feudalism," *American Historical Review*, XLVI (1941), 788–794; for later acceptance see e.g., White, *Medieval Technology*, p. 3.

Even medievalists who reject Brunner's very narrow definition of feudalism believe that significant changes in military tactics and organization were brought about by Charles Martel. R. S. Hoyt, *Europe in the Middle Ages*, 2nd ed. (New York, 1966), p. 121, a standard textbook, sums up the matter most succinctly: "Most historians have concluded that the outcome of this battle [Poitiers] taught Charles the value of having his own cavalry arm—a lesson whose immediate military results were to have profound consequences, ultimately, for the social structure of Europe." Cf. Walter Goffart, *The Le Mans Forgeries* (Cambridge, Mass., 1966), p. 8 n. 11.

Although Brunner's arguments that the war against the Muslims inspired Charles's revolution in military tactics and organization have been found wanting, the classic theory has been given new impetus by Lynn T. White, Jr., who has suggested an even more imaginative cause for the feudalization of Francia. White argues that mounted shock combat was made possible by the stirrup and that the introduction of the latter into Francia in the late seventh or early eighth century was the catalyst for a revolution in military tactics and for the development of feudalism. It is White's contention that Charles Martel probably recognized the usefulness of the stirrup and about 732 began to reform the military forces of Francia. Thus the half-naked levies of Frankish free men who are alleged to have characterized the military of the Merovingian era were replaced as the tactically decisive arm of Charles's forces by heavily armed horsemen who relied upon mounted shock combat and served as feudal retainers. White writes: "The Man on Horseback, as we have known him during the past millenium, was made possible by the stirrup, which joined man and steed into a fighting organism. Antiquity imagined the Centaur; the early Middle Ages made him the master of Europe." [2]

White supports the argument that cavalry using mounted shock combat was the decisive arm of Charles Martel's forces after the battle of Poitiers with three pieces of literary evidence. Following Brunner, he

2. White, *Medieval Technology*, pp. 1–38, 135–153. The acceptance of White's view of the importance of the stirrup to the early Carolingians is particularly noteworthy. The reviews in *Speculum*, XXXIX (1964), 360, and *American Historical Review*, LXVIII (1962), 93–94, by Marshall Clagett and Lynn Thorndike, respectively, leave White's arguments on the stirrup and mounted shock combat virtually unchallenged. Joseph R. Strayer, *Feudalism* (Princeton, N.J., 1965), p. 19; A. R. Lewis, *Emerging Medieval Europe A.D. 400–900* (New York, 1967), pp. 56, 59, 97; Jeffery Russell, *Medieval Civilization* (New York, 1968), pp. 147, 197; and Norman Cantor, *Medieval History*, 2nd ed. (London, 1969), pp. 218–219, all find the stirrup an important element in the development of heavy cavalry under Charles Martel and his successors.

For different views, see P. Sawyer and R. Hilton, "Technical Determinism: the stirrup and the plough," *Past and Present*, XXIV (1963), 90–100, who challenge the methodology White employs in evaluating his evidence; and J. D. A. Ogilvy, "The Stirrup and Feudalism," in *University of Colorado Studies*, X (1966), 1–13, who questions White's concept of mounted shock combat and its uses.

White's reliance on M. Baudot, "Localisation et datation de la première victoire remportée par Charles Martel contre les Musulmans," *Mémoires et documents publiés par la Société de l'École des Chartes*, XII, no. i (1955), 93–105, for setting the date of the battle of Poitiers in 733 is brought into question by the researches of M. Rouche, "Les Aquitans ont-ils trahi avant la bataille de Poitiers?" *Le Moyen Age*, LXXIV (1968), 5–26, who concludes from an exhaustive study of the Arabic sources that the battle did in fact take place in 732.

points out that in 758 Pepin changed the Saxon tribute from cattle to horses. He implies that Pepin did this to secure a supply of mounts for his cavalry.[3] In 748, however, Pepin took a tribute of 500 cows from the Saxons. This neglected evidence raises the question why, if the military revolution had been under way for more than a decade and a half in 748, were horses not taken from the Saxons in that year. In addition, the 300 horses taken in 758, while valuable (perhaps even worth as much as 2,100 solidi), would hardly be sufficient to support a great innovation in tactics; on the other hand, even a mayor or king who needed horses only for his household could always use 300 of them.[4]

Again following Brunner, White argues: "In 755 the Marchfield, the traditional muster of the Frankish army, was transferred to May, presumably because the number of cavalry had become so large that more forage was needed than was available in March." [5] The very existence of the "Marchfield," i.e., a traditional muster on the first of March, is a subject of scholarly debate. Many modern scholars as well as at least one important medieval observer, Hincmar of Rheims, who very probably knew more about the Franks than we know, contend that there was no Marchfield but a "field of Mars" or general muster for war which might be held at any time of the year.[6]

Finally, White follows Brunner in arguing that cavalry came to dominate the armies of Francia sometime before the battle of the Dyle in 891. The annalist of Fulda is alleged to have written concerning this battle: "'the Franks are unused to fighting on foot.'" [7] The *Annales Fuldenses* for 891, however, read on this point: ". . . Francis pedetemptim certare

---

3. White, *Medieval Technology*, p. 3.

4. *Fredegarii Chronicorum Liber Quartus cum Continuationibus*, ed. and trans., J. M. Wallace-Hadrill (London, 1960); hereafter references to Book IV are *Fred.*, and to the continuations *Fred. con't. Fred. con't.*, chap. 31: ". . . iure Francorum sese ut antiquitus mos fuerat subdiderunt et ea tributa quae Chlothario quondam prestiterant plenissima solutione ab eo tempore deinceps esse reddituros promiserunt." *Fred.*, IV, 74: "Quinnentas vaccas inferendalis annis singolis a Chlothario seniore censiti reddebant, quod a Dagoberto cassatum est." F. Kurze (ed.), *Annales Regni Francorum, Monumenta Germaniae Historica* (cited hereafter as *M.G.H.*), *SS in us. schol.* (Hanover, 1895): "DCCLVIII. Pippinus rex in Saxoniam ibat, et firmitates Saxonum per virtutem introivit in loco, qui dicitur Sitnia, et multae strages factae sunt in populo voluntates eius faciendum et honores in placito suo praesentandum usque in equos CCC per singulos annos." For the value of the horses see below, p. 60 n. 43.

5. White, *Medieval Technology*, pp. 3–4, 136–137.

6. *Ibid.*, 136–137, White discusses some of the pertinent literature. Cf. J. M. Wallace-Hadrill, *The Long-Haired Kings* (London, 1962), pp. 103, 154.

7. White, *Medieval Technology*, p. 3.

inusitatum est. . . . ." *Pedetemptim* does not mean "on foot" but to move forward slowly, step by step. It is essential for a proper understanding of the battle of the Dyle and the campaign of which it is a part to realize that the emphasis of *pedetemptim* is on the gradualness or slowness of the advance and not on its pedestrian nature. The swampy terrain at the Dyle made it impossible for Arnulf's forces to charge rapidly either on horseback or on foot through the morass in the face of a strongly positioned enemy. This is what the Franci were unused to doing and Arnulf seems to have been worried that their morale was not equal to such a challenge.[8]

The slow and gradual emphasis of *pedetemptim* is an accurate description of the tactical demands of the situation; tactically *pedetemptim* fits the context. Stylistically this is also the case for it is contrasted with *celeriter* in the previous sentence in which it is indicated how quickly Arnulf's

8. *Annales Fuldenses*, 891, ed. and trans. Reinhold Rau, *Ausgewählte Quellen zur deutschen Geschichte des Mittelalters* (Berlin, 1960): "Arnolfus ergo rex ob hos ulciscendum in Nordmannos cum Francis Alamannico exercitu inutile secum assumpto iter arripuit. Sed Alamanni quasi egrotantes a rege domum relapsi sunt; ipse cum Francis ad occidentem prospere profectus est. Nordmanni devasta ex maxima parte Hlotharici regni regione prope fluvio Dyla loco, qui dicitur Lovonnium, sepibus more eorum municione septa seduri consederunt. Ex inproviso enim rex et exercitus prevenere ad eundem locum. Transito igitur celeriter eodem fluvio nec mora meditatum est proelium applicari. Cunctanti namque regi, ne tam valida manus perclitaretur, qui interiacente palude ex parte una, ex altera circumfluente ripa non donatur facultas equitibus aggredi, oculis, cogitione, consilio huc illuc pervagabatur, quid consilii opus sit, quia Francis pedetemptim certare inusitatum est, anxie meditans, tandem heros primores Francorum advocans sic alloquitur patienter: 'Viri, Deum recolentes et semper sub Dei gratia patriam tuendo fuistis invincibiles; inspirate animis, si ab inimicis quandoquidem more paganissimo fuerentibus pium sanguinem parentum vestrorum effusum vindicari recolitis et sacra sub honore sanctorum creatoris vestri templa eversa iam in patria vestra cernitis, ministros eciam Dei summo gradu consistentes prostratos videtis. Nunc, milites, agite, ipsos sceleris factores ante oculos habentes, me primum equo descendentem, signa manu praeferentem sequinimi; non nostram, sed eius, quo omnia potest, contumeliam vindicantes inimicos nostros in Dei nominie aggredimur!' His incitati dictis, omnibus, senis et iuvenibus, par voluntas et audatia pedestre bellum aggredere datur; prius regem flagitantes, ut equitando eos procuraret, ne quid eius pugnantibus a tergo insidiis inimicorum timendum sit. Clamor a christianis in celum attollitur, nec minus pagani more suo clamantes, signa horribilia per castra movebantur. Evaginatis gladiis ex utraque parte, ut lapis ferro, in invicem ad invicem occursum est. Erat autem ibi gens fortissima inter Nordmannos Danorum, quae numquam antea in aliqua munitione vel capta vel superata auditur. Dure certatum est; sed non in diu subveniente gratia Dei victoria ad christianos concessit. Nordmanni fuge praesidium querentes, flumen, quod antea eis a tergo pro muro habebatur, pro morte occurrebat. Nam instantibus ex altera parte cede christianis coacti sunt in flumen praecipitari, coacervatim se per manus et colla cruribusque complectentes in profundum per centena vel milia numero mergebantur, ita ut cadaveribus interceptum alveum amnis siccum appareret."

forces arrived at the scene of the battle. It is unlikely, in addition, that the author of the *Annales* used *pedetemptim* in a corrupted sense to mean "on foot" since he knew the correct word *pedester*, and used it in the very next sentence.[9]

The annalist of Fulda's description of the battle of the Dyle indicates that Arnulf's mounted Franci pursued the Northmen to their fortified camp on the swampy banks of the Dyle and found that to engage them they had to dismount and slog step by step through the muck under a hail of missiles. Arnulf wondered if his troops would endure such an ordeal, one to which they were unaccustomed. Nevertheless the Franci advanced bravely, took the enemy position, and won the day.[10]

Even if, however, one were to accept the conclusions of Brunner concerning the Saxon tribute of 758, the Marchfield of 755, and the battle of the Dyle, they do not convincingly support the thesis that Charles Martel, who died in 741, created a revolution in military tactics.[11]

A detailed review of Charles Martel's post-733 military campaigns suggests serious reservations as to whether heavily armed horsemen engaging in mounted shock combat were in fact the decisive element of his armies. In 734 Charles led a naval expedition against the Frisians.[12] Concerning Charles's campaigns of 735 and 736 there is no tactical information,[13] but in 737 he laid siege to the fortified city of Avignon. Battering rams were brought into action and rope ladders were used to scale the walls. The city was taken. Charles then moved his forces against Narbonne and engines for its reduction were brought into place. Charles's forces also besieged the camp of Iussef ibn Abd ar Rahman by constructing a breastwork around it. Shortly thereafter Charles led his troops against an army led by Ukba ibn al Hadjdjadj, who was advancing to relieve his

9. *Ibid.*

10. *Ibid.* Cf. Eugen von Frauenholz, *Das Heerwesen der germanischen Frühzeit, des Frankenreiches un des ritterlichen Zeitalters* (Munich, 1935), p. 65, and Charles Oman, *A History of the Art of War in the Middle Ages*, 2nd ed., 2 vols. (London, 1924), I, 96.

11. The additional evidence examined by Brunner shows only that Carolingian armies, in the time of Charlemagne and later, occasionally fought and traveled on horseback.

12. *Fred. con't.*, chap. 17: ". . . Princeps audacter navale evectione praeparat; certatim alto mare ingressus navium copia adunata Unistrachia et Austrachia insulas Frigionum penetravit, super Bordine fluvio castra ponens." It should be noted that Charles's contemporaries regarded his efforts against the Frisians the most significant of his career. This point is brought out by White, *Medieval Technology*, p. 12. For the campaigns of Charles see T. Breysig (ed.), *Jahrbucher des fränkischen Reichs, 714–741* (Leipzig, 1869), *passim*.

13. *Fred. con't.*, chaps. 15, 18.

compatriot. On the swampy banks of the Berre in the valley of Corbières he defeated the Arabs, and those who tried to escape by boat or by swimming were cut down by Charles's men who took to boats in a successful effort to prevent the survivors' escape. In the same year Charles's troops had to retake Avignon.[14] In 738 Charles led a force against the Saxons, but no tactical details concerning this effort survive.[15] Charles's campaigns after the battle of Poitiers are imperfectly known. There is information about a naval invasion of the Frisian Islands, sieges of Avignon, Narbonne, and a military camp, and a battle on the swampy banks of the Berre which culminated in the use of light river craft. From these surviving examples, it seems fair to conclude, however, that heavily armed horsemen engaged in mounted shock combat were not the decisive arm of Charles's forces.

A detailed review of the campaigns of Pepin and Carloman show them to have been very like those of their father, Charles. In 741 Pepin and Carloman defeated a force at Bourges and then besieged and took the fortress of Loches. In the autumn of the same year they went against a group of Alamanni on the Danube. There is no tactical information con-

14. *Ibid.*, chap. 20: "Quique praepropere ad eandem urbem pervenientes tentoria instruunt, undique ipsud oppidum et suburbana praeoccupant, munitissimam civitatem obsedunt, aceiem instruunt, donec insecutus vir belligerator Carlus praedictam urbem adgreditur, muros circumdat, castra ponit, obsidionem coacervat . . . cum strepitu hostium et sonitum tubarum, cum machinis et restium funibus super muros et edium moenia inruunt, urbem munitissimam ingredientes succendunt, hostes inimicos suorum capiunt, interficientes trucidant atque prosternent et in sua dicione efficaciter restituunt . . . Carlus intrepidus Rodanum fluvium cum exercitu suo transiit, Gotorum fines penetravit, usque Narbonensem Galliam peraccessit, ipsam urbem celeberrimam atque metropolim eorum obsedit, super Adice fluvio munitionem in girum in modum arietum instruxit, regem Sarracinorum nomine Athima cum satellitibus suis ibidem reclusit castraque metatus est unidque. Haec audientes maiores natu et principes Sarracinorum, qui commorabantur eo tempore in regione Spaniarum, coadunato exercito hostium, cum alio rege Amormacha nomine adversus Carlum viriliter armati consurgunt, praeparantur ad proelium. Contra quos praefatus vir Carlus dux triumphator, super fluvium Byrra et vale Corbaria palatio occurrit. Illisque mutuo confligentibus Sarracini devicti atque prostrati, cernentes regem eorum interfectum in fugam lapsi terga verterunt; qui evaserant cupientes navale evectione evadere, in stagnum maris natantes, namque sibimet mutuo conatu insiliunt. Mox Franci cum navibus et iaculis armaturiis super eos insiliunt suffocantesque in aquis interimunt. . . . Urbes famosissimas Namausum, Agatem hac Biterris, funditus muros et moenia destruens igne subposito concremavit, suburbana et castra illius regionis vastavit." See also *Fred. con't.*, chap. 21. E. Lévi-Provençal, *Histoire de l'espagne musulmane*, 2nd ed., I (Paris, 1950), 63.

15. *Fred. con't.*, chap. 19.

cerning the victory at Bourges or the Alaman campaign.[16] In the winter of 743 the brothers defeated a Bavarian force on the banks of the Lech at Apfeldorf near Epfach. Pepin and Carloman led their troops through the marshy terrain surrounding the Bavarians' camp. There was no causeway and the unsuspecting enemy were caught by surprise and defeated.[17] Pepin led a force of picked men into the Swabian Alps and drove Duke Theudebald from his rocky retreat in 744.[18] Concerning the campaigns of the following year against the Gascons and the Alamanni there are no data on tactics available. In 748 Pepin used Wends and Frisians to fight the Saxons.[19] He led a large force across the river Inn and prepared river craft for a campaign against the Bavarians in 749.[20] The campaigns of Pepin and Carloman yield a siege at Loches, a winter battle in the swamps on the banks of the Lech, a sortie into the Swabian Alps, and preparations for a river campaign in Bavaria. Of the actions about which information survives, none gives the slightest hint that heavily armed horsemen engaged in mounted shock combat were the decisive arm of the armies of Charles Martel's sons, his successors as mayors of the palace.

Soon after becoming King, Pepin resumed his military activities. He sent a force to invest the fortified city of Narbonne in 752.[21] The following

16. *Ibid.*, chap. 25: ". . . Lucca castrum dirigunt atque funditus subvertunt, custodes illius castri capiunt. . . ." For Pepin's and Carloman's campaigns see H. Hahn, *Jahrbücher des fränkischen Reichs, 741–752* (Berlin, 1863), *passim.*

17. *Fred. con't.*, chap. 26: ". . . dederunt per loca deserta et palustria, ubi pons transiunde nullatenus adherat; nocteque inruentes divisis exercitibus eos inprovisos occupaverunt, commissoque proelio praedictus dux Odilo ceso exercitu suo vix cum paucis turpiter ultra Igne fluvium fugiendo evasit."

18. *Ibid.*, chap. 27: ". . . Pippinus cum virtute exercitus sui ab obsidione Alpiium turpiter expulit fugientem, revocatoque sibi loci ducato victor ad propria remeavit."

19. *Ibid.*, chaps. 28, 29, 31.

20. *Ibid.*, chap. 32: ". . . memoratus princeps super ripam Igni castra metatus, navale proelium praeparavit qualiter eos ad internitionem persequeretur."

21. B. von Simson (ed.), *Annales Mettenses priores* (hereafter cited as *Ann. Mett. Prior.*), 752, *M.G.H., SS. in us. schol.* (Hanover, 1895). Cf. E. A. Freeman, *Western Europe in the Eighth Century and Onward* (London, 1904), p. 108 n. 2. Although the *Annals of Metz* are somewhat garbled on this point, a siege of Narbonne at this time seems to have been consistent with Pepin's position. He had received the cities of Nîmes, Maguelone, Agde, and Béziers from the Gothic chief Ansemundus in 752 (G. Pertz (ed.), *Chronicon Moissiacensi* [hereafter cited as *Chron. Moiss.*], *M.G.H., Scr.* [Hanover, 1826], I, 294). Pepin had just become king and an attack on the Muslim-held Narbonne would seem to have been the appropriate gesture to solidify his position with the Christians in the area. The failure of the siege at this time seems to have been due to the Muslims' ability to supply Narbonne from the sea. For Pepin's reign see L. Oelsner, *Jahrbücher des fränkischen Reichs unter könig Pippin* (Leipzig, 1891), *passim.*

year he invaded Saxony and attacked a castrum on Mt. Iuberg.[22] Then in 755 and 756 he invaded Italy and his armies stormed Lombard fortifications on both occasions. Pavia was besieged by Pepin's forces and surrendered in the campaign of 756.[23] The next year Pepin sent another force to invest Narbonne.[24] He invaded Saxon territory in 758 and although no castra are mentioned, the sources do note that he overcame minor fortifications.[25] In 759 Pepin seems to have taken personal command of forces which had been besieging Narbonne during the preceding two years. Narbonne fell to the Carolingians in 759, and Pepin turned his attention to the rest of Aquitaine.[26] He besieged the fortress of Bourbon in the district of Bourges in 761, and after it fell he invested Clermont in the Auvergne.[27] The following year, with elaborate preparation, Pepin laid siege to and reduced the fortified city of Bourges. From there he went on to take the fortress of Thouars.[28] Pepin spent the remainder of his

22. *Annales Regni Francorum*, 753, and F. Kurze (ed.), *Annales qui dicunter Einhardi* (cited hereafter *Ann. q. d. Einhardi*), 753, *M.G.H., SS. in us. schol.* (Hanover, 1895). The former reads: "Hildegarius episcopus occisus est a Saxonibus in castro, quod dicitur Iuberg." See also *Fred. con't.*, chap. 35.

23. *Fred. con't.*, chap. 37: "Castra metatus est undique, omnia quae in giro fuit vastans partibus Italie maxime igne concremavit . . . castra Langobardorum omnia deripuit. . . ."Also chap. 38: "Rex Pippinus . . . partibus Italiae usque ad Ticinum iterum accessit et totam regionem illam fortiter devastans et circa muros Ticini utraque parte fixit tentoria. . . ." *Ann. q. d. Einhardi*, 756: ". . . Pippinus rex . . . cum exercitu Italiam intravit et Heistulfum in Papia civitate se includentem obsedit. . . ."

24. G. Pertz (ed.), *Annales Guelferbytani* and *Annales Nazariani*, 756 [757], *M.G.H., Scr.* (Hanover, 1826), I, 29: "Franci quieverunt, accepto custodes directos ad Arbonam." Cf. Freeman, *Western Europe*, pp. 227 ff.

25. *Ann. q. d. Einhardi*, 758: ". . . et quam is Saxonibus validissime resistentibus et munitiones suas tuentibus. . . ."

26. *Ann. Mett. Prior.*, 757-759; *Chron. Moiss.*, 759: "Franci Narbonam obsident." Freeman, *Western Europe*, p. 227 n. 1, seems to be accurate up to his denial of the campaign of 752. The entire effort may have begun with a siege in 752 and continued with harassment until 757 when serious operations were again undertaken which culminated in the fall of Narbonne in 759.

27. *Fred. con't.*, chap. 42: ". . . veniens Ligeris fluvium transmeato ad castrum cuius nomen est Burbone in pago Bitorivo pervenit. Cumque in giro castra posuisset, subito a Francis captus atque succensus est. . . . Usque urbem Arvernam cum omni exercitu veniens, Claremonte castro captum atque succesum bellando cepit. . . ."

28. *Ibid.*, chap. 43: ". . . cum universa multitudine gentis Francorum Bitoricas venit, castra metatusque est undique et omnia quae in giro fuit vastavit. Circumsepsit urbem munitionem fortissimam, ita ut nullus egredi ausus fuisset aut ingredi potuisset, cum machinis et omni genere armorum, circumdedit ea vallo. Multis vulneratis pluerisque interfectis fractisque muris cepit urbem. . . . Inde cum omni exercitu Francorum usque ad castro qui vocatur Toartius veniens, cumque in giro castra posuisset. . . ."

valry to Charles Martel. White argues that the traditional infantry
ons of the Franks disappeared in the eighth century and were
ced by a "longsword for horsemen" and a winged spear, the "novel
n" of which " is intelligible in terms of the new style of mounted
k combat with the lance at rest." [33] The inference that infantrymen as
Merovingians knew them disappeared and that they were replaced
cavalry is vitiated, however, by White's further statement that the
ority of fighting men in the armies of Charlemagne (and presumably
hose of Pepin and Charles Martel) were infantry.[34] But these infantry-
would have to be using the horsemen's longsword and the winged
ar which "is only intelligible in terms of mounted shock combat"
ause traditional infantry weapons had disappeared.

There is no reason to believe, however, that the longsword had any
cial cavalry value for the Franks. These weapons are found early in
Frankish period, and at least one archaeologist has concluded that
ey were primarily infantry weapons.[35] The winged spear may have been
"novel design" but it antedated the era of Charles Martel by several
nturies. It seems reasonable to conclude that men fighting on foot used
e longsword and the winged spear both before and after Charles
Martel's alleged revolution in military tactics. Thus this evidence supports
ntinuity rather than revolutionary change.[36]

From the linguistic evidence we see that the Old English word for
irrup, *stigráp* (Old Saxon, *stigerêp* and Old High German, *Stegareif*), is a
ombination of the elements *stig-e* ("climb") and *rap* ("rope"). Among the

33. White, *Medieval Technology*, p. 27.

34. *Ibid.*, pp. 5, 138.

35. E. Salin, *La civilisation mérovingienne*, III (Paris, 1957), 58. The evidence cited by
White, *Medieval Technology*, p. 146, shows the use of the longsword at least as early as the
sixth century. The proper archaeological work has not yet been done from which one can
safely argue, as does White, that the longsword was far more popular in the eighth century
than it was in the sixth or seventh centuries. Cf. Sawyer and Hilton, "Technical
Determinism," p. 93.

36. White, *Medieval Technology*, p. 147, presents abundant evidence to show that the
winged spear was used in pre-Carolingian days but argues that the winged spear was used
only for hunting in the period before Charles Martel's alleged reforms which were made
possible by the stirrup, which in turn made possible mounted shock combat, which then
made it possible to use the winged spear for military purposes. Ogilvy, "The Stirrup and
Feudalism," pp. 6–7, considers that White's arguments concerning the relation of the
winged spear to mounted shock combat are untenable. White's argument that the winged
spear was in general use in the eighth century is shown to be without foundation by recent
archaeological work; see note 50 below. See also Sawyer and Hilton, "Technical
Determinism," p. 93.

career hunting down Waiofar, the duke of Aq
occurred in southern Aquitaine, but there is
available concerning it.[29]

Between 752 and 762 the Carolingian armies
against the Saxons, Muslims, Lombards, and Aq
these sieges dwell upon the use of siege engines ar
with ladders.[30] In sieges, however, mounted troops
the flanks of raiding parties of footmen, cutting ol
and communications, and patrolling the lines so as
by the besieged to sally forth and burn the siege eng
this auxiliary role which cavalry can play in sieg
mention of them in the texts under discussion. T
siege warfare, moreover, depends primarily upon mer
men who bore the brunt of Pepin's campaigns and tl
brother fought on foot as the tactics of the situatio
elements of the armies of Charles, Pepin, and Carl
sidered to have been the decisive ones they surely v
which bombarded the walls of fortified positions an
stormed them. This seems to have been the judgme
temporary and enemy, Waiofar, duke of Aquitaine, wl
his garrisons from the fortified cities and castra in
breached their walls because he felt that Pepin would
them by siege.[31] Pepin not only made much of his siege
a great deal of faith in the defense of fortified positions a
expense and trouble to restore the fortifications dama
Pepin also garrisoned his fortifications.[32] From the mar
Charles, Pepin, and Carloman described by contempo
contemporaries there is not a shred of evidence to sugg
armed horsemen engaging in mounted shock combat wo
element of their armies.

Since the literary texts discussed above give no suppo
archaeological evidence has been cited to establish the gre

29. *Ibid.*, chaps. 44–52.

30. *Ibid.*, chaps. 20, 38, 43, 46.

31. *Ibid.*, chap. 46: "Videns praedictus Waiofarius princeps A
castro Claremonte rex bellando ceperat et Bitoricas caput Aquitania mun
cum machinis capuisset, et inpetum eius ferre non potuisset, omnes c
Aquitania provintia dictioni sui erant, id est Pectavis, Lemovicas, Sanct
Equolisma vel reliquis quam plures civitates et castella, omnes muros
prostravit. . . ."

32. *Ibid.*, chaps. 43, 44, 46, and *Annales Regni Francorum*, 766.

Latin words for stirrup, *scala* derives from the word for "ladder" while *scandile* and *scandula* derive from the verb "to climb," *scandere*. The Latin *stapha*, *stapes*, and *staffa* derive from the same germanic root as the modern English "step." This evidence would seem to indicate that the idea of mounting a horse was paramount in the minds of those who coined the various words for stirrup in the middle ages. Had the notion of mounted shock combat been paramount one might have expected a modernized form of *faber centauri* or some such construct to serve in lieu of the words which were in fact coined.[37]

White presents one interesting argument for the wide acceptance for any purpose, even nonmilitary, of the stirrup in Francia. Following Schlieben, White states: "The verbs *insilire* and *desilire*, formerly used for getting on and off horses, began to be replaced by *scandere equos* and *descendere*, showing that leaping was replaced by stepping when one mounted or dismounted."[38] This argument is based upon three sources, a poem by Hermoldus Nigellus, the *Annales Fuldenses* for 891, and the *Waltharius*, but these all date from the second half of the ninth century and they are less convincing when used as evidence for conditions of the eighth century. Further, the author of the *Waltharius* uses *desilire* and *descandere* interchangeably to describe "dismounting."[39] Finally, in the sixth century, Gregory of Tours generally uses *ascendere* and *descendere* to describe mounting and dismounting.[40] In short, the philological argument fails to support recognition of the importance of stirrups by Charles Martel and his contemporaries.

The earliest representation of a stirrup in western Europe comes from a manuscript illuminated at Saint Gallen sometime between 863 and 883. The illuminator of this manuscript, however, does not seem to have been overly impressed with the importance of stirrups and depicts some

37. *The Oxford English Dictionary* (Oxford, 1933), X, 982; and *Glossarium . . . Du Cange* (Paris, 1846), VI, 87, 93, 345. White, *Medieval Technology*, p. 142, suggests that the Romance and even the Germanic words for stirrup derive from *astraba*, which meant "pack saddle" and came to mean "foot rest." About 800, however, Carolingian glosses define *astraba* as "tabella ubi pedes requiesiunt." No hint is given of the stirrup's function or of shock combat some two generations after Charles Martel's alleged revolution.

38. A. Schlieben, "Geschichte der Steigbügel," *Annalen des Vereins für Nassauische Altertumskunde und Geschichtsforschung*, XXIV (1892), 180. White, *Medieval Technology*, p. 27.

39. K. Strecker (ed.), *Waltharius*, *M.G.H.*, *Poetae Latini Medie Aevi* (Weimar, 1951), lines 215–217; 638–639; 783–787; and Notker, *Gesta Karoli Magni Imperatoris*, ed. H. Haefele, *M.G.H.*, *S.S.R.G.*, N.S. XII (Berlin, 1959), I, 6.

40. Gregory of Tours, *Historiarum libri X*, IV. 3, 49; VI. 31; IX. 31; X. 9, ed. B Krusch and W. Levison, *M.G.H. Scr. rer. Merov.*, 2nd ed. (Hanover, 1937–51), I. 1.

horsemen with them and others without them. Carolingian manuscript illuminators throughout the late ninth century continue this inconsistent depiction of stirrups.[41] Before the appearance of stirrups in the St. Gall manuscript in the last third of the ninth century, Carolingian illuminators were consistent in ignoring them. For example, the illuminator of the Utrecht Psalter, ca. 830, who was not adverse to incorporating important technical innovations into his drawings, never once depicts a horseman with stirrups; this despite the fact that he draws scores of mounted warriors in battle.[42] From manuscript illuminations it might be concluded, at least tentatively, that stirrups did not impress the Carolingian world as an important technical innovation.

Early in the ninth century Charlemagne ordered a new recension of the law code of the Ripuarian Franks. In this new recension there is a list of weapons and horses with their values for compensation. Some historians see this as a list of the national arms of the Ripuarian Franks. Though marginal pieces of equipment like a sword sheath and greaves are included in the list along with the horses, *brunia*, helmet, lance, and shield, no stirrups are mentioned. But of even greater interest is the fact that this same list with its horses and armor appeared in the earliest recension of the code, which was compiled early in the seventh century, more than a century before Charles Martel's alleged revolution in tactics.[43]

41. Richard Stettiner, *Die illustrierten Prudentius-Handschriften* (Berlin, 1905), pls. 130 and 131; J. M. Clark, *The Abbey of St. Gaul as a Centre of Literature and Art* (Cambridge, 1926), p. 37; J. R. Rahn, *Das Psalterium Aureum von St. Gallen* (St. Gallen, 1878), pls. 9, 10, 15; and Adolf Merton, *Die Buchmalerei in St. Gallen vom neunten bis elften Jahrhundert* (Leipzig, 1912), pls. 56 and 57. H. Stern, "The Ivories on the ambo of the Cathedral of Aix-la-Chapelle," *The Connoisseur*, 153 (July, 1963), 166–171, argues that the horsemen depicted on these ivories date from the mid-eighth century. Their provenance, however, is Ommiad Egypt, and they could have been placed in the cathedral well after the period under discussion. White, *Medieval Technology*, p. 26, argues that the Apocalypse of Valenciennes, which heretofore had been considered to have been of Spanish provenance, should now be considered to have come from the German Alps. By accepting a date of shortly after the mid-ninth century White makes the stirrups depicted in this apocalypse the earliest representation of stirrups in *Francia*. This date may be correct, but this hardly demonstrates anything about the era of Charles Martel.

42. E. T. DeWald, *The Utrecht Psalter* (Princeton, 1933), pl. 58, for the rotary grindstone and *passim* for the horsemen. White, *Medieval Technology*, p. 169, for a discussion of the rotary grindstone as an innovation.

43. Brunner, "Der Reiterdienst . . .," pp. 13–16; and White, *Medieval Technology*, pp. 3–4. F. Beyerle and R. Buchner (eds.), *Lex Ribuaria, M.G.H., Leges*, III, Part ii (Hanover, 1954), 40, 11. "Equum . . . pro septem solid. tribuat. Equam . . . pro tre solid. tribuat. Spatam cum scoligilo pro septem solid. tribuat. . . . Brunia bona septem solid. tribuat. Helmo condericto pro sex solid. tribuat." I am inclined to view this as a list of movable

In turning to the literary sources of the Carolingian era, there are many instances where one might reasonably expect stirrups to be mentioned. Notker, the monk of Saint Gallen, tells of a newly appointed bishop whose horse was brought for him by his servants. They also brought along a mounting step so that the bishop would not have to leap upon his horse's back, as was the custom. Apparently the servants believed that a bishop should mount in a dignified manner. In any event, the bishop was a young man and regarded such a mounting step as suitable for the infirm; he thus leaped upon the horse in the traditional manner.[44]

In another instance the monk of Saint Gallen describes Charlemagne in full armor. He writes:

> Then the iron Charles could be seen, crested with an iron helmet, wearing iron gauntlets, his iron chest and broad shoulders protected by an iron breastplate, an iron spear was held high in his left hand, for his right always rested on his unconquered sword; his thighs were encased in flexible iron plates, though most others leave them unprotected by armor so that they may mount [their horses] more easily. What shall I say about the greaves? the entire army always uses iron ones. His shield appears to be nothing but iron. His horse was both in spirit and in color iron.[45]

---

property and not as a list of national arms. Included in this list are "bovem cornutum . . . pro duos solid. tribuat. Vaccam cornutam . . . pro unum solido tribuat." If stirrups had been commonly used and of notable value, one might expect them to have been included in the revised version of the code issued by Charlemagne.

44. Notker, *Gesta Karoli*, I, 6: "Qui cum laetus ad abeundum exiret et ministri eius iuxta gravitatem episcopalem caballum eius ad gradus ascensionum adducerent, indignatus ille, quod quasi pro infirmo eum habere voluissent, de plana terra ita super eum ascendit, ut vix se retineret in eo, ne in ulteriorem partem decideret. Quod per cancellos palatii rex prospiciens cito illum ad se vocari praecepit et sic illum allocutus est: 'Bone vir, celer es et agilis, pernix et praepes; utque ipse tu nosti, multis bellorum turbinibus undique serenitas imperii nostri turbatur, idcirco opus habeo tali clerico in comitatu meo. Esto igitur interim socius laborum nostrorum, dum tam celeriter ascendere potes caballum tuum.'" The manuscript tradition indicates as variant readings "super eum assiliit."

45. *Ibid.*, II, 17: "Tunc visus est ipse ferreus Karolus ferrea galea cristatus, ferreis manicis armillatus, ferrea torace ferreum pectus humerosque Platonicos tutatus; hasta ferrea in altum subrecta sinistram impletus. Nam dextra ad invictum calibem semper erat extenta; coxarum exteriora, quae propter faciliorem ascensum in alliis solet lorica nudari, in eo ferreis ambiebantur bratteolis. De ocreis quid dicam? Quae et cuncto exercitui solebant ferreae semper esse usui. In clipeo nihil apparuit nisi ferrum. Caballus quoque illius animo et colore ferrum renitebat."

Not only does the monk omit any mention of stirrups, but when he talks about mounting, he notes that customarily Carolingian horsemen did not wear armor on their thighs so that they could mount more easily.

The author of the *Waltharius*, mentioned above as a contemporary of the monk of Saint Gallen, was not averse to mentioning significant technical innovations in his work. He is, for example, the first writer in western Europe to mention the use of horseshoes. In the *Waltharius* there is abundant opportunity to mention stirrups but there is not a word about them.[46]

Such examples from the Carolingian sources could be multiplied, but the demonstration of a negative proposition, i.e., that the Carolingians did not appreciate the stirrup's military value and in fact tended to ignore it, needs more convincing evidence. Toward the middle of the ninth century Rabanus Maurus dedicated a revised version of Vegetius's *Epitoma rei Militaris* to King Lothair I. Rabanus departs from his model on several occasions. In one of these departures he makes additions to Vegetius's section on the use of wooden horses to help teach recruits to mount.[47] One would expect some mention of stirrups at this point if Rabanus had regarded them as being important. There is, however, not a word about stirrups here or at any other point in the work. Nor in fact is there any mention of shock combat or any reason to believe that cavalry were of great significance. These omissions would only be significant in a work devoted to military training and tactics if stirrups and mounted shock combat were of vital interest to the Carolingians. If such were not the case, as all the evidence seems to indicate, then Rabanus cannot be faulted for omitting notice of stirrups and mounted shock combat. It would have been strange indeed if he had mentioned either one.

The archaeological evidence for White's view deserves careful examination. It indicates that the stirrup became known in Europe by the late seventh or early eighth centuries, but it does not show that the use of the

---

46. *Waltharius*, lines 217, 639, 787, 1197, and 1280. In lines 1280 ff., preparation for a battle is described: "Dixit et a tergo saltu se iecit equino, / Hoc et Guntharius nec segnior egerat heros / Waltharius, cuncti pedites bellare parati. / Stabat quisque ac venturo se providus ictu / Praestruxit: trepidant sub peltis Martia membra." See line 1203 on horseshoes.

47. Rabanus Maurus, *De procinctu Romanae miliciae*, ed. E. Dümmler, *Zeitschrift für deutsches Alterthum*, XV (1872), 444 ff. See p. 448, for wooden horses used to practice mounting. Rabanus indicates (p. 450) that he has excluded from Vegetius's account those things which are not used in modern times. Cf. White, *Medieval Technology*, p. 149.

stirrup was common among horsemen or that it helped bring about the development of mounted shock combat.[48]

From the catalogue of a recent archaeological study it is possible to identify some 704 fighting men who were buried throughout eastern Francia from the late seventh through the early ninth century.[49] Compared with other evidence put forward on this subject this is a huge number.

As with any kind of archaeological data, great care must be taken to avoid misleading the reader as to the reliability of the evidence. The 704 warrior identifications mentioned above are not all sure; 187 of them are problematical for such reasons as damaged graves, primitive excavation technique, and poor reporting. Of the 704 gross figure, 147 have a knife as the only weapon and 36 have only equestrian artifacts and no weapon. Of the 704, 135 can be identified as equestrians, 85 of these are sure identifications and 50 are problematical.

Statistics can be manipulated to argue for or against almost anything, but the chart presented on p. 64 gives the reader an opportunity to make his own calculations. From the available data it would seem that a minimum of 13.9 percent of the sample of fighting men studied here were horsemen and a maximum of 23.6 percent were horsemen. The average of the seven "sure" percentages provides a figure of 17.1 percent horsemen and the average of the seven "gross" percentages provides a figure of 17.9 percent horsemen. It seems reasonable to conclude from the present sample of fighting men that less than 18 percent but more than 17 percent are identifiable as horsemen.

Of the total equestrian identifications only 13 have stirrups, 4 of these are sure identifications while 9 are problematical. Using any reasonable combination of figures, less than one percent of the equestrian identifications have stirrups. It seems that this evidence demonstrates, as conclusively

48. White, *Medieval Technology*, pp. 22–24, 27, 145–146. Sawyer and Hilton, "Technical Determinism," p. 91, questions the evidence on this point.

49. Frauke Stein, *Adelsgräber des achten Jahrhundert in Deutschland* (Berlin, 1967), I, 216–396, for the catalogue. The lack of coins in these finds makes dating beyond gross limits dangerous. Cf. Stein, *op. cit.*, pp. 8, 23 ff., 54 ff., 33 ff., and especially 104, where the paucity of evidence for reliable dates is graphically illustrated. To date the material found in the catalogue more precisely than late seventh through early ninth century is to go beyond the limits of the evidence in the overwhelming majority of cases. The dangers of being too precise in dating on the basis of limited evidence are pointed out by F. O'Rahilly, *Early Irish History and Mythology* (Dublin, 1946), pp. 440 ff., and Peter Sawyer, *The Age of the Vikings* (London, 1962), pp. 48 ff. I would like to thank Perry Onion for his help in compiling the statistics used here.

Chart

GROSS FIGURES

704 gross total
135 gross total equestrian figures

19.2% of gross identifications are equestrians.

133 gross identifications have knife only.
36 gross identifications have equestrian artifacts only.
14 gross identifications have only knives and equestrian artifacts.

704	704	704	135	135
−133	−36	−183	−36	−50
571	678	521	99	85

135 of 571 = 23.6%
99 of 678 = 14.6%
85 of 521 = 16.5%
99 of 571 = 17.3%
85 of 571 = 14.9%
99 of 521 = 19.0%

SURE FIGURES

517 sure total
85 sure equestrian total

16.4% of sure identifications are equestrian.

123 sure identifications have knives only.
15 sure identifications have equestrian artifacts only.
13 sure identifications have knives and equestrian artifacts.

517	517	517	85	85
−123	−15	−151	−15	−28
394	502	366	70	57

85 of 394 = 21.6%
70 of 502 = 13.9%
70 of 366 = 19.2%
57 of 366 = 15.6%
70 of 394 = 17.8%
57 of 394 = 14.5%

as any statistically significant sample can, that stirrups were not frequently buried with otherwise identifiable equestrians. Some scholars
might want to push the evidence even further and conclude that stirrups
were neither highly regarded nor frequently used; others might argue,

however, that stirrups were so highly prized and in such demand that they were not buried with their owners as were spurs.[50] If the latter were true, however, it would seem reasonable for stirrups to have been included in the list of equipment found in the ninth-century recension of the Ripuarian code.

This possibility of drawing diametrically opposed conclusions even from such a comparatively large corpus of data points up the dubious value of archaeological evidence for answering the kinds of questions posed by White. Further, the catalogue from which this evidence is drawn purports to list artifacts from *Adelsgräber*. Is it not strange that less than 18 percent of identifiable warriors labeled as "aristocrats" (or, as I would prefer, "rich") should be identifiable as equestrians? It is well known that even Merovingian aristocrats were mounted, and it is accepted that Carolingian aristocrats were mounted. One might then expect that close to 100 percent of identifiable male aristocrats or rich warriors of the eighth century should be identifiable as equestrians. Conversion to Christianity might account for a lack of artifacts in graves; but even after conversion warriors continued to be buried clothed. This generally means that the belt buckle, knife, and if a horseman the spurs, or at least one of them on the left foot, are found when the grave is excavated. Of the eighty-five sure equestrian identifications sixty-two or almost 73 percent have at least one spur. To return to the original point, however, of what value is archaeological evidence to determine the use of the stirrup, or to determine the percentage of horsemen, when the evidence is apparently so incomplete that it is only possible to identify some 18 percent of male aristocratic warriors as equestrians in the eighth century.

Even though the archaeological evidence presented here seems to support my contention that stirrups were little used by the Carolingians, I am inclined to regard these data as being of dubious value and prefer to rely upon the literary, pictorial, and philological evidence examined above. From these sources it seems clear that the stirrup was little appreciated and little used by the Carolingians during the eighth and ninth centuries. Further, heavily armed horsemen engaging in mounted shock combat were not the decisive arm of Charles Martel's post-733

---

50. Among the 704 warrior identifications discussed only thirteen winged spears are found. Two of these thirteen were found in conjunction with equestrian identifications and eleven with infantry identifications. These figures would seem to suggest that the winged spear was not in general use by horsemen from the time of Charles Martel onward. Cf. White, *Medieval Technology*, pp. 27, 147.

armies and those of his sons. These armies excelled in siege warfare in which horsemen play at most a limited role; and the horseman's role was so limited during the mid-eighth century that it goes virtually unnoticed by contemporary observers.

Since there was no military revolution under Charles Martel, it is necessary to re-examine his "seizures of Church land" in an effort to ascertain just what was happening. About 732 or perhaps a year later Charles seized the *honores* of Bishop Eucherius of Orléans and sent him and his followers into exile. Charles then parcelled out these *honores* among his followers (*satellites*).[51] A year later Charles invaded Burgundy and established some of his most able leudes within the boundaries of that kingdom to control the rebellious natives and to deal with Muslim raiders. Thus when things quieted down a bit he handed the Lyonais over to his *fideles* and confirmed these grants with charters.[52] Charles found it necessary, however, to make at least one more sortie into Burgundy before the end of the 730s in order to punish rebellious magnates.[53] During this period Charles took control of large amounts of church lands in the area of Vienne, Lyons, and Autun.[54]

Contemporaneously, the Abbot Teutsind of Saint Wandrille found it necessary to hand over a considerable portion of the lands of his monastery

51. W. Levison (ed.), *Vita Eucherii episcopi Aurelianensis*, *M.G.H.*, *Scr. rer. Merov.*, VII (Hanover, 1919), chap. 7: ". . . invidia circumfusi suggerentes Carolo principe ut beatum virum, cuius supra meminimus, cum omni propinquitate eius exilio deputaret honoresque eorum quasdam propriis usibus adnecteret, quasdam vero suis satellibus cumularet." Cf. B. Krusch (ed.), *Vita Remigii Episcopi Remensis Auctore Hincmaro*, *M.G.H.*, *Scr. rer. Merov.*, II (Hanover, 1886), p. 252.

52. *Fred. con't.*, chap. 14: ". . . Carlus princeps regionem Burgundie sagaciter penetravit, fines regni illius leudibus suis probatissimis viris industriis ad resistendas gentes rebelles et infideles statuit, pace patrata Lugdono Gallia suis fidelibus tradidit. Firmata foedera iudiciaria reversus est victor fiducialiter agens."

53. *Ibid.*, chap. 18.

54. G. Waitz (ed.), *Gesta Episcoporum Autisiodorensium*, *M.G.H.*, *Scr.*, XIII (Hanover, 1881), chap. 32: "Eius tempore res ecclesiasticae ab episcoporum postestate per eundem principem abstracte in dominatum secularium cesserunt; siquidem centum tantummodo mansis episcopo derelictis, quicquid villarum superfuit, in sex principes Baioarios distributum est, abbatie vero sigulis abbatibus dilargite." G. Pertz (ed.), *Chronica Adonis Archiepiscopi Viennensis*, *M.G.H.*, *Scr.*, II (Hanover, 1829), p. 319: "Idem Wilicarius, cum furioso et insano satis consilio Franci res sacras ecclesiarum ad usus suos retorquerent, videns Viennensem ecclesiam suam indecenter humiliari, relicto episcopatu, in monasterium sanctorum martyrum Agaunensium ingressus, vitam venerabilem duxit. Vastate et dissipata Viennensis et Lugdunensis provincia, aliquot annis sine episcopis utraque ecclesia fuit, laicis sacrilege et barbara res sacras ecclesiarum obtinentibus."

to the king's men (*homines regii*).[55] In a more general statement of what seems to have been Charles's policy, Adrevald of Fleury notes that the mayor having taken much church property added it to the fisc and then later distributed it to his own soldiers (*milites*).[56]

Among Charles's powerful contemporaries the seizure of church lands also seems to have been common. Eudo, duke of Aquitaine, tried to take church property in the Bourges area and give it to his followers; the patricians of Marseilles took land from Saint Victor of Marseilles; and Count Rathar extorted twenty-nine domains from the monastery of Saint Wandrille for which he paid a nominal yearly rent of sixty solidi.[57]

From the texts it is clear that important men seized revenue-producing lands from the church and perhaps from laymen and handed some of these lands over to their supporters. The appearance of such apparently anachronistic terms as *milites* is probably due to the fact that most of the texts which mention Charles's confiscations are from the later ninth century. In fact Fredegar's continuator is the only contemporary or near contemporary who deals with the problem, and he does not make explicit mention of the confiscation of church lands.[58]

It may be a distortion to view these seizures of lands as simply an episode in the battle of church and state with the former being despoiled by the latter. Bishop Eucherius, for example, seems to have opposed Charles's attempts to rule the Orléanais, and thus the latter, upon attaining victory, confiscated the former's *honores* and sent him and his followers into exile. The victor in dealing with the vanquished stripped him of his power and wealth. Whether the *honores* were personal holdings or church holdings cannot be ascertained with certainty. The true

55. S. Loewenfeld (ed.), *Gesta Abbatum Fontanellensium*, *M.G.H.*, *S.S.R.G.* (Hanover, 1886), chap. 10: "Nam poene tertiam partem facultatum abstulit suisque propinquis ac regliis hominibus ad possidendum contradidit, quae usque nunc de isto coenobio premanent ablatae, sicuti omnibus privilegia ac largitiones, quae inscriniis nostrii coenobii retinentur, revolventibus in promptu est; quae longum est narrare per singula."

56. O. Holder-Egger (ed.), *Miracula S. Benedicti Andrevaldi Floriacensis*, *M.G.H.*, *Scr.*, XV, Part I (Hanover, 1887), p. 483: "Denique rebus bellicis operosissime insistens, tyrannos per totam Franciam dominatum sibi vindicantes obpressit, ob eamque rem plurima iuri ecclesiastico detrahens praedia, fisco associavit ac deinde militibus propriis distribuere studuit."

57. B. Krusch (ed.), *Vita Austrigisili episcopi Biturgi*, *M.G.H.*, *Scr. rer. Merov.*, IV (Hanover, 1902), chaps. 6–10; *Gesta Abbatum Fontanellensium*, chap. 10; and M. Guérard (ed.), *Cartulaire de S. Victor de Marseille*, I (Paris, 1857), No. 31. M. Tangl (ed.), *S. Bonifatii et Lulli epistolae*, *M.G.H.*, *Epistolae selectae*, I (Berlin, 1916), Nos. 50 and 73. Goffart, *Le Mans Forgeries*, pp. 6–8.

58. Goffart, *Le Mans Forgeries*, p. 7.

ownership seems to be irrelevant. What is important is that Charles took the *honores*. In Burgundy, Charles conquered a large area, arranged for it administration and protection, and confiscated the wealth of his enemies and perhaps the wealth of those who had stood aloof in the contest for power.[59]

The sources indicate that Charles and his contemporaries took lands and movable wealth from their opponents, both lay and ecclesiastical, and used these assets to reward loyal supporters and to gain the support of additional followers. In addition to using the spoils of war to secure support, these men used their own lands as well. During this era of continual warfare and struggle for power it seems essential to view the service and support purchased by the magnates as military or paramilitary in nature. The using of wealth in the above manner and for the above purposes some scholars have argued was an innovation. They call this alleged innovation feudalism.[60]

The military forces of Charles's young nephew Theudoald were the personal followers, leudes, of Pepin II and Grimoald, Theudoald's grandfather and father.[61] A considerable amount of information survives concerning one of Pepin's leudes, a certain Dodo, who is described in the sources as being well off economically and as having a large number of armed dependent followers whom he provided with expensive weapons.[62] Indeed, Pepin II's fighting forces and those of his colleague Duke Martin were comprised of their followers (*sodales* and *socii*).[63] The loyalty of these men may well have been secured with gifts of church lands, for Saint

59. Many scholars have treated the problem of the confiscation of church land by Charles Martel. Two of the most important are E. Lesne, *Histoire de la propriété ecclésiastique en France*, II, Part I (Lille, 1922), and M. A. Pöschl, *Bischofsgut und Mensa episcopalis*, I (Bonn, 1908).

60. See above, n. 1.

61. *Fred. con't.*, chap. 8: ". . . contra Theudoaldum et leudis Pippino quondam atque Grimoaldo inierunt certamen, corruitque ibi non modicus exercitus. Theudoaldus itaque a sodalibus suis per fugam lapsus evasit."

62. B. Krusch (ed.), *Vita Landiberti Episcopi Traiectensis vetustissima*, M.G.H., *Scr. rer. Merov.*, VI (Hanover, 1906), chap. 11: "In diebus illis erat Dodo domesticus iam dicti principes Pipini, proprius consanguinius eorum qui interfecti fuerant, et erant ei possessiones multae et in obsequio eius pueri multi." See also chap. 13: "Et erat multitudo copiosa virorum pugnatorum ad bellandum, et erant induti lurices et cassidis, clipeis et lanceis gladiisque precincti et sagittis cum pharetris."

63. *Fred. con't.*, chap. 3: "Devicti cum sociis Martinus atque Pippinus in fugam lapsi sunt. . . . Qua in re illae credens eos, a Lauduno Clavato egressus cum sodalibus ac sociis ad Erchrego veniens, illic cum suis omnibus interfectus est." The author of the *Liber Historiae Francorum* (cited hereafter as *L.H.F.*), ed. B. Krusch, M.G.H., *Scr. rer. Merov.*, II (Hanover, 1888), chap. 46, calls this force an *exercitus*.

Boniface, writing in 742, laments that church property had been despoiled by secular magnates for at least sixty or seventy years.[64]

Pepin I, an important ancestor of Charles Martel, along with Bishop Chunibert of Cologne "skillfully and with suitable inducements drew the Austrasian magnates to their cause, and by treating them generously they gained their support and knew how to keep it." Thus they gained ascendancy in Austrasia over other important men.[65] Aega, a mayor of the palace for Neustria, strengthened his position by alienating lands from the royal fisc and giving them to the magnates whose support he coveted. Flaochad, upon succeeding to the mayorship of Burgundy, gained the support of the magnates by promising them in writing and by oath to protect them in their *honores* and dignity and to give them support.[66] Both these mayors, like Pepin I before them, secured the support of magnates who with their armed followers formed the basis of the mayors' fighting forces.[67] Two Neustrian mayors, Ebroin and Leudesius, relied upon their personal followings for military support, and the Burgundian Patrician Willebad also relied on magnates' followings to some extent.[68]

In this era of the *rois fainéants*, the *antrustiones*—"armed followers," including *pueri*, sworn to the king who served in a military or paramilitary capacity at the court or in the *centenae*—did not protect and serve the monarch but were in reality the supporters of the mayors of the palace, who controlled the fisc and supplied these *fideles cum armis suis* "with the means of their support." [69]

64. *Bonifatii . . . epistolae*, No. 50: ". . . de aecclesiastica religione, quae iam longo tempore, id est non minus quam sexginta vel septuaginta annos, calcata et dissipata fuit. . . ." Cf. Goffart, *Le Mans Forgeries*, pp. 6–8.

65. *Fred.*, IV, 85: ". . . Pippinus cum Chuniberto . . . omnesque leudis Austrasiorum secum uterque prudenter et cum dulcedene adtragentes, eos benigne governantes eorum amiciciam constringent semperque servandum."

66. *Ibid.*, for Aega's gifts and chap. 89 for Flaochad's promises.

67. *Ibid.*, chap. 90 for the mayors' armed forces.

68. *Ibid.*, for Willebad's followers and *Fred. con't.*, chap. 2 for Ebroin's and Leudesius's forces.

69. Formularies for the installation of *antrustiones* were drawn up and presumably used during the era of the *rois fainéants*. K. Zeumer (ed.), *Formulae Marculfi*, *M.G.H.*, *Formulae Merowingici et Karolini Aevi* (Hanover, 1886), I, 18: "Rectum est, ut qui nobis fidem pollicentur inlesam, nostro tuentur auxilio. Et qui illi fidelis, Deo propitio, noster veniens ibi in palatio nostro una cum arma sua in manu nostra trustem et fidelitatem nobis visus est coniurasse: propterea per presentem preceptum decernemus ac iobemus, ut deinceps memoratus ille inter numero antruscionorum conputetur. Et si quis fortasse eum interficere presumpserit, noverit se wiregildo suo soledos sexcentos esse culpabilem." But the king did not benefit from these retainers (*Fred.*, IV, 87, and *Fred. con't.*, chap. 2). See note 55 above p. 67, where church lands are given to the king's men. Deeds were still carried out

The last of the ruling Merovingian kings relied heavily upon the armed following of their leudes for military aid. Theudebert II was betrayed by his leudes who refused to fight and Queen Brunhild met a similar fate. Queen Fredegund secured the support of the important men of her son's kingdom with the distribution of rich gifts, and thus rallied sufficient military aid to defeat an invading force. Dagobert, whose *leudes in exercito* made his succession to his father's throne smooth, went so far as to seize church land and divided them among his followers (*milites*) to ensure their military support. An important magnate like Bishop Arnulf of Metz, a progenitor of the Carolingian house, owed his lord, King Dagobert, counsel and military aid (*consilium et solatium*).[70]

Clovis's grandsons took care to reward loyal followers and to purchase the support of additional followers. For example, Chilperic, immediately upon hearing of his father's death, distributed gifts from the royal fisc to ensure the loyalty and support of those men whom he thought would be most useful in ensuring his accession to the throne. In addition, Chilperic allowed his *fideles* to pillage estates and seize the lands of laymen and ecclesiastics within his kingdom, and thus he bought the support of important men and their followers with wealth which was not his to give. On one noteworthy occasion Chilperic purchased the loyalty of a certain Godinus, one of King Sigibert's followers. To pay for Godinus's support, which Gregory of Tours pictures in military terms, Chilperic gave him lands from the royal fisc. When Godinus did not perform on the field of battle in the manner in which he was required, Chilperic confiscated the estates which he had granted to him.[71]

---

in the king's name but the mayors had the power. Éginhard, *Vie de Charlemagne*, ed. L. Halphen, 3rd ed. (Paris, 1947), chap. 1. On the *antrustiones* see Maximin Deloche, *La trustis et l'antrustion royal sous les deux premiers races* (Paris, 1873); and on the *centena* see Wallace-Hadrill, *Long-Haired Kings*, p. 193 n. 1.

70. *Fred.*, IV, 27, 40, and 56 for Theudebert II, Brunhild, and Dagobert I; *L.H.F.*, chap. 36, for Fredegund; and B. Krusch (ed.), *Miracula Martini Abbatis Vertavensis*, *M.G.H.*, *Scr. rer. Merov.*, III (Hanover, 1896), chap. 7: "Rex Dagobertus Francorum rei publicae princeps cum multis et variis bellorum enentibus premeretur, de coenobiis sanctorum multa abstulit, quae suis militibus est." This text is of the same period as those which mention Charles's confiscations. At least one ninth-century observer was willing to blame Dagobert for the same thing which others chose to blame Charles. B. Krusch (ed.), *Vita Sancti Arnulfi*, *M.G.H.*, *Scr. rer. Merov.*, II (Hanover, 1888), chap. 17: ". . . volvit et suspicatus est prudens rex Dagobertus eum minus terrere, scilicet ut ab ipsius consilio vel solacio non discederet. . . ."

71. Gregory, *Historium*, IV, 22: "Chilpericus vero post patris funera thesaurus, qui in villa Brannacum erant congregati, accepit et ad Francos utiliores petiit ipsusque muneribus mollitus sibi subdidit." *Ibid.*, VII, 7: "Guntchramnus vero rex omnia quae

In 588 Guntram and his nephew Childebert II agreed in the Pact of Andelot that neither of them would bribe the other's leudes to defect, and neither king would accept the service of leudes who were desirous of defecting. In addition, lands and other wealth which had been granted to these men for their service and loyalty were not to be confiscated as long as they remained true to the oath of fealty which they had taken to their lord.[72]

Earlier, as well, it seems to have been common practice for magnates to employ armed retainers, for monarchs to secure the loyalty of these important men with gifts and to use their military force. Theudebert I was able to succeed his father, despite his uncles' opposition, because he secured the support of his leudes with gifts and thus had the muscle to enforce his claims to the throne of Austrasia.[73] Theuderic I after punishing the magnates of the Auvergne for their disloyalty granted estates in the area to his relative Sigivald so he could protect the area with his followers

---

fidelis regis Chilperici non recte diversis abstulerant ... restitutit. ..." *Ibid.*, V, 3: "Godinus autem, qui a sorte Sygiberthi se ad Chilpericum transtulerat et multis ab eo muneribus locopletatus est, caput belli istius fuit; sed in campo victus, primus fuga dilabitur. Villas vero, quas ei rex a fisco in territurio Sessionico indulserat, abstulit et basilicae contulit beati Medardi."

72. *Ibid.*, IX, 20: "Similiter convenit, ut secundum pactionis inter domnum Gunthchramnum et bonae memoriae domnum Sygiberthum initas leudes illi, qui domnum Gunthchramnum post transtitum domni Chlothari sacramenta primitus praebuerunt, et, si postea convincuntur se in parte alia tradidisse, de locis ubi conmanere videntur convenit ut debeant removeri. Similiter et qui post transitum domni Chlothari convincuntur domnum Sygiberthum sacramenta primitus praebuisse et se in alia parte transtulerunt, modo simile removantur. Similiter quicquid antefati regis eclesiabus aut fidelibus suis contulerunt aut adhuc conferre cum iusticiam Deo propiciante voluerint, stabiliter conservetur. Et quicquid unicuique fidelium in utriusque regno per legem et iusticiam redebetur, nullum praeiudicium paciatur, sed liceat res debetas possedere atque recipere; et si aliquid cuicumque per interregna sine culpa tultum est, audiencia habita, restauretur. Et de id, quod per munificentias praecedentium regum unusquisque usque transitum gloriosae memoriae domni Chlothari regis possedit, cum securitate possedeat. Et quod exinde fidelibus personis ablatum est, de praesenti recipiat. Et quia inter praefatus regis pura et simplex est in Dei nomine concordia inligata, convenit, ut in utroque regno utriusque fidelibus, tam pro causis publicis quam privatis quicumque voluerit ambulare, pervium nullis temporibus denegetur. Similiter convenit, ut nullus alterius leudis nec sollicitet nec venientes excipiat."

73. *Ibid.*, III, 23: "Cumque abissit, Theudoricus non post multos dies obiit vicinsimo tertio regni sui anno. Consurgentes autem Childebertus et Chlothacharius contra Theudobertum, regnum eius suferre voluerunt, sed ille muneribus placatis a leodibus suis defensatus est et in regnum stabilitus."

in the king's interest.[74] Clovis gave Melun to his loyal follower Aurelianus.[75]

Throughout the Merovingian era important men employed bands of armed retainers.[76] It was vital for any man who would rule in Gaul during this period, whether king or mayor, to have the support of large numbers of these magnates and their followers since such groups often formed a significant part of a ruler's military forces. Rulers and would-be rulers purchased such support with all kinds of wealth, movable and landed, their own and that taken from others, laymen and ecclesiastics alike. Charles employed techniques to secure such support similar to those used by rulers throughout the Merovingian era. If anyone still wishes to argue that Charles Martel's actions in these matters constituted feudalism, he would seem bound to argue that those of his predecessors also constituted feudalism.

In the foregoing pages some doubt has been cast upon the allegedly creative or innovative genius of Charles Martel. He did not grasp the importance of the stirrup, he did not make heavily armed horsemen using mounted shock combat the decisive arm of his military forces, nor did he even make cavalry the decisive arm of his military forces, and he did not provide for the explosive development of a new or little used technique for the securing of armed support called feudalism by some. In both military tactics and military organization Charles essentially continued to use techniques which were prevalent under his predecessors.

It seems desirable to try to explain why Charles Martel has been credited with so many significant policies when a study of the sources indicates that he was not an innovator. Charles not only thwarted the Muslims at Poitiers in 732, a deed given far too much prominence by eighteenth- and nineteenth-century historians, but he is also looked upon as a key figure in the Carolingian success story.[77] Thus it is only natural

74. *Ibid.*, III, 13: "Theudericus autem ab Arverno discendens, Sigivaldum, parentum suum, in ea quasi pro custodia dereliquid." Gregory, *Liber de passione et virtutibus sancti Iuliani martyris*, II, 14, ed. B. Krusch, *M.G.H., Scr. rer. Merov.*, I (Hanover, 1884): "Tunc Sigivaldus cum rege praepotens cum omni familia sua in Arverna regione ex regis jussu migravit. . . ."

75. *L.H.F.*, chap. 14.

76. Gregory, *Historium*, II, 42; III, 14, 15, 16, 35; IV, 12, 42; V, 14, 20, 24, 25, 49; VI, 2, 11, 16, 24, 26; VII, 3, 29, 38, 42; VIII, 8, 20; IX, 9, 10, 12, 20; X, 2; and *Fred.*, IV, 54, 55, 87, 90, are some instances of important men with armed followings which have not been previously cited.

77. White, *Medieval Technology*, p. 11.

for scholars to seek the origins of later medieval developments during the *floruit* of the man whose activities seemed to mark a point of departure from the past.

Nineteenth-century historians were intrigued by two problems: the failure of Germany to emerge from the middle ages as a unified state, and the emergence of the heavily armed knight who is portrayed as dominating the battle fields of medieval Europe and as forming the medieval nobility. Many historians believed that feudalism proved deleterious to stable government, and, in particular, that it accounted for the fragmentation of Germany into a mosaic of independent sovereignties. Nationalistic German historians tended to consider feudalism a Roman or French institution. French historians, however, contended that feudalism was a barbaric Germanic institution.[78] In the 1850s the legal historian Paul Roth, after re-examining the sources, was led to believe that feudalism was the product of the fusion of two institutions, the Germanic comitatus and the Roman precarium. He further argued that this union came about and flourished in the eighth century under the sponsorship of Charles Martel and his successors.[79]

The criticism of Roth's thesis was fierce. The main thrust of the opposition focused upon the question, why Charles Martel, the master of Francia, should have instituted a system which was so invidious and had such a negative effect upon centralized power.[80] Roth could not give his critics a satisfactory answer, but Brunner did. Charles, according to Brunner, saw the potential catastrophe of the Muslim advance and thus created a feudal cavalry of heavily armed knights (a new nobility) to save Francia. Great dangers could only be averted by extreme measures.

Thus with one theory Brunner explained the development of feudalism and the emergence of the nobility whose reason for being was military service. Such a simple answer to so many complex questions satisfied the very human craving for certainty, absolved the Germans from the guilt of gratuitously creating institutions which kept them from being a unified state, and demonstrated the honorable and Germanic origins of medieval nobility. Brunner's theory also prospered because historians who have accepted it have gone on to interpret later evidence in the light of it. The

78. Stephenson, "Origin of Feudalism," pp. 788–794.

79. Paul Roth, *Geschichte des Beneficialwesens von ältesten Zeiten bis in zehnte Jahrhundert* (Erlangen, 1850), pp. 1 ff., 105 ff., 146 ff., 203 ff., 313 ff., 392 ff., and 416 ff., and *idem*, *Feudalität und Unterthanverband* (Weimar, 1863), pp. 37 ff., 71 ff., 128 ff., 213 ff. For a discussion of Roth's ideas see Stephenson, "Origin of Feudalism," pp. 792–793.

80. Stephenson, "Origin of Feudalism," p. 794.

most important step in this direction has been the demonstration that two terms *vassaticum* (*vassus* and *vassalus*) and *beneficium* became associated on a large scale during the era of Charles Martel's sons. The earliest extant evidence showing the association of these terms appears in a charter issued by a Frankish magnate ca. 735. The usage of that charter indicates that these terms had been associated, at least on a small scale, from late in the seventh century, if not earlier. Though none of Charles Martel's documents exhibit the association of these terms, their usage became very popular under his sons, Pepin and Carloman, and common by the reign of Charlemagne.[81]

A vassal (*vassus, vassalus*) has been defined for the Carolingian era, in these contexts, as a free man in dependence to a lord whom he serves essentially in a military or paramilitary capacity. Vassalage (*vassaticum*) is simply the state of being a vassal. A *beneficium* in these contexts is generally defined as a piece of land (but can be anything of value) given on easy terms to a vassal in return for the above mentioned services. When *vassaticum* and *beneficium* are joined on a regular basis during the mid-eighth century some scholars consider feudalism to exist.[82]

By focusing upon these terms, however, historians have confused the problem. During the Merovingian era *vassi* (*vassali*) were slaves, and it would have been strange indeed to find large numbers of slaves in any era being granted noteworthy economic resources in return for service of any kind.[83] Thus to keep matters from further confusion it has been necessary to see that men in the Merovingian era performed service and acquired that place in society which during the Carolingian era became associated with men bearing the title *vassi*. Therefore in the preceding pages I have shown how it was common practice for the Merovingian monarchs and later the mayors of the palace to secure the military aid of important men, who led bands of armed followers, by granting them landed and movable wealth. The sources of this period do not describe this wealth with the term *beneficium*, but the activities of the persons involved make it clear that the wealth was exchanged for armed support and not for burdensome agricultural labor.

The widespread use and common association of the terms *vassus*

81. The best study of this evidence is F. L. Ganshof, "Note sur les origines de l'union de bénéfice avec la vassalité," *Études d'histoire dediées à la mémoire de Henri Pirenne* (Brussels, 1937), pp. 177–189. See also Ganshof, *Feudalism*, trans. P. Grierson, 2nd ed. (New York, 1961), pp. 16 ff.

82. Ganshof, *Feudalism*, pp. 1–50, and "Note sur les origines de l'union," pp. 182–188. See above n. 1.

83. Ganshof, *Feudalism*, p. 5.

(*vassalus* and *vassaticum*) and *beneficium*, during the mid-eighth century, to define relationships, in an apparently specialized manner, which had existed on a significant scale previously may have been determined by the efforts of Carloman, Pepin, and Saint Boniface to reform the church in Francia. The chapter of ecclesiastical property law developed in the councils of 743, 744, and 745 was written in part to ensure to the church sufficient revenue to carry on the business of reform. Thus it was necessary for the mayors and their supporters to recognize that the church had legal title to lands which were in lay hands, dating back perhaps to the reign of Dagobert I or even earlier. There was no real intention to restore possession of these lands to the church. A nominal rent was to be paid to the churches so that they would have a modicum of revenue to provide for their needs and legal title to right the wrongs of previous usurpations.[84]

Since the Carolingian mayors arranged this settlement the legal fiction was developed that the lands in question were held by the word of the mayor, later the king. Since only a small rent was paid to the church these estates were regarded as *beneficia*. The men who held these lands were the supporters of the mayors (in this era support was essentially military) and they came to be called vassals. The popularization of these terms, due to the arrangement of the above mentioned agreements with the church, soon meant their general application to men who functioned as armed supporters and were remunerated with economic resources without the burden of agricultural labor. This widespread use and association of the terms *vassus* and *beneficium* to describe long standing and widely developed techniques for securing armed supporters was a revolution, but only semantic and not substantial.

To conclude: Brunner's theory is inaccurate in its essentials. The decisive arm of the military forces of Charles Martel, and his sons, was not cavalry; infantry and artillery were their most useful units. The techniques used by Charles to secure armed support were the same as those used by his predecessors. The available source material does not support the theory that stirrups were used widely and made possible the extensive utilization of heavily armed cavalry in mounted shock combat. The stirrup, in fact, was all but ignored by the Carolingians. And finally, if one were to adhere to a definition of feudalism which can be constructed from the evidence of the period of Charles Martel's rule then one could find feudalism in the Merovingian era as well.

84. Goffart, *Le Mans Forgeries*, pp. 6 ff.

RELATIONS OF THE TWO JURISDICTIONS: CONFLICT AND COOPERATION IN ENGLAND DURING THE THIRTEENTH AND FOURTEENTH CENTURIES

W. R. Jones

University of New Hampshire

ACKNOWLEDGMENT

The author wishes to thank the Dean and Chapter of Canterbury, and their archivist, Dr. W. Urry, for permission to examine records in their keeping. He also expresses his sincere appreciation to the Central University Research Council of the University of New Hampshire for encouragement and assistance in completing this study.

RELATIONS OF THE TWO JURISDICTIONS: CONFLICT AND COOPERATION IN ENGLAND DURING THE THIRTEENTH AND FOURTEENTH CENTURIES

The conflict of the royal and ecclesiastical courts in later medieval England was generated by the expanding powers and pretensions of both jurisdictions. On the one hand, the canonists were trying to define as precisely as possible the extensive sphere of justice claimed by the church. The native English clergy were not always willing nor able to enforce papal and canonical ideals, but these did constitute a point of departure for the evolution of a spiritual jurisdiction in England. Energetic and strong-willed ecclesiastical statesmen, especially in the thirteenth century, tried to apply these principles to the English situation. In the middle of the thirteenth century in both England and France the laity were complaining about what they viewed as the church's aggressions in the area of law and justice. On the other hand, this same period saw the culmination of the dramatic growth of royal justice and the common law which distinguished England among the kingdoms of medieval Europe.[1] In England, unlike France where the baronage rivaled the kings for leadership in the struggle against ecclesiastical jurisdiction,[2] the claims of the

1. The latest discussion of the growth of royal law is found in D. M. Stenton, *English Justice between the Norman Conquest and the Great Charter, 1066–1215* (Philadelphia, 1964), pp. 22–114. See also H. G. Richardson and G. O. Sayles, *Law and Legislation from Aethelbert to Magna Carta* (Edinburgh, 1966), especially pp. 54–119. R. C. van Caenegem has traced the early history and development of the various kinds of royal writ, some of which concerned topics related to jurisdictional rivalry, in *Royal Writs in England from the Conquest to Glanvill*, Selden Society [SS] (London, 1959). Lady Stenton criticizes some of his conclusions in the work cited above.

2. There are some general statements concerning the jurisdictional conflict in France in P. Fournier, *Les Officialités au Moyen Age* (Paris, 1880), pp. 94–127; and O. Martin, *L'Assemblée de Vincennes de 1329 et ses Conséquences* (Paris, 1909), pp. 26–47, 223 ff. Matthew Paris quoted an agreement among the French nobles against ecclesiastical jurisdiction and attributed this movement to the inspiration of the Emperor Frederick II in *Chronica Majora*, ed. H. R. Luard, Rolls Series [RS], 6 vols. (London, 1872–83), IV, 591–593. Cf. the articles of grievance against ecclesiastical jurisdiction compiled by Philip Augustus and the French baronage in *Recueil des Actes de Philippe Auguste, roi de France*, ed. H.-F. Delaborde *et al.*, 3 vols. (Paris, 1916–1966), II, 489–491.

secular courts were ably stated and defended by the crown. The critical period of the jurisdictional conflict was that covering the reigns of Henry III, Edward I, and Edward II. During this era the crown and its courts invented new means or applied old ones for pushing back ecclesiastical jurisdiction in certain contested areas. Although the church had been forced to admit defeat in many respects by the end of Edward II's reign, the English prelates were still attempting to protect the church courts against other forms of royal aggression at the beginning of the fifteenth century.

Medieval political theory assumed that the temporal and spiritual powers should cooperate for their mutual advantage and for the general well-being of the Christian commonwealth. In the jurisdictional sphere in England princes and prelates showed a remarkable willingness to cooperate, to respect the rights of the other, and to avoid controversy. The royal courts readily admitted, for instance, that certain matters pertained exclusively to the church and refrained from interfering. All problems concerning the faith and morals of the laity or the correction of the clergy were surrendered to the church. In some instances the king's judges sent to the bishops for information and based their judgments on these findings. Generally speaking, the immunity of the clergy from trial and punishment in the royal courts was respected, and the king dutifully delivered criminous clerks to the church. In addition, the king's courts accepted the disqualification of suitors who had been excommunicated by the clergy. To the gratification of the bishops, the crown was usually willing to arrest and imprison unrepentant sinners until they had made their peace with the church. When, late in the fourteenth century, England was confronted with the worst outbreak of heresy the nation experienced during the entire middle ages, the crown actually exceeded the expectations of the bishops in lending its power and prestige to the repression of false belief. The church and clergy were expected to show similar respect and restraint. The Christian prince was viewed as the defender of the faith and as the guardian and helpmate of the clergy in promoting true belief. In its respect for the role of the secular ruler and its avoidance of conflict with temporal authority the English church was simply complying with the teachings of the canonists regarding the loyalty due the Christian magistrate and with conciliar legislation forbidding it to interfere with secular jurisdiction.[3]

There were historical precedents as well as theoretical principles

3. J. A. Watt, *The Theory of Papal Monarchy in the Thirteenth Century* (New York, 1965), pp. 29, 196.

reinforcing the spirit of restraint, tolerance, and compromise, which usually guided their relations with one another. From the Norman Conquest to the reign of Henry II jurisdictional conflict was occasional and relatively unimportant.[4] The Becket episode was quite unnecessary and did not alter greatly the relations between the royal and ecclesiastical courts. During the next two centuries, when disagreements sometimes became heated or protracted, the two jurisdictions displayed the ability, nevertheless, to limit the conflict to a few areas and to cooperate in several others. Viewing the jurisdictional controversy of the thirteenth and fourteenth centuries in the broadest terms, their day-to-day relations were not significantly different from what they had been a century previously—"a normally gentle process of adjustment."[5] As the two jurisdictions grew and came into closer contact with each other, they sometimes conflicted; but the opposition of the royal to the ecclesiastical courts in England was never total, inevitable, nor invariable.

There was no question of a war all along the line between the spiritual and the temporal power. The king never disputed that many questions belonged of right to the justice of the church, nor the bishop that many belonged to the justice of the king. But there was always a greater or less extent of border-land that might be more or less plausibly fought for.[6]

Half a century before F. W. Maitland composed this description of the jurisdictional controversy in medieval England, Archdeacon W. H. Hale had come to a similar conclusion through his study of the act books of the diocese of London in the fifteenth and sixteenth centuries.[7] Every modern

4. F. Barlow, *The English Church, 1000–1066: A Constitutional History* (Hamden, Conn., 1963), pp. 3–4, 115–116, 137–153, 255–276; C. Morris minimizes the importance of William the Conqueror's decision to separate the two court systems in "William I and the Church Courts," *English Historical Review* [*EHR*], LXXXII (1967), 458–463; C. R. Cheney, *From Becket to Langton: English Church Government, 1170–1213* (Manchester, 1956), pp. 107–108; H. G. Richardson and G. O. Sayles, *The Governance of Mediaeval England from the Conquest to Magna Carta* (Edinburgh, 1963), pp. 285 ff. Tract nine of the Anonymous of York argued the freedom of the clergy from secular courts and the independence of ecclesiastical jurisdiction from the laity, N. F. Cantor, *Church, Kingship, and Lay Investiture in England, 1089–1135* (Princeton, 1958), p. 245.

5. Cheney, *From Becket to Langton*, p. 118.

6. F. Pollock and F. W. Maitland, *A History of English Law before the Time of Edward I*, 2nd ed., 2 vols. (Cambridge, 1911), II, 198.

7. *A Series of Precedents and Proceedings in Criminal Causes Extending from the Year 1475 to 1640 Extracted from Act-Books of Ecclesiastical Courts in the Diocese of London*, ed. W. H. Hale (London, 1847), pp. xx–xxi.

scholar who has examined the relations of the jurisdictions has commented on the limited and occasional nature of the conflict.[8] The issues over which they disagreed were actually few in number and sometimes of only limited importance within the context of the total jurisdiction of each. Each side conceded much to the other. Vast areas of jurisdictional competence never figured in the struggle; and the existence of several troublesome issues never led to a direct and total confrontation.

Sometimes controversy arose from the uncertainty or ambiguity surrounding certain types of cases or the multiplicity of issues they contained. Depending on how they were viewed and by whom, they might legitimately be claimed for one jurisdiction or the other and sometimes for both. Medieval English church courts, for example, tried a large number of cases concerning tithes, pensions, and other customary religious payments, and the royal courts admitted their right to do so. Whenever it appeared, however, that the tithes in question amounted to a large part of the total value of the clerical benefice and that a decision by the church court would prejudice the patron's right to present to a particular living, then the royal jurisdiction could intervene to protect its exclusive authority over pleas of patronage. In some cases, where the tithes had been sold or commuted for a money payment, the church court might be accused of encroaching on the royal jurisdiction over debt and lay chattels. The best example of the dual nature of certain kinds of cases is provided by those many cases of debt which the church presumed to try by virtue of its jurisdiction over breach of faith and the royal and municipal courts decided as pleas of debt and contract. Similarly, the church always insisted on punishing assault upon the persons of the clergy. On the other hand, it was sometimes challenged in doing so because the crime seemed to fall within the scope of the royal law of trespass. The two jurisdictions were occasionally able to draw neat and satisfactory distinctions, as in the case of their agreement to allow the royal courts to confiscate the chattels of dead usurers and to let the church courts punish live ones.[9] At other

8. Tout makes the same point in his introduction to the *Register of John de Halton, Bishop of Carlisle, A.D. 1292–1324*, ed. W. N. Thompson and T. F. Tout, Canterbury and York Society [CYS] (London, 1913), p. xl; Cheney, *From Becket to Langton*, pp. 107–108, 118.

9. This agreement is contained in the statute of 1341, *Statutes of the Realm, presented by Command of His Majesty King George the Third . . . from Original Records and Authentic Manuscripts*, 11 vols. (London, 1810–24), I, 296; hereafter cited as *SR*. The petition of the clergy is printed in *Rotuli Parliamentorum; ut et petitiones, et placita in Parliamento Tempore Edwardi R. I [ad finem Henrici VII]*, 7 vols. (London, 1767–77), II, 133; hereafter cited as *Rot. Parl.* Since the time of Charlemagne church and state had both opposed usury: J. T. Noonan, *The Scholastic Analysis of Usury* (Cambridge, Mass., 1957), pp. 15–16.

times they admitted a dual jurisdiction, as that over the crime of perjury, which was a nuisance that both wanted to stamp out. But in several instances the issues eluded clear and easy definition, and it was difficult, if not impossible, to divide jurisdictional competence.

The conflict of jurisdictions could also result from the greater versatility and ingenuity of one law, which enabled it to attract suitors to its courts, whatever the rights or pretensions of the other. Despite the existence of the royal prohibitions against trying a plea of debt in a church court, the inadequacy of the common law, with its rather stringent requirements of pleading and proof, encouraged many people to take cases of petty debt to the ecclesiastical courts. The willingness of the church courts to enforce verbal agreements under the guise of punishing breach of faith greatly enhanced their usefulness for the average person. To cite another example, the broad jurisdiction of the church over testamentary matters contrasted favorably with the crown's relative indifference to the English will until the end of the thirteenth century. Until Edward I's reign the state seemed to have abandoned to the church the testament and jurisdiction over its interpretation, validation, and enforcement. Ecclesiastical jurisdiction over the office of the testamentary executor and over testamentary debt was only challenged from the reign of Edward I forward as the common law came more and more to appreciate the importance of the executor and its obligation to assist him in the performance of his duties.

The conflict was not entirely the product of competing laws, as, for example, when both jurisdictions claimed to try cases of bastardy or patronage. Frequently it was the result of disagreement over procedures which were quasi-judicial or administrative. The history of the legal process called "caption" illustrates this. During the thirteenth and fourteenth centuries the crown frequently arrested and imprisoned excommunicates at the request of the higher clergy until they declared their willingness to submit to ecclesiastical justice. This practice was vital for enforcing ecclesiastical judgments and for defending the integrity of the church's authority, and the crown usually complied with the expectations of the bishops. The *gravamina* of the period, however, repeatedly denounced the violation of caption, the unwarranted release of excommunicates, and the exemption of certain persons from the full rigor of the law. What the church viewed as the automatic duty of the state, the crown saw as a privilege dependent on royal grace. Whenever it seemed that law and order would be better served, the crown reserved the right to deny caption, to release prisoners, or to ignore the legal disabilities accompanying excommunication.

The dispute over benefit of clergy focused also on procedural details rather than on first principles. During the thirteenth and fourteenth centuries the crown usually surrendered criminous clerks to the church for trial and punishment. The church's complaints that clerical immunity was being violated resulted from the crown's efforts to impose procedural checks on its enjoyment or to eliminate abuse. Likewise, the common lawyers admitted that certain matters pertained exclusively to the church and its courts, and royal judges sent to the bishops for information concerning the status of an ecclesiastical benefice, the qualifications of a presentee, the interpretation of a will, or the validity of a marriage contract. The royal courts succeeded in devising ways for avoiding reference to the church when there was the likelihood that canonical opinion might run counter to the principles of the common law or prejudice the royal view of what was right and just. The sworn inquest or jury was occasionally substituted for the writ to the bishop as a means for acquiring the necessary information. The origin of jurisdictional controversy in procedural practices can be illustrated by the crown's custom of distraining the bishops to produce their unwilling subordinates in royal courts. Although secular authorities defended this procedure as necessary and just, the higher clergy bitterly resented being placed in such an uncomfortable and sometimes costly position.

Finally, the efforts of the king's courts to capture control of all aspects of the right to confer an ecclesiastical benefice led not only to the abolition of the church's right to try cases of patronage and to the curtailment of its jurisdiction over rival presentees claiming the same benefice but also to the restriction of the bishops' freedom to exercise certain administrative powers. The king's courts and chancery invented and applied a number of actions designed to bend the bishop to the royal will and to force him to admit and institute to benefices in accordance with royal needs and the demands of the common law.

In the jurisdictional conflict as in the other disputes between church and state in England, the crown had the advantage. Its superiority was based on the effective coercive power of the king and his courts, which was expressed by the royal writ of prohibition and the machinery of constraint and intimidation that this action could bring to bear against the church courts. Except in those instances when the crown and its courts acceded to the claims of the church and, for one reason or another, refrained from acting, the crown usually got its way. This harsh fact of life was as evident in the jurisdictional conflict as it was in respect to the other issues debated between church and state—elections to bishoprics, papal provisions, and the taxation of the clergy. Although Bishop Robert Grosseteste of Lincoln, complaining against royal prohibitions, denied the ability of the secular power on its own authority to draw the line separating the jurisdictions, the crown was doing so frequently and effectively in his own day.[10] By Edward I's reign, at the latest, the church had been forced to admit the right of the king's courts to delimit the scope of ecclesiastical justice; and Archbishop John Pecham and his successors among the leaders of the English church focused their efforts upon preventing the abuse of this discretionary power.[11] In short, the English church courts were obliged to live within the context of a situation determined by the superior physical power and the resourcefulness of the crown and its courts.

The symbol of and principal instrument for the curtailment of ecclesiastical jurisdiction was the royal writ of prohibition.[12] Medieval English kings were accustomed to command any number of things to be done or not to be done. This discretionary authority, which was being enlarged and enhanced during the later middle ages in England, was applied to the jurisdictional struggle through the various prohibitory writs available to defendants in the church courts who wanted to delay or defeat actions against themselves or their interests by ecclesiastical judges. Like so much else in the history of English law and legal institutions they appeared in Henry II's time and were probably the result of that burst of judicial creativity which marked the latter part of his reign. By means of the writ of prohibition, the king commanded the ecclesiastical judge and the plaintiff in the Court Christian to stop prosecuting a particular case which was alleged to belong to the royal courts, or, in some instances, to delay further action on a plea until the king's courts had decided another, exclusively secular issue that had been raised. The punishment for refusing to comply with the king's command was attachment and distraint of the plaintiff and the judge to appear before a royal court to

10. See the letter to Archbishop Edmund in *Roberti Grosseteste Episcopi Quondam Lincolniensis Epistolae*, ed. H. R. Luard, RS (London, 1861), p. 220; hereafter cited as *Epistolae Grosseteste*. For a characterization of Grosseteste's views, see *Robert Grosseteste, Scholar and Bishop*, ed. D. A. Callus (Oxford, 1955), pp. 178–215.

11. D. Douie, *Archbishop Pecham* (Oxford, 1952), p. 118; for petitions of the clergy concerning the writ of prohibition in the fourteenth century, *Rot. Parl.*, II, 151, 357, 373, etc.

12. For the history of the prohibition see the articles by G. B. Flahiff, "The Use of Prohibitions by Clerics against Ecclesiastical Courts in England," *Mediaeval Studies*, III (1941), 101–116; and "The Writ of Prohibition to Courts Christian in the Thirteenth Century," *Mediaeval Studies*, VI (1944), 266–313; VII (1945), 229–290. I have summarized his discussion of the writ of prohibition in the twelfth and thirteenth centuries.

answer for the implied contempt—by no means a negligible threat. Apparently, if the church court believed that it was within its rights and that the case was truly a spiritual one, then it could ignore the command and proceed to judgment. There was, however, the problem of convincing the crown of the justice of its conduct, and the danger of having to pay a fine to the king for contempt and damages to the injured party. The safer approach was to request the annulment of the writ of prohibition. Bracton mentions the possibility of consulting the royal judges in order to obtain the revocation of an illicit prohibition.[13] By the end of the thirteenth century the Statute of Consultation gave statutory form to the writ of consultation (*de consultatione*) so-called, which quashed the prohibition and allowed the church to continue prosecuting the original plea.[14] Throughout the thirteenth and fourteenth centuries, however, the bishops repeatedly denounced the difficulties and delays which they encountered in obtaining consultations and the failure of the crown to punish false or malicious users of the writs and to compensate the judge and the plaintiff in the church court for the expense and discomfort they had suffered. Mingled with these grievances were complaints against the lax issue of prohibitions in the first place. Evidently, the church was never convinced that the royal courts and chancery exercised caution in dispensing the writs.

The writ of prohibition was the most effective means for expressing the royal claim to try a particular type of case. The fact that prohibitions were available to whomever desired them encouraged private persons to use them in ways which defeated or frustrated the pretensions of the church courts. At the beginning of the thirteenth century there existed writs of prohibition against trial by a church court of a plea of lay fee (*de laico feodo*), of advowson or the right to present to an ecclesiastical benefice (*de advocatione*), and of debt and lay chattels (*de catallis et debitis*), not connected, that is, with testament or matrimony (*nisi sunt de testamento vel matrimonio*). Royal prohibitions were popular with a considerable number of people of all conditions and professions. The earliest surviving *Curia Regis* rolls frequently cite their use.[15] Chancery and the king's courts, complying with popular demand, added new ones and tried to make the

13. Bracton, *De Legibus et Consuetudinibus Angliae*, ed. G. E. Woodbine, 4 vols. (New Haven, 1915–42), IV, fol. 405b; hereafter cited as Bracton.

14. *SR*, I, 108.

15. *Curia Regis Rolls of the Reigns of Richard I and John [and Henry III]* preserved in the *Public Record Office*, 14 vols. (London, 1922–61), *4 Henry III*, pp. 28, 150, 174, 209, 211, 222, 223, 229, 235, 236, 258, 285; hereafter cited as *CRR; CRR, 9–10 Henry III*, Nos. 211, 805, 1027, 1258, 1778, etc.

old writs more effective and more easily available. At the beginning of the thirteenth century the prohibitions of lay fee and of advowson had long been classed among the cursory writs (*de cursu*) of the register, which meant that they were available for routine use free of charge, or, perhaps, for a small fee to the chancery clerks for inscribing them. Between 1220 and 1230 the prohibition of lay chattels was listed as a cursory writ; and the prohibition against trying a case of trespass in a church court (*de transgressione*) was identified as a cursory writ by the end of the thirteenth century. In addition to the four cursory prohibitions of lay fee, advowson, lay chattels, and trespass, there were other prohibitions of a special kind, which were classed as writs *de praecepto* and which forbade the church courts to try cases of defamation, rape, and several other less prominent matters. Writs of prohibition were applicable against plaintiffs in the Courts Christian and against native ecclesiastical judges and papal judges delegate. The church's efforts to cope with them were never particularly successful. Early in Edward I's reign, and probably in response to efforts by the bishops to discourage their use by threat of excommunication, the crown invented the variant of the prohibitory writ of course known as *ex relatu plurium*.[16] This kind of prohibition, which covered all of the contested cases, concealed the identity of the purchaser, who was often a cleric, by making the king a party to the plea. It was brought to the Court Christian and prosecuted by its purchaser, who acted as the king's agent on this occasion. *Ex relatu plurium* was invented to protect the defendant in the ecclesiastical court, who wanted to challenge its jurisdiction but who feared retaliation by the church. The bishops never succeeded in convincing the king of the injustice of such writs, and they were ultimately forced to rely entirely upon the crown's discretion, sense of fair play, and self-restraint in issuing them.

The growth of the common law and the canon law made conflict likely or at least possible. Nevertheless, the conflict of jurisdictions was primarily the result of the activities of individual suitors, especially the purchasers of royal prohibitions. The existence of these writs and others, readily available to private persons, encouraged both laymen and clerks, high and humble, to use them for self-serving purposes. Despite the invention of the writs of prohibition by the crown as a means for asserting the jurisdictional claims of the king's courts, they were acquired and prosecuted by that host of private persons who saw it to their advantage to do so. The jurisdictional struggle in medieval England was the result of the actions of a fairly large number of people—prelates, priests, nobles,

16. Flahiff, "Use of Prohibitions by Clerics," pp. 109–115.

and commoners—motivated by nothing more exalted than self-interest and expediency, who brought the two jurisdictions into conflict in the hope of their own gain or reward.

Neither the clergy nor the laity were united among themselves in defending one jurisdiction or in opposing the other. Both laymen and clerks of all ranks took their legal problems to whomever could solve them regardless of rival claims and pretensions. Laymen were willing to seek the protection or help of the church courts when it was to their advantage to do so. Often suit in a temporal or spiritual court was simply a prelude to or, perhaps, a consequence of litigation in the other. On the other hand, the idealists among the higher clergy were seldom able to obtain the compliance either of their colleagues or of their subordinates with the high-flown principles of the gravamina or the teachings of the canonists.[17] Churchmen, both secular and religious, purchased writs of prohibition. Prelates and priests alike were willing to sue in the royal courts on doubtful matters.[18] It is very apparent from the episcopal injunctions against violating the jurisdictional rights of the church and from the spiritual censures periodically decreed against violators that the bishops, the authors of the gravamina, never succeeded in uniting the clergy in the defense of the church courts.

The popes of the thirteenth and fourteenth centuries could seldom be counted on to support strongly the claims of the English ecclesiastical courts except when papal interests themselves were threatened. The relations of Rome with English sovereigns, on the one hand, and with the English church, on the other, were usually determined by considerations of expediency. On those few occasions when the papacy took notice of the claims of the English church courts and of alleged royal encroachments, it seldom showed a desire to press the struggle to the limit or to risk a dangerous confrontation with the crown. Pope Alexander III's decree claiming all pleas of patronage for the church remained a dead letter in England; and later popes had no desire to renew the struggle. In Henry III's reign the high church position on jurisdictional matters was represented by men like Bishop Grosseteste of Lincoln rather than the popes of the period. That kings like Henry III and Edward I believed that appeals to Rome might be to their advantage in the jurisdictional struggle indicates that they did not assume that the interests of the English church and the papacy inevitably coincided. King Henry III, for instance, appealed to Rome against Archbishop Boniface of Savoy's canons of 1261,

17. F. M. Powicke, *The Thirteenth Century: 1216–1307* (Oxford, 1953), pp. 467–469.
18. See the remark of C. R. Cheney, *Hubert Walter* (London, 1967), p. 10.

several of which dealt with jurisdictional matters. Although Pope Urban IV said that he saw nothing wrong with them and urged the king to be just to the church, out of deference to the crown he refused to confirm them.[19]

In like manner, the reluctance of the papacy to support the pronouncements of Archbishop Pecham at Reading in 1279 and at the Council of Lambeth in 1281 on behalf of ecclesiastical liberties and the rights of church courts, proves that the pope did not see himself invariably committed to the defense of English ecclesiastical jurisdiction. The divergence of the interests of the English bishops from those of Rome is very evident in the jurisdictional controversy. The native bishops, for instance, were not especially interested in supporting such explicitly papal claims as the freedom to execute papal mandates within the kingdom or to cite clerics outside it. On the other hand, the bishops stressed in the gravamina presented to the crown such matters of primarily local interest as the government's failure to arrest and detain excommunicates at the request of the bishops rather than a problem which worried the papacy— the denial of the privilege of caption to papal judges delegate.[20] Even when Rome intervened to support the jurisdictional pretensions of the English church courts its efforts were, at best, half-hearted. On those occasions when the papacy showed greater determination, its conduct was usually prompted by a concern for its own interests or needs. Although the popes of the fourteenth century succeeded in consolidating their control of the churches of Christendom, papal power was usually exercised in defense of its own jurisdictional claims rather than on behalf of the English church courts, except when their interests were identical or, through delegation, the jurisdictions coincided. Revenues and sinecures were much higher on the list of papal priorities than the jurisdictional claims of English bishops and archdeacons; and the relations of the papacy with the English church were usually determined by papal ambitions in respect to taxation, provisions to benefices, and the appointment of the higher clergy. The policy of conciliation, restraint, and compromise, which seemed to guide the popes of the fourteenth century in their negotiations with English sovereigns, surely dissuaded them from pressing too ardently for the recognition of the jurisdictional claims of the English church.[21]

19. J. W. Gray, "Archbishop Pecham and the Decrees of Boniface," in *Studies in Church History*, ed. G. J. Cuming, II (London, 1965), 215–219.

20. J. W. Gray makes this point and places the Stubbs-Maitland controversy in a new perspective in "Canon Law in England: some Reflections on the Stubbs-Maitland Controversy," in *Studies in Church History*, ed. G. J. Cuming, III (Leiden, 1966), 61–64.

21. W. A. Pantin, *The English Church in the Fourteenth Century* (Cambridge, 1955), pp. 3–4, 97.

The English church responded in several ways to the jurisdictional challenge posed by the king's courts. About the middle of Henry III's reign the bishops began the practice of compiling lists of grievances, the gravamina, for presentation to the crown. The surviving gravamina, which date from about 1239 to 1399, frequently mention matters of jurisdictional disagreement.[22] Like the English laity, the clergy recognized the value of timing their efforts to coincide with royal requests for taxation or with political crises of one sort or another. However, the church found it necessary, as did baronage and commons, to resort to more forceful methods of protecting itself against royal oppression. On several occasions in the reigns of Henry III and Edward I the bishops applied spiritual sanctions to the defense of ecclesiastical jurisdiction against royal encroachment and violations instigated by private persons. The church also tried to protect itself by obtaining legislation on its behalf. During the thirteenth and early fourteenth centuries the crown usually avoided giving written replies to the petitions of the clergy, and it was always difficult to hold the king and his ministers to the royal promises. Beginning in Edward II's reign the higher clergy sought, with only limited success, to obtain the incorporation of the king's favorable answers into royal statutes, which, they hoped, would guarantee their enforcement. None of these approaches—petitionings, spiritual censures, or statutes—were totally satisfactory, however, as methods for preventing the violation of the jurisdictional claims of the church.

The official grievances of the clergy indicate the major topics of dispute as well as the arguments adduced by one jurisdiction or the other in defense of its claim to try certain types of cases. The earliest surviving gravamina date from about 1239.[23] The English bishops may have seized the opportunity afforded by the presence of the cardinal legate Otto in England to petition Henry III for the redress of grievances. Although the gravamina of ca. 1239 contain complaints of a nonjurisdictional kind, they go to the heart of the jurisdictional controversy by denouncing the use of prohibitions and the practices of compelling bishops to answer before laymen for the exercise of their office and of requiring clerics to submit to the civil and criminal jurisdiction of the king. The gravamina of

22. See my article, "Bishops, Politics, and the Two Laws: the *Gravamina* of the English Clergy, 1237–1399," *Speculum*, XLI (1966), 209–245.

23. *Councils & Synods with Other Documents Relating to the English Church*, Part II: *1205–1313*, ed. F. M. Powicke and C. R. Cheney (Oxford, 1964), pp. 280–284; hereafter cited as *Councils & Synods*. F. M. Powicke, *King Henry III and the Lord Edward*, 2 vols. (Oxford, 1947), I, 351–353; D. M. Williamson, "Some Aspects of the Legation of Cardinal Otto in England," *EHR*, LXIV (1949), 163 ff.

1239, which may have been presented to the king again in 1240 and are similar to another list of grievances dating from 1253, bear the unmistakable imprint of the ideals and opinions of Bishop Grosseteste of Lincoln.[24] Grosseteste's exalted idea of the priestly office and of the duties of the Christian bishop are reflected in the gravamina of 1239 and 1253, which attempted to reduce to a minimum the authority of laymen over clerics and which denied the right of the secular authority to define the scope of ecclesiastical justice or to judge bishops for the performance of their spiritual duties.[25]

There is no evidence that these earliest gravamina were ever answered by the crown or that the higher clergy succeeded in remedying the specific grievances which they expressed. The practice of petitioning the king was, however, resumed later in Henry III's reign. The pressing financial needs of the crown and the growing unrest of the baronage provided the circumstances surrounding the compilation and presentation of the gravamina of 1257.[26] This list contained fifty articles and focused on jurisdictional disagreements. The refusal of the sheriffs to arrest excommunicates at the demand of the bishops, repeated violation of sanctuary and benefit of clergy, and interference with the testamentary jurisdiction of the church were denounced, along with that perennial abuse, the use of prohibitions to impede the operation of the church courts. Another list of grievances dates from the period marked by the London council of 1257 and the Lambeth council of 1261, and it contains what appear to be the official responses of the crown to the clerical complaints.[27] The most important advancement by the church in the jurisdictional controversy of Henry III's reign was, however, the decision made in 1257 and repeated in the councils of 1258 and 1261 to apply spiritual sanctions to the defense of ecclesiastical jurisdiction.

In 1257 the custom of pronouncing spiritual censures against the violators of ecclesiastical liberties was applied to the jurisdictional conflict when the provincial council of London, under Archbishop Boniface, proposed to use such sanctions in defense of the church courts.[28] The ten proposals from 1257 urged the ecclesiastical judges to resist royal intrusion and to respond, if necessary, by excommunicating the violators of the jurisdictional rights of the church. If an ecclesiastical judge, for example,

24. *Councils & Synods*, pp. 284, 469–472.
25. Callus (ed.), *Robert Grosseteste*, pp. 150 ff., 179 ff.
26. *Councils & Synods*, pp. 539–548. See Powicke, *Henry III and the Lord Edward*, I, 343 ff.
27. *Councils & Synods*, pp. 687–692.
28. *Ibid.*, pp. 537–539.

were prohibited from trying a case of tithes or of breach of faith on the grounds that it concerned the advowson of a benefice or was a plea of lay fee and lay chattels, he was admonished to ignore the writ. Should he be attached to answer in the king's court for the implied contempt, he and his colleagues were counseled to excommunicate the royal justices and others responsible for this infraction of ecclesiastical liberties. Similarly, spiritual sanctions were to be employed to defend the jurisdiction of the church courts over purely spiritual cases like personal actions involving clerics, to prevent the distraint of prelates to produce their clerical subordinates in secular courts, and to force the release of imprisoned ecclesiastical judges guilty of violating royal prohibitions. The proposals of 1257 depended upon the bishops for their enforcement, and the higher clergy were urged to unite in the defense of common interests. They did not become official legislation of the English church, however, until they were revised and incorporated into the canons of the Council of Merton and Westminster in 1258.

The canons of 1258 instructed prelates and other ecclesiastical officials to refuse to comply with royal writs which called them to explain their performance of such purely spiritual functions as admitting and instituting to benefices, excommunicating persons, or trying pleas of tithes, perjury, breach of faith, and the like.[29] The higher clergy were instructed to write in a respectful manner to the king explaining why the king's command could not be obeyed. If the secular authority continued to press the matter to the point of attaching the accused prelate, then the offending sheriff, royal officials, and even the chancery clerks who had inscribed the writ were to be excommunicated. If they were churchmen they were to be deprived of their clerical livings and disqualified from holding a benefice for a period of five years. If this did not suffice to halt royal oppression, then the lands and residences of the king within the diocese were to be placed under interdict; in especially grievous cases this interdict might be extended to the whole realm. Bishops were told to cooperate by imposing the sanctions in their dioceses, and the archbishops were to constrain the timid. In two dozen separate provisions, many of them dealing with jurisdictional issues, the church announced its intention of applying spiritual censures to the defense of the jurisdictional prerogatives of the church courts. Henceforth, the problems arising out of the unwillingness of the secular authority to arrest and imprison obdurate excommunicates, to respect benefit of clergy and the right of sanctuary, to allow the prelates free exercise of their authority over faith and morals, and to permit

29. *Ibid.*, pp. 572–583.

the church to enjoy its testamentary jurisdiction, were to be dealt with in more forceful ways than mere petitioning. The provisions of 1258 were republished in a revised form in the canons of 1261, which the provincial Council at Lambeth enacted into formal legislation of the English church.[30] Although Pope Urban IV temporarily refused to confirm them, they were republished on several occasions and were considered to be authentic.[31]

The struggle on behalf of the church courts was renewed in Edward I's reign by Archbishop Pecham, an especially able and energetic primate, who was committed to the reform of the church and the defense of ecclesiastical justice.[32] Pecham resumed in 1280 and 1285 the custom of petitioning for the redress of the clergy's grievances.[33] The success of the crown and its courts in forcing the church to accept the fact of the king's right to decide the limits of jurisdictional competence is revealed by the differing attitudes of Robert Grosseteste and John Pecham toward the writs of prohibition. Whereas Grosseteste rejected them out of hand, Pecham tried to eliminate their abuse by securing the crown's promise to punish persons using them unjustly and to expedite the process of their annulment.[34] The gravamina of 1285 requested that a commission of royal judges resident at Westminster be empowered to grant consultations and that the prelates be permitted to punish fraudulent users of the writs. The enactment of the Statute of Consultation, which gave statutory form to the method of quashing a prohibition, probably represented a victory for the church.[35]

On the other hand, Pecham returned to the more forceful methods of opposing royal encroachment on ecclesiastical jurisdiction devised by Archbishop Boniface and the higher clergy of the previous reign. At the Councils of Reading in 1279 and Lambeth in 1281 he republished, with a few additions of his own, the earlier legislation decreeing spiritual sanctions against violators of ecclesiastical jurisdiction.[36] The Council of Reading confirmed the enactments of Otto, Ottobono, and Boniface.

30. *Ibid.*, pp. 669–685.

31. Pecham believed that they had been confirmed by the pope; Boniface's canons were applied in Dublin and York, renewed by Archbishop Stratford, and quoted as authoritative legislation of the church by William Lyndwood. See *Councils & Synods*, p. 662.

32. Douie, *Archbishop Pecham*, pp. 48, 95 ff.

33. For the gravamina of 1280, see *Councils & Synods*, pp. 873–886; for those of 1285, see *ibid.*, pp. 956–964.

34. Douie, *Archbishop Pecham*, pp. 118–119.

35. *SR*, I, 108.

36. For the articles of excommunication of 1279, see *Councils & Synods*, pp. 848–850; for those of 1281, see *ibid.*, pp. 905–907.

Pecham augmented the canons of 1261 with certain new articles of excommunication. One of these declared the excommunication *ipso facto* of persons who used writs of prohibition to interfere with the lawful jurisdiction of the church over purely spiritual cases. The other articles excommunicated those royal officials who denied writs of caption, who released excommunicates before they had satisfied the church, or who seized ecclesiastical properties during wardship. The archbishop outraged the king by ordering, in addition, the posting of copies of Magna Carta in the churches. Edward reacted immediately. At the November Parliament of 1279 he forced Pecham to withdraw the offending clauses and to revoke the order for the posting of the charter. Nevertheless, they were later, with the exception of the one concerning Magna Carta, included in the Lambeth legislation of 1281. Henceforth, the most notorious infractions of ecclesiastical justice stood condemned by the declarations of two English primates. It would seem, moreover, that this custom of retaliating by spiritual censures against the use of royal prohibitions was having the desired effect. It was in Edward I's reign that the royal government devised the writ, *ex relatu plurium*, which enabled its users to escape ecclesiastical punishment.

The reign of Edward I was a time of trial for the church courts.[37] The attitude and conduct of the crown and its courts show that the secular power was making a serious effort to restrict the church courts to matrimonial and testamentary matters where the laity and their chattels were concerned. The extortions of ecclesiastical judges constituted an article of the *Quo warranto* inquiries, and apparently the royal judges were receiving the indictment of ecclesiastical judges accused of trying several types of borderline cases. In 1285 the bishops denounced certain chapters of the second Statute of Westminster which seemed to challenge their jurisdiction over testamentary matters, corodies, tithes, and vicarages.[38] In the summer of 1285 the crown announced its intention of enforcing a policy of stringent restriction of the church courts to testamentary and matrimonial matters and explicitly moral crimes. Two royal justices, Richard Boyland and William Rothing, were sent into the diocese of Norwich to entertain complaints against ecclesiastical courts. This investigation was painfully thorough and extended to encroachments upon royal jurisdiction com-

37. Douie, *Archbishop Pecham*, pp. 309–321. For the events of this period, see also G. O. Sayles and H. G. Richardson, "The Clergy and the Easter Parliament of 1285," *EHR*, LII (1937), 220–234; E. B. Graves, "Circumpsecte Agatis," *EHR*, XLIII (1928), 1–20. The best edition of *Circumspecte agatis* is to be found in the Graves article.

38. *Councils & Synods*, pp. 964–965.

mitted since the beginning of the reign. It was shortly broadened to cover a general inquiry into the misdeeds of ecclesiastical judges in the eastern counties. The general edict and its ruthless enforcement by the royal justices constituted the most serious and efficient attack on the church courts hitherto undertaken. A crisis was narrowly averted by Edward I's decision, announced from Paris in the writ *Circumspecte agatis*, to relax the persecution and to define as precisely as possible the rights of the church courts in those jurisdictional areas which had been the focus of the recent controversy. It is unlikely that *Circumspecte agatis*, which later generations viewed as an important statute, eliminated all doubt concerning these types of cases; but it did signal the state's decision to abandon the frontal attack on ecclesiastical jurisdiction in preference for the old piecemeal approach of the past.

Fortunately for the English church one great archbishop was followed by another, when Robert Winchelsey succeeded John Pecham in the see of Canterbury in 1293. At his first council convened after his arrival in England, the higher clergy, under Winchelsey's leadership, took up the jurisdictional controversy in a·list of over fifty articles of grievance drawn heavily from the petition of 1280.[39] There is some evidence that the English church hoped to enlist the aid of the papacy in the defense of its jurisdictional pretensions and that Rome was sympathetic with its plight.[40] The struggle on behalf of the church courts was temporarily deflected by the dispute provoked by *Clericis laicos*, although the political crises of the latter part of Edward I's reign offered opportunities for renewed efforts. In 1300–1301 both baronage and bishops presented petitions to the king in the expectation that the times were favorable to winning concessions, and it seems that Winchelsey and the clergy intended to petition again in 1305.[41] The death of Edward I and the succession of Edward II in 1307 was followed by an especially ambitious attempt to petition for the redress of the church's jurisdictional grievances. At the provincial Council of London and Lambeth in 1309 the clergy compiled a long list of grievances based upon a discussion of the earlier petitions of 1280 and 1301. Winchelsey prefaced the petition with a letter surveying the history of jurisdictional relations since William the Conqueror's decision to separate the courts down to the present time, and reminding the new king

39. *Ibid.*, pp. 1138–1147; Powicke, *Thirteenth Century*, pp. 671–673; 704–705, 717–718.

40. See the petition addressed to Boniface VIII in 1295 in *Registrum Johannis de Pontissara, Episcopi Wyntoniensis, A.D. MCCLXXXII–MCCCIV*, ed. C. Deedes, CYS, 2 vols. (London, 1913–24), I, 203–204. See also *Councils & Synods*, p. 1267.

41. *Councils & Synods*, pp. 1206–1218, 1227.

of his and his ancestors' promises in their coronation oaths to keep the liberties of the English church inviolate.[42] Winchelsey, like Pecham before him, denounced the writ *ex relatu plurium*, whereby suitors covertly challenged the jurisdiction of church courts, and he urged both the punishment of false use of the writ and the compensation of the ecclesiastical judge and the plaintiff in the church court for their injuries. The political crisis involving Thomas of Lancaster and the baronage provided the opportunity for another effort on behalf of ecclesiastical jurisdiction. The eleventh chapter of the Ordinances of 1311 gave the ecclesiastical judge and the plaintiff damages for having been victimized by a writ of prohibition; and this victory must have been the result of the close association of Winchelsey with Earl Thomas and the baronial program of reform.[43] After the death of Archbishop Winchelsey in 1313 none of the leaders of the English church, with the possible exception of John Stratford in Edward III's reign, were of the stature of a Grosseteste, a Pecham, or a Winchelsey. The higher clergy continued the struggle, however, and the Articles of the Clergy in 1316 marked an important advance in the church's method of contending with the royal jurisdiction.

The repetition of particular complaints, which had supposedly been remedied by earlier concessions, shows that the church never succeeded in holding the crown to its promises or in obtaining the compliance of the king's courts and his ministers with royal assurances that the legitimate jurisdictional rights of the church would be respected. In the jurisdictional area, as in so many other fields of medieval administration, there was the real problem of bringing the actions of local government into conformity with official policy, and this difficulty was aggravated by the uncertainty and ambiguity of many areas of rivalry. Throughout the thirteenth and fourteenth centuries the bishops repeatedly denounced the excesses and outrages of sheriffs and royal bailiffs, who were apparently ignoring the promises made in reply to the gravamina. Further, the crown had successfully avoided on several occasions committing itself by written replies. Beginning in 1316 with the so-called Articles of the Clergy the church succeeded in having the favorable replies to its grievances incorporated into parliamentary legislation. Subsequently, in 1341, 1344, 1352, 1376, and in 1377, certain favorable responses to clerical gravamina were given statutory form.[44] The political crisis of Edward III's reign,

42. *Ibid.*, pp. 1269–1274.

43. *SR*, I, 160; T. F. Tout, *The Place of the Reign of Edward II in English History* (Manchester, 1936), pp. 77 ff.

44. The statutes enacted in response to clerical petitioning are found in *SR*, I, 171–174, 295–296, 302–303, 325–326, 398; II, 5. The clerical petitions are in *Rot. Parl.*, I, 350; II, 129–130, 151–152, 244–245, 357–358, 373; III, 25–27.

which extended from 1341 to 1343, and the accession of Richard II
in 1377 probably seemed opportune for petitioning for the redress of
grievances and the enactment of statutes favorable to the pretensions of
the church, although the gravamina presented in 1327 and 1399 to the
new kings, Edward III and Henry IV, were not incorporated into
statutes.[45]

The jurisdictional conflict during the reigns of Edward III and
Richard II narrowed its focus to certain topics determined by new
pressures and conditions. Old matters occasionally came up for discussion, and twice the bishops asked that the "statute" of *Circumspecte
agatis* be confirmed; but the gravamina and the statutes show that the
jurisdictional controversy had become more limited and had shifted to
certain new areas of disagreement. Some of the problems of the past—
such as the denial or disregard of caption or some of the specific abuses
associated with writs of prohibition—were seldom mentioned. It is very
evident that at this late date the higher clergy had been forced to accede
in many instances to the demands of the royal courts. On the other hand,
the church courts were experiencing pressure in some new areas. During
the course of the fourteenth century the church repeatedly criticized royal
intrusion upon its jurisdiction over customary religious payments,
especially pensions based on tithes. The efforts of the clergy to impose
upon the laity their definition of the tithe of ceduous wood (*sylva cedua*)
and to enforce payment by canonical process doubtlessly aggravated
relations in this area. It would seem that whenever the church courts were
attempting to force the payment of money or decide cases of chattels they
were experiencing opposition and sometimes worse. Another area of controversy in the latter part of the fourteenth century concerned the clergy
themselves. The political crisis of Edward III's reign, which began in
1341, had entailed the arrest and punishment of a large number of royal
officials, some of whom were clerics, in ways which seemed to flout Magna
Carta and benefit of clergy. The problem of law enforcement, which led
the royal authorities to arrest churchmen on general charges of lawlessness
and brigandage, combined with the new legislation concerning treason in
1352, seemed to jeopardize the principle of the immunity of the clergy
from trial and punishment by laymen. Finally, the custom of granting
conditional consultations, which permitted the acquisition of new prohibitions after the annulment of the first, was repeatedly condemned as an

45. For the petition of 1327, see *Rotuli Parliamentorum Anglie Hactenus Inediti,
MCCLXXIX–MCCCLXXIII*, ed. H. G. Richardson and G. O. Sayles, Camden Society,
Ser. 3, LI (London, 1935), pp. 106–110; hereafter cited as *Rot. Parl. Inediti*. For the petition
of 1399, see *Concilia Magnae Brittaniae et Hiberniae . . .*, ed. D. Wilkins, 4 vols. (London,
1737), III, 240–245; hereafter cited as Wilkins.

unwarranted and novel abuse. New areas of controversy or variations of the older ones are reflected in the gravamina from the reigns of Edward III and Richard II and occasionally in the statutes which the church hoped would remedy its complaints.

Although the gravamina are very useful for identifying the specific areas of jurisdictional rivalry from the middle of Henry III's reign to the accession of Henry IV, nevertheless, the actual conflict occurred in the course of trying certain types of cases or applying certain judicial or administrative procedures in the royal and ecclesiastical courts. The jurisdictional conflict, on both sides, was a day-to-day, almost casual affair, which must be traced in several kinds of cases that were tried by one court system or the other and sometimes by both. Writ registers, statutes, legal treatises, and the royal replies to gravamina reveal the rationale underlying royal claims and the opinions of the common lawyers. On the other hand, the success of the crown in enforcing its claims depended on the willingness of private persons to seek royal justice and on the ability of the king's courts to dispense it. The records of cases tried in the royal courts and the reports of opinions and procedures given by the Year Books are especially helpful in understanding both the topics of jurisdictional controversy and the practices adopted by one jurisdiction or the other to enforce its claims.

Regrettably, the actual functioning of the courts of the archbishops, bishops, archdeacons, and their officials has not received the same attention as has been given to the king's courts and the common law during the later middle ages. We are, for instance, still awaiting a volume from the Selden Society on select pleas in the church courts comparable to their learned editions of royal plea rolls and Year Books. Despite recent attempts to explore the working of the ecclesiastical courts in England, much remains undone and even unattempted.[46] The paucity of printed

---

46. Most helpful for the study of the English ecclesiastical courts in the later middle ages is B. L. Woodcock, *Medieval Ecclesiastical Courts in the Diocese of Canterbury* (London, 1952). See also the articles by J. Sayers, "Canterbury Proctors at the Court of 'Audientia Litterarum Contradictarum,'" *Traditio*, XXII (1966), 311–345; "The Judicial Activities of the General Chapters," *Journal of Ecclesiastical History [JEH]*, XV (1964), 18–32, 168–185; and C. Morris, "A Consistory Court in the Middle Ages," *JEH*, XIV (1963), 150–159. R. Brentano has described the interaction of papal and metropolitical jurisdiction in *York Metropolitan Jurisdiction and Papal Judges Delegate (1279–1296)* (Berkeley and Los Angeles, 1959). In *Two Churches* (Princeton, 1968), pp. 74 ff., 132 ff., the same author compares ecclesiastical jurisdiction in thirteenth-century England and Italy. For the court of the commissary at York, see J. S. Purvis, *A Medieval Act Book, with some Account of Ecclesiastical Jurisdiction at York* (York, n.d.).

court records from the thirteenth and fourteenth centuries forces the historian to search out his evidence in a variety of nonjudicial sources, both ecclesiastical and secular.[47] The bishops' registers published by the indefatigable editors of the Canterbury and York Society and the several county record societies contain much material bearing on the jurisdictional conflict. The body of the canon law and the works of individual canonists are, like royal statutes and the treatises of Bracton, Fleta, and Britton, useful for explaining the theoretical claims of English ecclesiastical justice, although the reasons for its success in withstanding the aggression of royal jurisdiction can be discerned only by examining some specific cases which the church managed to reserve to itself.

The limited and very specific nature of the jurisdictional conflict is clearly revealed by the several kinds of cases and the procedural

---

47. Most of the printed ecclesiastical court records are of rather late date and are usually extracts or abridgments, therefore, of only limited value. In addition to William Hale's *A Series of Precedents and Proceedings in Criminal Causes . . . from Act-Books of Ecclesiastical Courts in the Diocese of London . . .*, see *Depositions and other Ecclesiastical Proceedings from the Courts of Durham extending from 1311 to the Reign of Elizabeth*, ed. J. Raine, Surtees Society (London, 1847); *Acts of Chapter of the Collegiate Church of SS. Peter and Wilfrid, Ripon, A.D. 1452 to A.D. 1506*, ed. J. T. Fowler, Surtees Society (Durham, 1875); *Norwich Consistory Court Depositions, 1499–1512 and 1518–1530*, ed. E. D. Stone and B. Cozens-Hardy, Norfolk Record Society (London, 1938); J. S. Purvis, *Introduction to Ecclesiastical Records* (London, 1953); E. R. Brinkworth, "The Study and Use of Archdeacons' Court Records: Illustrated from the Oxford Records (1566–1759)," in *Transactions of the Royal Historical Society* [*TRHS*], Ser. 4, XXV (1943), 93–119; F. G. Emmison, "Abstract of an Act Book of the Archdeacon of Huntingdon's Court," in *Transactions of the East Herts Archaeological Society*, VIII (1928–33), 26–42, 187–194; F. S. Hockaday, "The Consistory Court of the Diocese of Gloucester," in *Transactions of the Bristol and Gloucestershire Archaeological Society*, XLVI (1924), 195–287; W. J. Pressey, "The Records of the Archdeaconries of Essex and Colchester," in *Transactions of the Essex Archaeological Society*, N.S., XIX (1927–30), 1–21; V. B. Redstone, "Records of the Sudbury Archdeaconry," in *Proceedings of the Suffolk Institute of Archaeology and Natural History*, XI (1903), 252–300; M. D. Slater, "The Records of the Court of Arches," *JEH*, IV (1953), 139–153; two articles by the former librarian of the Dean and Chapter of Canterbury, C. E. Woodruff, are "Notes from a Fourteenth Century Act Book of the Consistory Court of Canterbury," and "The Records of the Archdeaconry and Consistory of Canterbury," in *Archaeologia Cantiana*, XL (1928), 53–64; and XLI (1929), 89–105; F. W. X. Ficham, "Notes from the Ecclesiastical Court Records at Somerset House," *TRHS*, Ser. 4, IV (1921), 103–139; A. P. Moore, "Proceedings of the Ecclesiastical Courts in the Archdeaconry of Leicester, 1516–1535," *Associated Architectural Societies Reports and Papers*, XXVIII, part i (1905), 117–220; XXVIII, part ii (1906), 593–662; *An Episcopal Court Book for the Diocese of Lincoln, 1514–1520*, ed. M. Bowker, Lincoln Record Society (Lincoln, 1967).

interrelationships which were the focus of controversy.[48] Among the most prominent of these were the following:

1. The success of the royal courts in establishing their exclusive competence over the patronage of ecclesiastical benefices led also to their restriction of the church's jurisdiction over cases concerning the possession of benefices contested between clerics, over certain kinds of tithes cases, and even over admissions and institutions to ecclesiastical livings. The requirement that royal judgments be kept inviolate limited the bishops' freedom to exercise important administrative functions of the episcopal office.

2. The ambition of the king's courts to capture for themselves all cases of real property soon led to the abolition of the church's jurisdiction over certain types of landed property, which a previous age had granted it, and also to the curtailment of its testamentary and matrimonial jurisdiction.

3. Although the crown was usually prepared to recognize and respect spiritual censures and to lend its assistance to their enforcement, controversy sometimes erupted when such sentences of excommunication seemed to jeopardize the rule of law or to be contrary to royal rights and the judgments of the king's courts. What the higher clergy viewed as an absolute duty of the Christian magistrate, the English sovereigns and their courts saw as a gracious act of assistance limited by the needs of law enforcement and the demands of justice.

4. The jurisdictional competence of the church over tithes, pensions, and other customary religious payments was sometimes challenged by royal writs of prohibition when it appeared that the church was trying cases which were actually pleas of debt or contract. Whenever the Courts Christian presumed to try cases concerning the chattels of the laity, except when such were explicitly connected with testamentary and matrimonial matters, they ran the risk of being stopped by a royal prohibition.

5. On the other hand, the greater attractiveness of the canon law drew a considerable number of cases of petty debt to the church courts, which compelled restitution by virtue of punishing breach of faith (*fidei laesio*). The intrinsic advantage of canon law in such cases offset the existence of the royal prohibition *de catallis et debitis*, whereby

48. A brief but useful survey of the jurisdictional conflict in the thirteenth and fourteenth centuries is offered by I. J. Churchill, *Canterbury Administration*, 2 vols. (London, 1933), II, 520–534.

private persons asserted the claim of the king's courts to this kind of case.

6. The decision of the king's courts in Edward I's reign to pay more attention to the enforcement of the English will brought them into competition with the church in an area of law and justice long ago abandoned to the ecclesiastical jurisdiction. This competition of the two jurisdictions arose from their efforts to enforce testamentary debt by providing judicial actions for and against the executor in their respective courts.

7. The enthusiasm of the king's courts and royal officials for maintaining law and order sometimes seemed to jeopardize the principles of benefit of clergy and sanctuary, although controversy resulted from efforts to eliminate abuses rather than from an attack on the rights themselves.

8. The general willingness of the two jurisdictions to cooperate is revealed by their combination to stamp out perjury in the law courts. Yet the crown took a dim view of the use of the canon law of defamation to interfere with the accusation of criminals before the king's justices.

9. A number of procedural difficulties continued to trouble relations between the jurisdictions in the later middle ages. The bishops, for example, bitterly resented being forced to produce the lesser clergy of their dioceses before royal judges or to collect from them monies due the crown. On the other side, the church courts were occasionally criticized for using lay juries for their own purposes or for imposing pecuniary penances as punishments for spiritual crimes.

These are the major topics which figured in the lists of official grievances of the church and clergy during the thirteenth and fourteenth centuries. Occasionally one or two of them were dramatized by the personalities or policies of particular statesmen. Henry III, for example, vigorously opposed both the methods and the effects of a thorough scrutiny of public morals undertaken by some of the higher clergy during his reign. On one occasion it seemed that Edward I was launching a special attack on ecclesiastical jurisdiction over lay chattels. On the other hand, the conflict concerning ecclesiastical jurisdiction over certain kinds of real property was over by the middle of Henry III's reign, although dispute over tithes and pensions was probably more intense during the fourteenth century than earlier. Conflict was always aggravated when the rights or interests of the crown were involved, as was the case frequently in respect to patronage. Generally speaking, however, the jurisdictional controversy assumed the form of a steady pressure by the courts of the king on the courts of the church—a pressure generated by private suitors or by the requirements of particular judicial and administrative procedures.

I. THE STRUGGLE OVER THE ECCLESIASTICAL BENEFICE: ADVOWSON AND PATRONAGE

In their effort to enforce the claim of the Constitutions of Clarendon to exclusive jurisdiction over patronage, the king's courts and chancery invented several actions and procedures which severely limited the church's authority over the benefice and its possession by clerics. Some of these innovations appeared in the late twelfth century. During the thirteenth and early fourteenth centuries they were applied so as to vindicate the royal claim to try all cases touching the right to present to ecclesiastical livings.[49] Until the middle of the fourteenth century, when the challenge of papal justice encouraged the crown to experiment with new means for defending the royal jurisdiction, these were: (1) the availability to defendants in the Courts Christian of royal prohibitions *de advocatione* prohibiting the church courts from trying pleas of patronage; (2) the existence of other prohibitory writs which either ordered the church court to stop trying a case concerning a benefice disputed between clerics until the king's court had decided the question of the right to patronage or else ordered the church to cease prosecuting a plea which could conceivably end in a judgment contrary to a prior royal judgment; (3) the invention and popularization of royal actions of a possessory nature which attracted patrons and their presentees from the courts of the church to those of the crown; (4) the extension of the definition of the right to patronage to cover cases involving the right to bestow a significant portion of the value of the benefice in tithes and oblations; (5) the creation of several royal writs which had the effect of limiting the bishops' freedom in admitting and instituting to benefices; and (6) the use of the lay jury as a means for determining the status of a benefice. The effect of these actions was to force the church to surrender pleas of patronage to the crown and also to impose rather stringent restrictions upon the exercise of the judicial and

---

49. In English law the term *advowson* was used to signify the ownership or possession of the right to present a candidate to a clerical benefice and was early equated with real property. The most thorough investigation of the jurisdictional conflict over advowson is the article by J. W. Gray, "The Ius Praesentandi from the Constitutions of Clarendon to Bracton," *EHR*, LXVII (1952), 481–509.

administrative authority of the bishop in other, explicitly spiritual areas. The right of the church courts to decide between two clerics claiming possession of the same benefice was drastically limited; and the ex officio authority of the bishop as diocesan was subjected, at least theoretically, to the superior will of the king's courts. By the end of the thirteenth century the crown had enforced its jurisdictional claims upon the English church. Yet this was the very time when the Roman Curia was replacing the native ecclesiastical courts as the principal jurisdictional rival of the crown in respect to the ecclesiastical benefice. The multiplication of papal provisions to English benefices and the growth of papal jurisdiction during the fourteenth century led to the creation of more dramatic ways for asserting the jurisdictional pretensions of the crown. The antipapal legislation of Edward III's reign was considerably less innovative than has sometimes been supposed. The Ordinances and Statutes of Provisors and Praemunire were based upon the old assumption that pleas of advowson belonged solely to the royal courts. The methods which were applied to defend this jurisdictional claim were simply an extension of the theory and practice of the royal prohibition. Their importance lay in their dramatization, in response to lay criticism in England, of the new situation created by the emergence of the papacy as the Patron Paramount and Universal Ordinary of the Western Church.

At no time did the king and his courts aspire to abolish entirely the church's control over the possession by the clergy of their sources of income or their tenure of clerical offices. Nor did the English church seriously attempt to enforce during the thirteenth and fourteenth centuries the jurisdictional claim to total authority over patronage declared by Pope Alexander III in 1180. Yet the possibility of considerable disagreement always existed.

The very nature of the ecclesiastical benefice, which seemed to span the temporal and spiritual worlds, contributed to confusion and provoked controversy. Both the canonical and secular concepts of the benefice and of the right to its patronage arose in the aftermath of the Investiture Controversy. In the course of the twelfth century the proprietary right of laymen to churches of their endowment or foundation, the *Eigenkirchen* of an earlier time,[50] had been quietly transformed into the claim to patronage.

50. For the *Eigenkirchen* see U. Stutz, "The Proprietary Church as an Element of Mediaeval Germanic Ecclesiastical Law," in *Studies in Mediaeval History*, Vol. II: *Essays: Mediaeval Germany, 911–1250*, ed. G. Barraclough (Oxford, 1938); H. Boehmer, "Das Eigenkirchentum in England," in *Texte und Forschungen zur Englischen Kulturgeschichte: Festgabe für Felix Liebermann* (Halle, 1921), pp. 301–353; *Domesday Monachorum of Christ Church, Canterbury*, ed. D. Douglas (London, 1944), pp. 5–14.

The patron presented a candidate to the bishop, who, after examining the rights and qualifications of the parties concerned, admitted the presentee to the benefice and confirmed his possession of the properties attached to it. The right of patronage was, under the title of advowson, quickly accommodated to medieval notions of real property, and in England was viewed as a tangible thing—something to be bequeathed, bartered, or abused.[51] On the other hand, annexed to the revenues or the landed estate constituting the material substance of the benefice was a spiritual office, often with the care of souls. It was the primary goal of the Gregorian reformers to establish effective control of the clergy in order to achieve the moral and spiritual regeneration of the Latin church.[52] Accordingly, the church insisted that the ultimate decision as to the admission of the clergy to their offices should rest with itself and that only tolerably well-qualified and deserving persons should occupy responsible positions in the clerical hierarchy.[53]

This distinction between the spiritual office and the substance of the benefice required that there be a similar distinction between the jurisdictions concerned with its spiritual or temporal aspects. The dual nature of the act of presenting a cleric to a benefice, whereby the patron expressed his right to the advowson and whereby also the presentee was given a claim to a particular living, attracted the attention of both jurisdictions. The ultimate responsibility of the church for the moral and spiritual qualifications of its members and the derivation of the revenues of a benefice from such explicitly spiritual sources as tithes and oblations likewise seemed to reinforce the church's argument to have a role in the disposition of ecclesiastical offices and incomes. Efforts to define these respective spheres of authority and responsibility were made difficult by virtue of the fact that both jurisdictions offered advantages to the average suitor, whose choice of one or the other was usually dictated by considerations of expediency or self-interest rather than by sympathy for the official pretensions of church or state.

In England during most of the twelfth century both royal and ecclesiastical courts were trying cases concerning the right of presenting to ecclesiastical benefices with few signs of conflict or controversy. This age of peaceful cooperation and self-restraint was ended by Henry II, Becket,

51. Pollock and Maitland, *History of English Law*, II, 136.

52. A. Fliche surveys the course of the struggle over lay investiture of the clergy and the evolution of reformist doctrine in *La Réforme Grégorienne*, 3 vols. (Louvain, 1924–37), especially I, 23–39, and II, 205–262.

53. For the evolution of canonical opinion, see P. Thomas, *Le Droit de Propriété des Laïques sur les Eglises et le Patronage Laïque au Moyen Age* (Paris, 1906), pp. 105–148.

and Alexander III, who drew the lines of future battle. The first chapter of the Constitutions of Clarendon claimed cases of advowson for the king's courts;[54] whereas Pope Alexander III, in a famous letter which found a place in the *Decretals*, defined advowson as a purely spiritual thing belonging properly to the jurisdiction of the church.[55] Both jurisdictions were stimulated to develop ways for achieving their ambitions, although there was still a sufficient degree of doubt and tolerance to enable them, for some time at least, to continue cooperating in deciding cases of this kind.[56]

By Ranulph Glanvill's time the royal prohibition against trying a case of advowson in a church court existed as a means for asserting the jurisdictional pretensions of the crown; and, apparently, this was having an effect. After the earliest decades of the thirteenth century, there are relatively few citations on the surviving *Curia Regis* rolls of prohibitions *de advocatione* where the issue being debated was exclusively that of patronage.[57] The English church begrudgingly submitted to the will of the crown. Bishop Grosseteste of Lincoln complained that the secular power unjustly (*contra justitiam*) tried pleas of patronage—a usurpation which the church was forced to tolerate.[58] Some versions of Boniface's constitutions of 1261 alluded unsympathetically to the *de facto* jurisdiction of royal courts over pleas of patronage;[59] and the canonist Hostensius noted that Alexander III's decretal was not observed in England.[60] By the middle of the thirteenth century, at the latest, the church courts had lost the struggle over advowson per se, and the conflict of the two jurisdictions had moved to other areas.

At the end of the century the canonical ideal of the church's jurisdiction over pleas of patronage was argued on the occasion of a suit between Edward I and Nicholas of Ely, bishop of Winchester, for the advowson of the cathedral priory of St. Swithun's. During the course of this affair, the bishop first took exception to the composition of the assize and then he appealed to Rome, saying that the partition of a church was a purely

---

54. *Select Charters and Other Illustrations of English Constitutional History*, ed. W. Stubbs, 6th ed. rev. (Oxford, 1942), p. 164; hereafter cited as *Select Charters*.

55. *Decretals*, II, 1, 3, in *Corpus Iuris Canonici*, ed. E. Richter and E. Friedberg, 2 vols. (Leipzig, 1879–81).

56. Cheney, *From Becket to Langton*, pp. 109–117.

57. *The Treatise on the Laws and Customs of the Realm of England Commonly Called Glanvill*, ed. G. D. G. Hall (London, 1965), IV, 13–14; hereafter cited as Glanvill; Flahiff, "Writ of Prohibition (i)," pp. 274–276; Gray, "Ius Praesentandi," p. 486.

58. *Epistolae Grosseteste*, p. 228.

59. See the collation notes in *Councils & Synods*, p. 672.

60. Quoted by Gray, "Ius Praesentandi," p. 487 n. 3.

spiritual matter. His successor, Bishop John Pontissara, continued the battle by arguing against the competence of secular courts to decide questions of this kind. Quoting the canons in defense of his stand, Pontissara insisted that laymen should not presume to try pleas of advowson which were purely spiritual in nature, especially when the defendant was a cleric like himself. That the case concerned the patronage of a cathedral priory attached to the episcopal office also seemed to reinforce its spiritual nature. Whatever the customs or corruptions of England, the bishop insisted, the crown was guilty of a usurpation of justice. "Pretera usurpare intelligitur qui talia vendicat coram judice seculari. Cum jurisdictio seculariis super hujusmodi spiritualibus, spiritualibus annexis usurpacio censeatur a jure." [61]

Pontissara's argument notwithstanding, it would appear that the church had bowed to royal jurisdiction on this point. The gravamina of the clergy during the second half of the thirteenth and the fourteenth centuries make no mention of the church's claim to try cases of patronage when advowson itself was the principal issue, but concentrate on defending the jurisdiction of the church courts over tithes, which affected the right of advowson, or over suits between presentees contending for possession of the same benefice. The magnitude of the crown's victory in England is revealed by comparison with conditions elsewhere. In France Philip Augustus had compromised with the church, and French ecclesiastical courts continued thereafter to play an important role in the trial of cases of patronage. [62] In Wales and Ireland during the thirteenth century the church retained a considerable jurisdictional competency in this respect; and in Scotland ecclesiastical jurisdiction over patronage was virtually unimpaired during the same period. [63]

The controversy over the ecclesiastical benefice during the thirteenth and fourteenth centuries centered on issues other than that of advowson as such. Glanvill reveals the other, correlative question by citing a royal prohibition which ordered the church court to stop trying a plea between two clerics seeking possession of the same living until a royal court had pronounced on the question of the right to present. [64] This writ was interlocutory in nature, and it implied that the church courts could legitimately try cases of benefices disputed between churchmen—a type of case that canonists called pleas of parsonage—so long as the right to the

61. *Registrum J. Pontissara*, II, 681–682.
62. Thomas, *Le Droit de Propriété*, pp. 168–169.
63. Gray, "Ius Praesentandi," p. 487 and n. 2.
64. Glanvill, IV, 12–13.

advowson of the benefice was not raised. Should this occur, however, the defendant in the Court Christian or his patron could obtain the intervention of the royal court on the grounds that the Court Christian was presuming to try a purely temporal plea. Glanvill's interlocutory writ did not permanently halt action by the church court. There remained the possibility that the case would be resumed in the ecclesiastical court once the royal court had pronounced on the question of patronage. By Bracton's time, however, the royal courts had hedged ecclesiastical jurisdiction with further restrictions. Bracton quotes an example of a royal prohibition which was final and peremptory. This writ summarily commanded the ecclesiastical judge and the plaintiff in the Court Christian to cease trying a plea between clerics concerning the possession of a benefice which could conceivably end in the annulment of a royal judgment on the advowson.[65] It was obviously designed to protect the integrity of royal justice and to prevent the church courts from challenging or rejecting the judgments of the king's courts on advowson by virtue of their jurisdiction over cases of parsonage. Although Bracton admitted the right of the church to try cases of this kind where both parties were clerics and the patronage was not at issue, nonetheless, these writs of prohibition threatened to remove such pleas from the church courts, unless, that is, the plaintiff or judge ordinary could prove that the prohibition had been falsely obtained or that it did not suit the circumstances of the case. Until the surviving ecclesiastical court records of the thirteenth century have been thoroughly studied, it will be impossible to estimate the effectiveness of these writs for curtailing ecclesiastical jurisdiction over the benefice. Formularies for the church courts continued during the thirteenth and fourteenth centuries to cite forms of action whereby clerics could sue for the removal of a rival or prove their rights to possess a benefice in an ecclesiastical court.[66] On the other hand, the records of the diocesan court of Canterbury at the end of the fourteenth century do not contain a single example of a plea of parsonage or of a disputed benefice.[67] The English church courts were doubtlessly experiencing a loss of jurisdiction, but this may have resulted as much from the extension of papal jurisdiction as from the aggression of royal justice.

65. Bracton, IV, fol. 403.

66. See William of Drogheda's *Summa Aurea*, chaps. 284–331, in *Quellen zur Geschichte des Romisch-Kanonischen Processes im Mittelalter*, ed. L. Wahrmund, 3 vols. (Innsbruck, 1905–16), II, 239–254; Brit. Mus. Add. MS. 32089, which is a fourteenth-century act book, cites (fols. 79–80) this action: "Libellus ubi unus et presentatus ad ecclesiam plenam et incumbens non habeat ius et presentatus petit de admitti et incumbens remoti."

67. Woodcock, *Medieval Ecclesiastical Courts*, pp. 79–92.

The royal writ of prohibition was the most obvious and, perhaps, most effective means for limiting ecclesiastical jurisdiction over the benefice. On the other hand, the common law and the king's courts had to go further than simply denying ecclesiastical jurisdiction in order to seal the domination by the crown of this area of law and justice. Shortly before the beginning of the thirteenth century a variety of new writs, rules, and precedents were invented and enforced in order to strengthen the crown's claim to have the last word in cases of advowson. The effect of these judicial innovations was to enhance considerably the usefulness of the common law, and to attract the attention of many suitors away from the church courts to the king's courts. Prominent among the new actions were the possessory assizes of *darrein presentment* and *quare impedit* and the action initiated by the writ, *quod permittat presentare*, which was a variant of the old writ of right of advowson. During the early part of the thirteenth century these common law actions, most of which made their appearance in the late twelfth century, were cutting deeply into the jurisdictional competence of the church to decide cases concerning benefices disputed by rival patrons and their presentees.

The English church courts had been very popular during the twelfth century for patrons and presentees seeking to prove claims to present to or possess ecclesiastical benefices. This earlier popularity was doubtlessly due to the greater ingenuity and flexibility of the canons as contrasted with the more limited common law actions. It is possible that the growth of the common law was the result of its imitation of more sophisticated canonical forms of action.[68] The first new writ to appear was that known as *darrein presentment*, which initiated an action in the king's courts for possession or seisin of the advowson as distinguished from the proprietorship or right to it, which previously could have been claimed only by hereditary succession. The same trend which encouraged the substitution of a possessory action, *novel disseisin*, for the recovery of seisin of real property for the older claim to a proprietary right, also promoted the popularity of a common law action for claiming seisin of the advowson in contrast to the hereditary right to it. In both instances the more limited

68. The influence of canon law on secular possessory actions is still disputed. Lady Stenton in her *English Justice*, pp. 22–23, ascribes the concept of seisin to the influence of the False Decretals; but van Caenegem, *Royal Writs*, pp. 290–304, 370, argues that novel disseisin came from earlier, explicitly secular actions. See also F. Joüon des Longrais, "La portée politique des réformes d'Henry II en matière de saisine," *Nouvelle Révue Historique de Droit Français et Étranger*, Ser. 4, XV (1891), 547 ff.; Gray, "Ius Praesentandi," p. 485, and references cited in n. 2.

forms of action, which elevated possession to a position of judicial importance almost equal to ownership, proved immensely valuable for suitors in the king's courts.

Darrein presentment considerably facilitated proof of a patron's claim to present to a benefice by allowing him to assert a previous presentation by himself or an ancestor. But *darrein presentment*, which required proof of a prior presentation, was unavailable to patrons by gift, purchase, or judgment who were unable to assert such a claim in defense of their pretensions. The records of the king's courts at the beginning of the thirteenth century convey the impression that the common law was searching for ways of broadening its coverage of pleas of advowson disputed between patrons and their presentees. Claimants to the advowson were resorting to a number of different common law actions to prove their right to present to a vacant benefice or to challenge a rival patron. A variant of the writ of right of advowson called *quod permittat presentare* or *quare non permittat presentare* was being used in the first decades of the thirteenth century.[69] Presentees, on the other hand, were sometimes being required to answer in the king's courts as to their patrons' right to the advowson, *quo advocatu teneat se in ecclesia*.[70] At other times both patrons and their presentees were claiming their rights by a possessory action which became increasingly popular in the thirteenth century.

This possessory action, which was initiated by the writ *quare impedit*, marked a major advance in common law interest in the ecclesiastical benefice.[71] *Quare impedit*, as Bracton observed, offered the only hope of justice to the patron who could not prove a prior presentation in support of his claim.[72] It enabled the plaintiff to assert his possession of the advowson by arguing that the benefice had become vacant at a particular time and that he had the right to exercise the patronage by virtue of the fact that he or an ancestor had acquired it by judgment or purchase, although his right had never been manifested by an actual presentation. It required the defendant to admit the past vacancy of the benefice and to counter with a better claim to the patronage, which he had already exercised by appointing to the living. *Quare impedit* could be sued by patrons or their

69. *CRR, 4 Henry III*, pp. 40, 43, 56, 160, 178, 215, 297; *CRR, 7–9 Henry III*, Nos. 213, 410, 552, 1218, 1235, 1395, 1594, 1677, 1684, 1766, 1820, 2595.

70. *CRR, 3–5 John*, pp. 100, 129.

71. For early examples, see *CRR, 5–7 John*, pp. 210, 340. Before the appearance of *quare impedit* an action similar to it could be brought by plaint: *Select Cases of Procedure without Writ under Henry III*, ed. H. G. Richardson and G. O. Sayles, SS (London, 1941), p. cv, and references in n. 5.

72. Bracton, III, fols. 246b–247.

presentees.[73] It required both plaintiff and defendant to claim possession of the advowson, although there was a tendency to allow its use against a bishop if he had collated to a benefice by lapse.[74]

During the second half of the thirteenth century *quare impedit* was sharpened in its effectiveness by legislation. The Provisions of Westminster in 1259,[75] as confirmed by the Statute of Marlborough in 1267,[76] gave the action the mesne process of attachment and distraint in order to force the defendant to come to court. In the event of the latter's default he suffered the loss of the presentation to the plaintiff on this occasion. In order to prevent the bishop from collating to the benefice according to the six-month period of grace afforded the patron by the Lateran Council of 1179,[77] the second Statute of Westminster in 1285 provided that the argument that the benefice was filled by the bishop's presentation should not be accepted as an adequate defense if the writ had been acquired within the six months following upon notification of vacancy even though the plea had not been terminated within this period.[78] This was obviously designed to limit the privilege of the bishops to collate to empty livings on the basis of their diocesan authority. Further, the statute awarded the successful plaintiff on *quare impedit* damages estimated at twice the annual value of the benefice if he had lost his presentation to the bishop by lapse, or at half the annual value if he had not.[79]

Quare impedit affected the jurisdictional conflict only indirectly insofar as it offered patrons and their presentees an attractive alternative to possessory actions available in the church courts. Since the writ did not raise the question of jurisdictional competency, the gravamina seldom mentioned it. When they did so, it was usually to criticize its use by the

73. According to the Year Books one had to claim in the advowson in order to impede: *Year Book* [*YB*] *5 Edward II* [*1311*], ed. G. J. Turner and T. F. T. Plucknett, SS (London, 1944), pp. 170–173. Chief Justice William Bereford was of the opinion that there was no basis for a suit against the parson when the latter disclaimed in the advowson; Bracton, III, 247b–248.

74. *Quare impedit* was sued against the bishop because he had refused to hold the inquest *de iure patronatus;* however, it was said that this was a case for the Court Christian: *YB 5 Edward II* [*1311*], pp. 123–126; the year book for Easter term, *40 Edward III*, describes suit on *quare impedit* against a bishop for failing to admit a presentee because of canonical disqualifications. See *Les Reports des Cases en Ley, Que Furent argues a Quadragesimo ad Quinquagesimum Annum des Tres Haut & Puissant Prince Roy Edward le Tierce* . . . (London, 1679), pp. 25–26.

75. *SR*, I, 9.   76. *Ibid.*, p. 23.

77. Pollock and Maitland, *History of English Law*, I, 148.

78. *SR*, I, 76. The same statute also extended action on *quare impedit* to cover the advowson of vicarages, *ibid.*, p. 77.

79. *Ibid.*, p. 76.

king himself to lay claim to the patronage of benefices of the advowson of bishops, which had been vacated during periods of royal wardship of the episcopal temporalities.[80] The royal claim was based upon the doctrine of the regalian right, the *droit de regale* or *ius regalium*, which was being enhanced and enforced during the late thirteenth and the fourteenth centuries, and which enabled the king to exercise the rights of patronage attached to the temporalities of tenants-in-chief, both laymen and clerics, during periods of royal guardianship.[81] Combined with the doctrine that the lapse of time does not defeat the king's claim, the *ius regalium* considerably increased the rights of patronage claimed by the crown by permitting it to search out claims to present, sometimes of a remote and distant kind.[82] Presentations by the king on the basis of the regalian right conflicted with efforts of the bishops to exercise the rights of patronage attached to their offices and also to enforce the decree of the Third Lateran Council in 1179, which encouraged them to collate to vacant benefices of the advowson of laymen or clerks after the failure of the true patron to exercise his right within a six-month period of grace.[83]

Quare impedit was very handy for asserting royal rights to the patronage of benefices which were normally of the advowson of others. The higher clergy in England vehemently denounced both the usurpation of their rights of patronage and the infringement of the conciliar decree, but such

80. *Rot. Parl. Inediti*, p. 110; *Rot. Parl.*, II, 245.

81. M. Howell, *Regalian Right in Medieval England* (London, 1962), pp. 167 ff., 207 ff.; W. E. L. Smith, *Episcopal Appointments and Patronage in the Reign of Edward II* (Chicago, 1938), pp. 57 ff.; A. Deeley, "Papal Provisions and Royal Rights of Patronage in the Early Fourteenth Century," *EHR*, XLIII (1928), 497–527.

82. The doctrine is contained in the so-called "*Praerogativa regis*," *SR*, I, 226. For an example of the application of this maxim see *Placitorum in Domo Capituli Westmonasteriensi Asservatorum Abbreviatio, Temporibus Regum Ric. I. Hen. III. Edw. II.* (London, 1831), p. 339; hereafter cited as *Placitorum Abbreviatio*. The earl of Chester had some difficulty claiming this prerogative for himself: *Calendar of Close Rolls Preserved in the Public Record Office* [*Edward I–Henry IV*], 34 vols. (London, 1892–1938), *1323–27*, pp. 44–45; hereafter cited as *CCR*. In the fourteenth century the king asserted, in defense of his claim to the patronage of benefices by regalian right, that he was exempt from the ordinary rule of lapse: Howell, *Regalian Right*, pp. 183–184.

83. C.-J. Hefele and H. Leclercq, *Histoire des Conciles d'après les Documents Originaux*, 11 vols. (Paris, 1907–52), vol. V, part 2, p. 1100; Decretals, III, 38, chaps. 3, 22. In 1340 Bishop John Grandisson of Exeter was not allowed to disclaim in the advowson when he presented by lapse, although a majority of the royal justices admitted his right to do so. The bishop appealed to the King's council and a discussion held at the Hilary Parliament of 1340 was adduced in favor of his stand. For the background to this interesting case, see *CCR, 1339–40*, p. 401; and *Register of John de Grandisson, Bishop of Exeter, A.D. 1327–1369, with Some Account of the Episcopate of James de Berkeley, A.D. 1327*, ed. F. C. Hingeston-Randolph, Episcopal Registers of the Diocese of Exeter, 3 parts (London, 1894), I, 64–65. See also the request of the bishops in 1352, *Rot. Parl.*, I, 244 (article 12).

complaints focused upon substantive losses rather than jurisdictional claims. Nevertheless, *quare impedit* was a real thorn in the side of the English bishops. One of the charges made against the Despensers in 1327 was that they had urged Edward II to use the writ to usurp rights of patronage, threatening the bishops with the loss of their temporalities if they did not submit.[84] In 1391 Pope Urban VI compared *quare impedit* with the detested *praemunire facias* in estimating its evil effects on episcopal rights and urged the nuncio, Nicholas of Nonantola, to work for the abolition of both actions.[85] As late as 1399, on the occasion of Henry IV's accession, the English prelates were still complaining against the writ. In this year the gravamina requested the king to renounce its use in favor of the practice of proving his claims to patronage in such cases in the bishops' consistory courts or by appeal in the Court of Arches, the provincial court of the archdiocese of Canterbury.[86] There was, of course, no likelihood at all that such a request would have been honored at this late date.

The English bishops and the church courts continued to exercise controls of one kind or another over the ecclesiastical benefice during the thirteenth and fourteenth centuries. This authority was both judicial and administrative, and assumed a variety of shapes. It could, for instance, take the form of the ex officio right of the bishop to admit and institute candidates to benefices. In other cases it could be manifested in individual acts of arbitration or administrative decision. And, despite the growth of the common law of advowson, it could still be expressed through judicial action and litigation between clerics in church courts both English and foreign. Eventually the royal courts were obliged to take notice of the existence of these powers and prerogatives, most of which were attached to the office of the bishop, and which were sometimes exercised in ways which tended to delay, frustrate, or reject the judgments of the king's courts in pleas of advowson.

The methods adopted by the royal courts to tighten their authority over pleas of patronage led them to intervene to prevent the trial in church courts of such ostensibly spiritual matters as the right to or possession of tithes and other customary religious payments. The common lawyers justified this intrusion as necessary in order to protect the value of the advowson and the integrity of the patron's right to present to a benefice. On the other hand, the church complained against the pre-

84. *Rot. Parl.*, II, 8, 11; *Rot. Parl. Inediti*, p. 118.

85. *Diplomatic Correspondence of Richard II*, ed. E. Perroy, Camden Society, Ser. 3, XLVIII (London, 1933), pp. 89–90.

86. Wilkins, III, 241.

sumption of laymen in meddling with such spiritualities as tithes and oblations under the pretext that the worth of the patronage was affected by decisions of the ecclesiastical courts. During the course of the thirteenth and early fourteenth centuries the common lawyers and the church in England were attempting to define relations between the two jurisdictions so as to leave relatively unimpaired the ecclesiastical jurisdiction over tithes and yet to protect the competence of the king's courts in pleas of advowson.

The value of an ecclesiastical benefice derived from various sources— glebe lands, tithes, and a variety of customary ecclesiastical payments called oblations, obventions, and mortuaries. Obviously any action, judicial or administrative, which restricted or qualified these sources of income would considerably affect the attractiveness of the benefice as a possession and the value of its patronage. From early in Henry III's reign some patrons were obtaining writs of prohibition to halt the trial of tithes cases in the church courts on the basis of the allegation that their rights as patrons were thereby reduced or threatened. Glanvill does not mention tithes in quoting those examples of interlocutory writs which were designed to prevent further litigation in a church court until the question of the advowson had been decided in a royal court. By Bracton's day, or even before, the king's courts and chancery were making available to patrons royal writs of prohibition touching advowson when it appeared that the trial of a case of tithes in the Courts Christian might affect adversely the value of advowson. In the thirteenth and early fourteenth centuries it would appear that the majority of prohibitions delivered to church courts and ordering them to cease trying a plea of advowson did not concern advowson at all, but were, rather, designed to prevent litigation on tithes which threatened to diminish the worth of the benefice and the patron's right.[87]

The earliest gravamina condemn this intrusion and also protest the unwillingness of the royal judges to specify precisely the proportion of the total value of the benefice which could properly be litigated in the ecclesiastical courts. The gravamina of 1239 requested the denial of prohibitions to patrons who used them to prevent clerics from recovering their tithes in the Courts Christian on the grounds that the advowson of certain churches was being diminished.[88] Evidently some patrons, at the instigation of their presentees, were interfering with suits in the church courts for the spoliation of tithes by means of prohibitions *de advocatione*. This situation was the result of the efforts of some clerics to collect tithes

87. Flahiff, "Writ of Prohibition (i)," p. 276.
88. *Councils & Synods*, p. 281 (article 11).

outside of their native parishes; and it was doubtlessly complicated by the partition of benefices to create vicarages or chapels and the appropriation of livings to monastic houses. Archbishop Boniface's constitutions published in 1261 admonished the prelates to unite in opposing this kind of jurisdictional intrusion. The judges and plaintiffs in the Courts Christian were instructed to ignore prohibitions ordering them to stop prosecuting a tithes case on the pretext that the advowson was in jeopardy. Should they be attached or arrested, the prelates were counseled to excommunicate the bearer of the prohibition and the secular judge who refused to heed their warning.[89] In the gravamina compiled for presentation to the crown in 1280, the church again complained of royal interference with the trial of cases of tithes, oblations, obventions, and mortuaries. The royal reply defended the jurisdiction of the king's courts over tithes cases arising out of the right of advowson (*originem habens de iure patronatus*), which concerned as much as a third of the total goods of a benefice.[90]

A new factor was introduced into discussions concerning tithes and advowson when the second Statute of Westminster in 1285 provided patrons with the writ of right of advowson of tithes, whereby they could sue in the royal courts for the recovery of the advowson of such spiritual payments.[91] The intent of the statute was to distinguish the tithes from their advowson, thus creating a double action; but the church opposed this innovation which, it said, would have the effect of abolishing ecclesiastical jurisdiction over less than a third or a quarter of the tithes and of preventing poor suitors from getting their just deserts because of the expense of the two law suits.

The ambiguous reply of the crown to this complaint was not especially promising.[92] The gravamina of 1295 referred back to the distinction made by the Statute of Westminster by arguing against the issuance of the prohibition, *indicavit*, to prevent the trial in a church court of a tithes case wherein merely their possession and not the right to the patronage was disputed.[93] The next article of the same petition criticized the rationale underlying the use of prohibitions in this way. The prohibition of advowson could not logically apply, it was argued, in cases concerning the possession of tithes or where their value amounted to less than a quarter of the worth of the benefice. Anyone who despoiled another of tithes and then proceeded to sue that person in a royal court for the right to the advowson before he had restored them was in an absurd and illegal position:

89. *Ibid.*, pp. 672–673.   90. *Ibid.*, p. 875.
91. *Ibid.*, p. 975 (article 9).   92. *Ibid.*, p. 967 (article 8).
93. *Ibid.*, p. 1140 (article 16).

"alioquin quilibet spoliaret alium decimis et in omni tali spoliatione oportet agere de iure patronatus ante restitutionem, quod esset absurdum et etiam contra legem terre, quia disseisitus licet ius non habeat in re ipsa spoliata tamen restituitur." [94] The innovation of the Statute of Westminster did not constitute a serious invasion of canonical jurisdiction. The Year Books of Edward III's reign, for example, cite only about half a dozen cases of advowson for tithes.[95] But the gravamina of 1300/1301 once more denounced this interference, and the complaint was repeated in the petition of 1327.[96]

There was some confusion as to what proportion of the total value of the benefice constituted a threat to the patron's right. In royal replies to the gravamina of 1280 and 1300/1301 the figure one third was cited as the ratio which should decide jurisdictional competence.[97] The writs of prohibition quoted in the grievances of 1295, 1300/1301, and 1327, however, indicate that the king's courts were claiming jurisdiction over tithes cases concerning a quarter or more of the value of the benefice.[98] Although the Articles of the Clergy in 1316 had stated that the prohibition should apply only against suits for the spoliation of tithes amounting to a fourth or more of the goods of the benefice,[99] the clergy were still complaining against royal intrusion in cases of less than this amount at the end of Edward III's reign. The statute of 1376 repeated the promise that the prohibition of advowson would be granted only in those cases wherein a quarter or more of the value of the living was involved.[100] This uncertainty doubtlessly worked to the disadvantage of ecclesiastical jurisdiction by encouraging suitors to challenge church courts presuming to try tithes cases in any amount.

The authority of the bishop to admit a clerical candidate to a benefice or to deprive him of its possession was one of the most important duties attached to the episcopal office. It embodied and enforced the ideals of the great reformers of the church, who sought to use such controls in order to assure the moral and spiritual qualifications of persons holding religious office. By the thirteenth century the English church had devised formal methods for investigating the qualifications of the presentee to a benefice and had distinguished certain steps in the process of admitting him to his duties and to the enjoyment of the income which enabled him to perform

94. *Ibid.*, pp. 1140–1141 (article 17).
95. N. Adams, "The Judicial Conflict over Tithes," *EHR*, LII (1937), 7 n. 3.
96. *Councils & Synods*, pp. 1210–1211 (article 9).
97. *Ibid.*, pp. 875, 1211.   98. *Ibid.*, pp. 1140, 1211; *Rot. Parl. Inediti*, p. 107.
99. *SR*, I, 171.   100. *Rot. Parl.*, II, 357.

them.[101] The usual way for filling a vacant benefice was, first, the presentation of a candidate by the patron acting in response either to his knowledge of the vacancy or on the basis of the bishop's notification to him. Secondly, the presentee was formally examined as to his claim and his qualifications to possess the benefice. Although the bishop himself was legally responsible for this inquiry, during the thirteenth century it was usually performed by a delegate. In compliance with the bishop's order, the archdeacon of the district in which the benefice was located, or the archdeacon's official, or, as was more customary, the rural dean summoned the rural chapter to a certain place where, after due notice had been given, the inquiry was held. In the thirteenth and fourteenth centuries two subjects of investigation could be distinguished or else combined into a single hearing. One of these concerned the qualifications of the presentee. The other investigated every aspect of the benefice and the presentation: the vacancy of the church and the time of its vacation; the possessor of the patronage and whether or not his right was legal or contested; the existence of pensions or other obligations encumbering the benefice; and, finally, the total worth of it. The inquiry concerning the fact of the vacancy and the claim of a particular presentee was known as the inquest *de iure patronatus* and was recognized to pertain solely to the bishop. In the see of Durham during Bishop Richard Kellawe's episcopacy some twenty questions were put to a jury,[102] although often the rural chapter itself gave testimony. If all were found acceptable—the legality of the patron's claim, the canonical qualifications of the presentee, and the legal status of the benefice—then the candidate might be given temporary custody while the bishop was notified of the absence of any impediment to his admission. Upon receipt of the information disclosed by the inquest the bishop then proceeded to exercise his authority to admit the candidate. This administrative procedure was distinguished by three steps: first, the acceptance of the candidate by the bishop or his delegate; second, his institution into the spiritual office; and, third, his investiture with the properties or revenues attached to it.[103]

101. See J. W. Gray's transcript of Bodley MS. Rawlinson D. 893, fol. 114b, in "Ius Praesentandi," p. 509. For an explanation of the procedure of admitting and instituting to ecclesiastical benefices, see Churchill, *Canterbury Administration*, II, 106–111; and R. M. Haines, *The Administration of the Diocese of Worcester in the First Half of the Fourteenth Century* (London, 1965), pp. 85 ff., 148 ff.

102. *Registrum Palatinum Dunelmense: The Register of Richard de Kellawe, Lord Palatine and Bishop of Durham, 1311–1316*, ed. T. Duffus Hardy, RS, 4 vols. (London, 1873–78), I, 182.

103. Thomas, *Le Droit de Propriété*, pp. 144–148, ascribed this formalization of the procedure of admission to clerical efforts to oppose lay investiture by distinguishing the spiritual office from the material living.

The king's courts respected the spiritual nature of the inquest *de iure patronatus*.[104] They customarily accepted its findings as certified by the bishop, and based their judgments on its conclusions. Yet care was taken to prevent fraud or collusion. If the bishop were himself party to the plea in the king's courts, the royal judges could send to the metropolitan for information concerning the benefice or the presentee.[105] The canonical qualifications of a deceased cleric could be put to a lay jury as a matter of fact, since, it was said, he could not be examined by the bishop.[106] The king's courts took a dim view of the bishop who used his office to defeat the rights of a patron by judgment of the royal courts. In Easter term, *40 Edward III*, a year book states that a bishop was amerced on a *quare impedit* for refusing to institute a presentee on the grounds that he was insufficiently learned, although he was later admitted while the plea was still pending.[107] The decision of the king's court was that if the candidate had once been found to be qualified to assume office, then it was understood that he had always been so. The refusal of the inquest *de iure patronatus* was, on the other hand, admitted to belong to the bishop; and aggrieved clerics in the king's courts were told to sue before the bishop for their examination,[108] or else take their appeal to the metropolitan.[109] Whenever there was the possibility of rejecting a royal judgment, an appeal to the king was possible. In 1335 two presentees petitioned in Parliament against the taking of an inquest which might be prejudicial to rights declared in the king's courts.[110] For the most part, however, the royal courts did not meddle with this aspect of episcopal authority. Since the inquest was administrative rather than judicial in character, and because it was so clearly an intrinsic part of the diocesan office, it was seldom questioned.

The authority of the bishop over admissions and institutions enabled him to enforce or defeat the rights of patrons and their presentees. In the case of those patrons and presentees whose claims were based upon judgments of the king's courts, the effect of exercising or failing to exercise this authority was to fulfill or reject royal decisions. The crown became

104. *YB 32–33 Edward I*, ed. A. J. Horwood, RS (London, 1864), pp. 179, 213–215; *Registrum Roberti Winchelsey, Cantuariensis Archiepiscopi, A.D. 1294–1313*, ed. R. Graham, CYS, 2 vols. (London, 1956), I, 491–493; *YB 5 Edward II [1311]*, p. 124.
105. *YB 32–33 Edward I*, pp. 124, 179.
106. *Les Reports des Cases en Ley . . .*, Easter term, 40 Edward III, pp. 25–26.
107. *Ibid.*
108. *YB 5 Edward II [1311]*, p. 124.
109. *YB 32–33 Edward I*, pp. 213–215.
110. *Rot. Parl.*, II, 94.

acutely aware of this fact, and the common lawyers set to work to hedge episcopal authority with restrictions. To prevent the bishop from admitting and instituting a candidate while a benefice was still being litigated in a royal court, the variant of the prohibitory writ called *ne admittas* could be issued to him. Especially in respect to the possessory action, *quare impedit*, it was usual for the plaintiff in the king's court to cause a *ne admittas* to issue to the bishop, commanding him not to admit a rival presentee until the royal judgment had been rendered. If the bishop ignored this command he was liable to the patron or his presentee on the action, *quare incumbravit*, which called him to answer for having admitted and instituted a presentee contrary to the *ne admittas*. This was an entirely new action, distinct from the suit for possession of the advowson.[111] After judgment in the king's court on a plea of patronage, the writ *ut admittas* issued in favor of the presentee by judgment. *Ut admittas* commanded the bishop to admit and institute the successful presentee.[112] These royal writs, *ne admittas* and *ut admittas*, had the effect of binding the bishop to exercise his administrative powers in accordance with judgments of the king's courts.

The bishops apparently complied with such commands in a large number of instances. There is, however, evidence to suggest that the *ut admittas* did not inevitably lead to the actual admission of the lawful patron's candidate immediately after judgment. In cases where the benefice had been filled with another than the true patron's presentee, the canonists urged the patron to present (or re-present) the incumbent, who had been previously admitted and was in possession of the living. In this way the lawful right of the patron and the judgment of the king's court were respected without disturbing the incumbent.[113] Further, the considerable number of agreements about pensions and tithes recorded in the bishops' registers suggest that amicable arrangements could be worked out under the supervision of the bishop or his delegate so as to satisfy the contending parties.[114] The common lawyers seemed to have viewed the writ *ut admittas* as something less than an absolute command. Bracton suggested that rival presentees could fight it out for possession of the benefice in a church court. At any rate, there was the possibility that the

111. Gray, "Ius Praesentandi," pp. 494–495.

112. For an example of the writ, see Bracton, III, fol. 248.

113. Gray, "Ius Praesentandi," pp. 501–506.

114. For an example of the creation of an annual pension in favor of one of the contending parties in a case of disputed advowson, see *Rotuli Ricardi Gravesend Episcopi Lincolniensis, A.D. MCCLVIII–MCCLXXIX*, ed. F. N. Davis, C. W. Foster, and A. Hamilton Thompson, Lincoln Record Society (Lincoln, 1925), pp. 139–141.

patron by judgment of the king's courts might not receive his rights on a particular occasion. Patrons by royal judgment were, accordingly, without secular remedy until the invention of an action which called the bishop to account for not admitting a presentee and threatened him with penalties for the contempt which was implied by his refusal to exercise his office.

The crown was obliged to take notice of a situation which could and did have the effect of annuling its judgments. Early in King John's reign a writ designed to avoid this danger was making its appearance. When, for instance, a patron had successfully defended his right to present to a vacant benefice by actions pursued in a royal court, an *ut admittas* issued from the court to the bishop, informing the latter to admit and institute a particular presentee. If the bishop failed to comply, he could be called to appear in a royal court to answer the question *quare non vult recipere idoneam personam*, or, as it was later phrased, *quare non admisit idoneam personam*.[115] By means of the writ to admit, the king's courts commanded the bishop to exercise his office in accordance with the decisions of the royal courts; and by means of the action on *quare non admisit* threatened him with punishment for failing to do so.

Quare non admisit, like attachment on the prohibition, transformed the issue into one of contempt of the royal jurisdiction.[116] According to Bracton, the bishop might excuse himself by pleading that the church was litigious at the time of the reception of the *ut admittas* or else by alleging a disqualification of the patron or his presentee.[117] The excommunication of the patron or the deficiency of knowledge or morals of the candidate were accepted as satisfactory answers to the charge,[118] although the royal courts would not admit the binding nature of spiritual censures launched against the plaintiff, if it were obvious that he had been excommunicated at the instigation of his present adversary.[119] The royal courts required the bishop to plead a specific disqualification of the clerical candidate, i.e., that he was under age, insufficiently learned, or illegitimate.[120] If the plaintiff

115. An early case from Michaelmas, 1201, is printed in *Select Civil Pleas*, ed. W. P. Baildon, SS (London, 1890), p. 40; and others in *CRR, 3–5 John*, pp. 43, 272, 312, and *CRR, 5–7 John*, pp. 28, 95, 112. See also Gray, "Ius Praesentandi," p. 504 n. 6.

116. Note the wording of the charge against the archbishop of York in Trinity term, 23 Edward I, published in *Select Cases in the Court of King's Bench under Edward I*, ed. G. O. Sayles, SS, 3 vols. (London, 1936–54), III, 137.

117. Bracton, III, fol. 252.

118. *YB 12–13 Edward III*, ed. L. O. Pike, RS (London, 1885), p. 299.

119. *YB 20 Edward III [Part I]*, ed. L. O. Pike, RS (London, 1908), p. 219, provides an example.

120. See the discussion on a *quare incumbravit* in Hilary term, 1304, printed in *YB 32–33 Edward I*, pp. 33–35.

alleged the contrary, the issue had been reached. In the fourteenth century two courses of action were open. The question could be sent to the metropolitan for certification, or it might be put to a lay jury as a question of fact. Although the majority of common lawyers argued for the spiritual nature of pleas of this sort, there were some in the king's courts who were prepared to argue for the suitability of juries for deciding them.[121] If it were said that a particular presentee had not been canonically qualified at some time in the past, although he was at the present time, this question might be put to a jury.[122] The royal courts were doing this in regard to the question of past vacancy, and it would have been natural to use it in similar situations.[123] Another answer which was available to the bishop was that the benefice was full by a prior presentation, and the plaintiff could sue on the plea "dolosa fuit presentatio, clandestina institutio, et inquisitio non solemnis."[124] The effect of the *quare non admisit* was, therefore, to raise serious doubts concerning the validity of admission, of which the inquest *de iure patronatus* was a vital part. The archbishop of York, Walter Giffard, writing to Henry III to explain his refusal to admit the king's presentee to a church, said that the living was occupied by another, whose right and the right of whose patron, were declared by canonical inquest; since, therefore, the church ought not to be governed more by secular laws than by the canons, he will not oust the incumbent to satisfy the royal command.[125]

The Year Books clearly indicate that the royal courts frowned at an answer of the plenarty of a benefice by another's presentation when put forward in opposition to the king's claim. On a *quare non admisit* between the king and the bishop of Lincoln in *19 Edward III*, the attorney for the king said that the bishop should have declared the church vacant and to have instituted the king's clerk in order to satisfy the royal writ. Afterwards the bishop would be liable to the ousted clerk in the Court Christian on a plea of spoliation. Justice Richard Willoughby, on the other hand, believed that the best course of action would have been to admit the king's clerk, and allow the rival presentees to battle it out for final possession in

121. King v. Archbishop of York, Easter term, 1346, in *YB 20 Edward III [Part I]*, p. 371.

122. *Les Reports des Cases en Ley*, Easter term, 40 Edward III, pp. 25–26.

123. T. F. T. Plucknett, "Execrabilis in the Common Pleas," *Cambridge Law Journal*, I (1923), 67 ff.

124. Bracton, III, fol. 252.

125. *Register of Walter Giffard, Lord Archbishop of York, 1266–1279*, ed. W. Brown, Surtees Society (Durham, 1904), pp. 221–222. The king's presentee in this case appealed to the pope, and the incumbent threatened to do so (pp. 4–5, 222–224). For the background to this interesting case, see *ibid.*, pp. 85, 86; and *CCR, 1268–72*, pp. 92–95.

an ecclesiastical court.[126] Both judges were attempting to see that royal writs were enforced, and yet preserve the dignity of the ecclesiastical courts. Events elsewhere reveal, however, that the church courts could have been prevented from acting in both instances. In 1304 Edward I ordered the official of the court of Canterbury to stop prosecuting the bishop of Worcester for having admitted the king's clerk in obedience to a judgment of the royal courts.[127] The king said that his judgments must be executed and that those whose duty it was to perform such tasks should not suffer thereby. Secondly, as regards the suit between the presentees, a prohibition *de advocatione* was always available whereby the king's presentee might halt action in the Court Christian. Whenever the king was a plaintiff on a *quare non admisit*, the prevailing opinion in the royal courts was that the bishop, whose role in this respect could even be compared with the sheriff, had done wrong in not executing the royal writ to admit.[128] In a case between the king and the bishop of Exeter in 1345 the bishop was charged with not having declared a vicarage void before admitting the king's presentee, with the result that the clerk was not actually in possession of the living.[129]

One of the safest excuses which was permitted the bishop in reply to a *quare non admisit* was that the benefice was litigious at the time of presentation.[130] Obviously, it might be said, he was barred from acting so long as the patronage was in doubt. The royal courts were, however, very careful to prevent collusion or dishonesty. If the king's title had once been declared by his courts, in spite of the fact that there were other actions pending, the bishop was expected to admit upon receipt of the writ.[131] Furthermore, an appeal to an ecclesiastical court was never recognized as binding upon the bishop, unless this appeal were licensed by the king himself.[132] During a discussion on a *quare non admisit* in 1339 several of the king's judges agreed that it might be wise to legislate against the possibility of the bishop's initiating false litigation in order to get the presentation by lapse.[133]

126. *YB 19 Edward III*, ed. L. O. Pike, RS (London, 1906), pp. 169, 173.

127. *CCR, 1302–1307*, pp. 222–223.

128. *YB 19 Edward III*, p. 169. The record for a case in Easter term, 20 Edward III, speaks of the bishop as "minister domini Regis in hoc casu." See *YB 20 Edward III [Part I]*, p. 169 n. 1.

129. *YB 19 Edward III*, p. 219.

130. *YB 12–13 Edward III*, pp. 295–297.

131. *YB 20 Edward III [Part I]*, pp. 163–165, makes this point.

132. Bracton, III, fol. 251b; for an example of such a license, see *Calendar of the Patent Rolls Preserved in the Public Record Office [Henry III–Henry IV]*, 41 vols. (London, 1901–16), *1345–48*, pp. 367–368; hereafter cited as *CPR*.

133. *YB 12–13 Edward III*, p. 299.

Quare non admisit placed the bishops under great handicaps. In 1348 the archbishop of York had to obtain the special pardon of the monarch for failing to admit his presentee to a church, for the royal courts usually awarded damages to the aggrieved plaintiff and a large fine to the king for the contempt.[134] In Edward I's reign the temporalities of the archbishop of York were seized into the hands of the king until he acquitted himself of a fine of £10,000, which he had been amerced on a *quare non admisit*.[135] In 1352 the higher clergy under Archbishop Stratford's leadership appealed to the king in Parliament for the privilege of making a reasonable fine instead of suffering the loss of their temporalities.[136] The bishop of Exeter was treated relatively leniently when in 1352 he was permitted to settle for the payment of £200.[137] Contempt of the king's justice, which was what *quare non admisit* implied, remained a very serious charge, particularly when the royal rights were involved. The writ was available to all, however, and suit could be brought by the presentee in his patron's name, as was the case in many of the disputed royal presentations. Its advantages were obvious, even to the clergy, who used it to protect their own rights of patronage.[138] Because of its nature, *quare non admisit* never enjoyed the popularity of *darrein presentment* or *quare impedit*. It was always an extreme measure for use in particularly difficult instances. This is why a great deal more is heard about it in the gravamina of the clergy than the actual number of recorded cases would lead one to expect.[139]

During Henry III's reign the church repeatedly criticized this manner of questioning the integrity of episcopal authority.[140] Bishop Grosseteste, arguing the superiority of canon law to secular justice and the sanctity of the bishop's office, denounced the practice of forcing prelates to answer for performing or refusing to perform duties attached to their spiritual offices, such as the dedication of churches, the confirmation of monastic elections,

134. *CPR, 1348–50*, p. 118.

135. *Select Cases in the Court of King's Bench under Edward I*, III, 137.

136. *SR*, I, 326.

137. Public Record Office [PRO], King's Bench [KB] 27/359, 25–5d. The judgment of the court was confiscation of the temporalities; and then the bishop prayed the king to make fine, which was granted.

138. See the case of the Abbot of Tewkesbury v. Bishop of Worcester in *YB 33 [Michaelmas] and 34–35 Edward I*, ed. A. J. Horwood, RS (London, 1879), pp. 45 ff.

139. Gray, "Ius Praesentandi," p. 505 and n. 3.

140. See article 7 of the gravamina of 1239 in *Councils & Synods*, p. 281; the fourth proposal for the protection of ecclesiastical liberties of the London council of 1257 (*ibid.*, p. 534); the first provision of the council of 1258 (*ibid.*, p. 573); the first article of the gravamina of 1261 (*ibid.*, p. 687).

and admitting and instituting clerics.[141] The common law action initiated by the writ, *quare non admisit*, was specifically cited as being very offensive to the higher clergy. Boniface's canons of 1261 explained the official attitude of the bishops toward such royal practices. The sixth canon stated that the bishops would admit presentees by judgment of the king's courts to those benefices which were canonically vacant; however, it insisted upon their right to refuse admission to a living which was legally filled. In such instances the right of the patron by royal judgment might be safeguarded by allowing him to present the incumbent, but the bishops should not be forced to explain or justify the exercise of their holy office.[142] During the fourteenth century the higher clergy changed their tactics somewhat by arguing for the purely spiritual nature of pleas of plenarty, which would have given the church the exclusive right to judge the authenticity of admissions and the legality of claims to possess ecclesiastical livings, and by seeking to impose limits upon the exercise of regalian right.[143]

Royal control of all aspects of the law of advowson extended during Edward I's reign to encompass litigation concerning vicarages, which canonists had always viewed as purely spiritual things. The custom of appropriating benefices to monastic foundations resulted in a diminution of religious services, which the church tried to counter by requiring the creation of vicarages to replace those livings which had been drawn to other uses. The reformers among the English clergy of the thirteenth and fourteenth centuries emphasized the importance of the establishment of a vicarage, usually supported by a portion of the tithes of the original living, to continue the performance of the services owed by the latter.[144] The basis of the vicarage, which derived from an agreement concerning tithes, implied, at least in ecclesiastical eyes, its purely spiritual character, and the church claimed exclusive jurisdiction over cases concerning its possession. In 1285 the higher clergy complained against the common law action for the recovery of the advowson of a vicarage which was created by

141. *Epistolae Grosseteste*, pp. 227–228.

142. *Councils & Synods*, p. 674.

143. For instance, article 12 of the gravamina of 1327 in *Rot. Parl. Inediti*, pp. 109–110; chapter 2 of the statute of 1340, *SR*, I, 293; and for the grievances of 1352, see article 66, *Rot. Parl.*, II, 245, which became the sixth chapter of the statute, *SR*, I, 326.

144. See statute 112 of the Statutes of Salisbury, 1217–19 (*Councils & Synods*, p. 96); canon 21 of the Council of Oxford in 1222 (*ibid.*, pp. 112–113); statute 24 of the Statutes of Winchester in 1224 (*ibid.*, p. 130); statute 74 of Worcester in 1240 (*ibid.*, p. 314); statute 68 of the Statutes of Chichester in 1245–52 (*ibid.*, p. 465); canon 22 of the legatine council convened by Cardinal Ottobono in 1268 in London (*ibid.*, p. 771).

the second Statute of Westminster.[145] Subsequently, many contested claims to the advowson of vicarages were drawn within the orbit of royal jurisdiction, regardless of the complaint and criticism of the church; and all of the common law actions available for asserting the patron's right to the advowson of benefices were also available to persons claiming to appoint to vicarages.

During the course of the thirteenth and fourteenth centuries the royal courts developed methods for avoiding reference to the church in matters which, though admittedly spiritual in nature, might oblige them to render judgments contrary to the predilections or presuppositions of the common law and secular custom. The best known of these conflicts of substantive law was that concerning the legal definition of bastardy. The desire of the common lawyers to avoid accepting the church's more humane and liberal notion of legitimacy prompted the king's courts to couch the question of a suitor's legitimacy in terms capable of being submitted to a lay jury as a question of fact. The sworn inquest was also employed in the conflict over the ecclesiastical benefice to allow the royal courts to obtain information necessary for the delivery of judgments in conformity with the jurisdictional pretensions of the crown. The plaintiff on the possessory writ, *quare impedit*, for example, had to allege the vacancy of the benefice which he claimed in order to use this particular action. If his opponent answered that it was filled, then the issue at law had been reached. The common lawyers admitted that the question of the vacancy of a benefice was a purely spiritual one, which could be determined only by the church.[146] Under the designation "pleas of plenarty" so-called, such questions were directed to the bishop and royal judgments were based upon his findings.[147] The higher clergy argued that this procedure was

145. The chapter of the statute which gave *quare impedit* for the recovery of the advowson of vicarages is in *SR*, I, 77. The complaint of the clergy is printed, *Councils & Synods*, p. 965 (article 8). The royal response to this grievance (article 9, in *ibid.*, p. 967) stated that the patronage of vicarages claimed by a layman should be tried in the royal courts; the church could still judge cases of vicarages of the patronage of clerics.

146. Bracton, III, fol. 247b; *Britton*, ed. F. M. Nichols, 2 vols. (Oxford, 1865), II, 204. A case from Trinity term, 2 Edward III, was referred to the ordinary because, as it was said, "huiusmodi cause cognicio ad forum spectant ecclesiasticum," PRO, Common Pleas [CP] 40/274, 85. In Easter term, 10 Edward II, the justices sent to the bishop for the following information: whether or not the church was full, by whom and at whose presentation, and the time of occupancy: *YB 10 Edward II [1316–17]*, ed. M. D. Legge and W. Holdsworth, SS (London, 1935), p. 97. See also the king's reply to the twelfth article of the grievances of 1327, in *Rot. Parl. Inediti*, pp. 109–110.

147. *YB 10 Edward II [1316–17]*, pp. 33, 34, 97, 200; *YB 11 Richard II [1387–88]*, ed. I. D. Thornley and T. F. T. Plucknett, Ames Foundation [AF] (London, 1937), pp. 76–77.

necessary and just. Writing to the chancellor and two royal judges in 1296, Archbishop Winchelsey insisted on the purely spiritual nature of such questions: "Ad quem vero judicem ecclesiasticum vel secularem pertineat de vacacione vel plenitudine ecclesiarum agnoscere bene nostis."[148]

The gravamina of 1327 state, however, that the royal courts had been deciding questions of vacancy and plenarty, when the king himself was plaintiff, without reference to the bishop as diocesan.[149] Evidently the crucial question was being rephrased so that it was made cognizable by a jury. The jurymen were asked not if the benefice were full but rather if it were vacant or not, thereby ignoring the jurisdiction of the church and rejecting the bishop's certificate of admission. Although the royal responses to this complaint promised that pleas of plenarty, strictly speaking, belonged to the church, apparently, the substitution of the lay inquest for the bishop's certificate continued.[150] In a Year Book from *20 Edward III* a royal judge concluded that "plenarty will be tried by the Court Christian, but void or not void will always be tried here." [151] The prelates continued to complain against this invasion of ecclesiastical jurisdiction. The statute of 1352, which promised that the vacancy of a benefice should be determined by the church, represented a concession to the ecclesiastical point of view.[152] The primary motivation for the use of the lay jury in a way which flouted ecclesiastical pretensions doubtlessly derived from the efforts of the crown to act upon rights of patronage which had accrued to it by virtue of the *droit de regale*. The king's claim rested simply upon the fact of the voidance of a benefice of the advowson of a tenant-in-chief during a period of royal wardship of the temporalities; and the kings were adamant in insisting that their regalian rights had priority over conflicting presentations by episcopal successors or by the popes. As we might suspect, the jurisdictional conflict was most intense in cases wherein the material interests of the crown itself were directly involved.

The jurisdictional conflict over the ecclesiastical benefice was aggravated during the last quarter of the thirteenth century and during the fourteenth century by the growing popularity of papal provisions and the prominence of Roman jurisdiction. The Roman Curia and the jurisdiction exercised by papal judges delegate replaced the courts of native bishops

148. *Registrum R. Winchelsey*, I, 61.
149. *Rot. Parl. Inediti*, pp. 109–110.
150. Plucknett, "Execrabilis in the Common Pleas," p. 67, and n. 6. For examples, see *CPR, 1343–45*, p. 318, *CPR, 1348–50*, p. 125.
151. *YB 20 Edward III [Part II]*, ed. L. O. Pike, RS (London, 1911), p. 396.
152. *SR*, I, 326.

and archdeacons as the principal rivals of the king's courts in respect to litigation concerning the benefice. The significance of this aspect of the conflict and its novelty is easily exaggerated. The focus of the controversy had shifted somewhat. It had certainly grown more intense. But the nature of the competition remained unchanged. For some time the royal jurisdiction continued to apply the same safeguards to the defense of its jurisdictional pretensions, and the antipapal legislation of Edward III's reign was considerably less innovative than has sometimes been assumed. It was, in essence, simply an extension and refinement of the theory and practice of royal control represented by the writ of prohibition *de advocatione*.[153]

The conflict over appointments to English benefices was not waged generally over the whole area of ecclesiastical patronage but concentrated, rather, on certain types of ecclesiastical livings, such as cathedral prebends, canonries, and archdeaconries, and on benefices of the patronage of certain persons, especially the bishops. The popes seldom presumed to provide to churches of the advowson of laymen, but preferred to lay claim to churches and livings to which bishops normally presented, in the expectation that the prelates would be both more compliant and defenseless.[154] Yet these efforts to present to benefices of the patronage of English bishops led to a collision with the kings, who claimed a similar privilege by virtue of the developing theory of regalian right. Controversy centered on competing claims to present to the same type of living, which, having been vacated while the temporalities of prelates were in royal wardship, the crown pretended to fill by its regalian right, and, which the popes reserved to themselves by virtue of their authority as Patrons Paramount.[155] This competition had an important material side. It was the result of the growing needs of church and state for sinecures to reward their loyal clerical servants. The stimulus for papal provisions and royal presentations alike came as much from promptings from below as from theoretical pretensions expressed from above.[156]

We should probably not exaggerate the extent of the conflict, at least insofar as the popes and the kings were concerned. In reality they showed a remarkable ability to compromise in exploiting the resources of the

153. Pantin, *English Church*, p. 87.

154. *Ibid.*, pp. 54, 59–61.

155. G. Mollat, *Collation des Bénéfices Ecclésiastiques sous les Papes d'Avignon* [*1305–1378*] (Paris, 1921), pp. 21–86, 227–269.

156. G. Barraclough, *Papal Provisions: Aspects of Church History Constitutional, Legal, and Administrative in the Middle Ages* (Oxford, 1935), pp. 158–159, 162–163; Howell, *Regalian Right*, p. 180.

English church. Royal candidates were often collated by the popes, and, seemingly, the laity were never convinced that the crown was sufficiently energetic in preventing and punishing papal intrusion. The advantage always lay, of course, with the crown.[157] Royal candidates usually got their way whether their appointments were couched in the form of papal letters of provision or royal writs.[158] The demands of political expediency or the dictates of current policy decided whether or not the crown would oppose or accept particular papal acts. The antipapal attitudes and actions of the fourteenth century might well represent the sentiments of the laity rather than real worries of the crown.[159] On the other hand, the royal jurisdiction was well prepared, both ideologically and procedurally, to cope with the challenge from abroad. The royal claim to absolute jurisdiction over advowson had been firmly established in the thirteenth century. The English church had been compelled to accept this fact, and the popes were expected to recognize it. This was the point that Edward III was trying to make in a letter to the pope in 1342, when he wrote: "omnes causae super iure patronatus quorumcumque beneficiorum, in dicto regno existentium, in curia nostra, coram justitiariis nostris, et non alibi, placitari debent, sententialiter discuti et finiri." [160]

Long before the special legislation of Edward III's reign against papal provisions and suit at Rome, the English crown had armed itself with weapons equally effective against church courts domestic as well as foreign. The writs and actions which were employed to defend the integrity of royal justice against the Courts Christian within the realm could also be applied against jurisdiction exercised from abroad. Bracton quoted a version of the *indicavit* which was used in Henry III's reign to prevent a

157. A. Hamilton Thompson, *The English Clergy and Their Organization in the Later Middle Ages* (Oxford, 1947), p. 38, remarks: "The royal power in fact loomed so prominently in dealings where king and pope were jointly concerned that Henry VIII's task in severing the ties which bound the English Church to Rome was materially lightened by the passive attitude into which the Holy See had fallen where the will of the Crown was in question."

158. Pantin, *English Church*, p. 68.

159. The attitude of the English laity toward papal provisions and other manifestations of papal power within England has never been thoroughly investigated. See *ibid.*, pp. 65–75, for a statement of this question. Antipapal sentiment and action in thirteenth-century England is also described in H. MacKenzie, "The Anti-Foreign Movement in England, 1231–1232," in *Anniversary Essays in Mediaeval History by Students of Charles Homer Haskins*, ed. C. H. Taylor (Boston, 1929), pp. 183–203.

160. T. Rymer, *Foedera, Conventiones, Litterae, et Acta Publica inter Reges Anglicae et Alios . . .*, 4 vols. (London, 1816–69), vol. II, part 2, p. 1208; hereafter cited as *Foedera*. Quoted by Pantin, *English Church*, p. 66.

judge ordinary from proceeding further in a plea which had been initiated by a papal citation.[161] In the reign of Edward I the temporalities of the archbishop of York were confiscated for instituting a papal provisor to a benefice, the patronage of which had been declared by the king's court to belong to the crown on this occasion.[162] In 1309 Archbishop William Greenfield of York excused himself to the pope for failing to execute a papal mandate by citing the terrible punishment of forfeiture of temporalities and even imprisonment that could befall him as they had befallen his predecessors, John Romeyn and Thomas Corbridge.[163] Prior to the enactment of the Statute of Praemunire in 1353 no new actions were added to those which had long been available to persons desiring protection against papal provision or suit at Rome. An examination of the *Rex* membranes of the plea rolls of the court of King's Bench following the ordinances of 1343 and 1344 and the statute of 1351 reveals that the vast majority of cases against papal intrusion were simple attachments on the prohibition,[164] which, like the new laws, made the charge that of contempt of the king's justice and the punishment that of imprisonment and forfeiture.[165] It was still possible for a patron to deliver a prohibition to the bishop or other ecclesiastical judge in order to avoid disputes and delays;[166] and the writ *ex relatu plurium* retained its value as a shield from retaliation by ecclesiastical authorities.[167] Although the ordinances of 1343 and 1344 and the statute of 1351 did not add any new weapons to the arsenal of the crown, they did possess a significant propaganda value.[168]

161. Bracton, III, fol. 250b. Brit. Mus. Add. MS. 35179, fol. 75, calls the writ *judicatur.* See the remarks of Innocent III to John in *Selected Letters of Pope Innocent III Concerning England, 1198–1216*, ed. C. R. Cheney and W. H. Semple (London, 1953), p. 50.

162. *Select Cases in the Court of King's Bench under Edward I*, III, 136 ff.

163. This letter is in the *Register of William Greenfield, Lord Archbishop of York, 1306–1315*, ed. A. Hamilton Thompson, Surtees Society, 5 vols. (Durham, 1931–38), IV, 209–211.

164. PRO, KB 27/342, 25, 30d, 31, 40, which are pleas of attachment on the prohibition against suit at Rome for Michaelmas term, 19 Edward III.

165. In 1329 an Irish royal justice was released from prison and a fine of £500 remitted for causing papal letters of excommunication to be published in the king's court. See *CPR, 1327–30*, p. 475; also *Placitorum Abbreviatio*, p. 338.

166. PRO, KB 27/342, 29d. In response to the request of the commons in 1351 for legislation against suit at Rome, the spokesmen of the crown said that there was already adequate remedy, *Rot. Parl.*, II, 228.

167. PRO, KB 27/342, 25.

168. For the ordinance and statute against provisors in 1343 and 1351 see *Rot. Parl.*, II, 143–145, and *SR*, I, 316–318. For the ordinance and statute of 1344 and 1353 against suit at Rome see *Rot. Parl.*, II, 153–154; *SR*, I, 329. For the petition of 1347 against suit at Rome see *Rot. Parl.*, II, 172–173; and for the petition and statute of 1363 see *Rot. Parl.*,

It has long been known that the Statute of Praemunire in 1353 merely speeded up the mesne process of attachment and distraint which preceded the rendering of judgment on defaulters in the king's courts.[169] The new prerogative writ, *praemunire facias*, which had made its appearance under entirely different circumstances earlier in the fourteenth century, informed the accused of the charges against him.[170] It was designed to cope with the elusive and often troublesome person, the papal provisor, who could not easily be distrained by seizing his personal properties or attached through his bishop or ecclesiastical superior. Although the crown had long used and continued to use, even after the enactment of the statute of 1353, the writs of prohibition to lay claim to advowson and other contested cases, the new action created by the statute provided a solution to the problem of getting a person to appear in court. It required that the defendant be publicly warned two months prior to the scheduled hearing in the king's court. If he did not appear, the royal court could proceed immediately to judgment, followed by declarations of forfeiture and outlawry. The statute did not establish any additional penalties. It continued the customary penalties and procedures of the old writ of prohibition, now expedited by action on the new writ of warning, *praemunire facias*. Further, the new action did not supplant the earlier methods of dealing with the problem; nor was it intended to do so, since it was created specifically to deal with fugitives from justice.

Although *praemunire facias* became known as a means for preventing suits at Rome on papal provisions, it could apply to cases of contracts and pensions,[171] trespass,[172] and exemption from ordinary jurisdiction.[173] Later it was extended to cover suitors accused of applying to Rome for exemption from the payment of tithes.[174] Although in the fourteenth

II, 283–285, and *SR*, I, 385–387. In 1416 a statute, *SR*, II, 193–194, gave the successful plaintiff on *praemunire facias* damages computed at three times the value of the benefice.

169. E. B. Graves, "The Legal Significance of the Statute of Praemunire of 1353," in *Haskins Anniversary Essays*, ed. Taylor, pp. 57–80, which is a condensation of his unpublished doctoral dissertation, "Studies on the Statute of Praemunire of 1353" (Harvard University, 1929). For a critical treatment of the statute of 1393, see W. T. Waugh, "The Great Statute of Praemunire," *EHR*, XXXVII (1922), 173–205. See also the comments of Pollock and Maitland, *History of English Law*, II, 591–593.

170. In 1306 a writ called *praemunire facias* was used to obtain information concerning advowson and the custody of lands, *Rot. Parl.*, I, 208.

171. PRO, KB 27/341, 50.

172. *CPR, 1396–99*, pp. 106–107.

173. Library of Dean and Chapter, Canterbury, Register N, fol. 177, for a writ of *praemunire facias* concerning an exemption by papal bull from ordinary jurisdiction.

174. *SR*, II, 121–122.

century *praemunire facias* was directed principally against jurisdiction exercised from abroad or by papal judges delegate, it placed the native prelates in an unenviable position between popes and kings.[175] The only protection the higher clergy of England received was contained in the Statute of Praemunire in 1393, which extended the penalties of outlawry and forfeiture to those who caused the translation or excommunication of bishops who had acted in compliance with the judgments of the king's courts.[176]

A number of conclusions emerge from a consideration of the jurisdictional conflict over the benefice. Popes and canonists never conceded the right of laymen to decide questions of patronage. In Henry III's reign, however, the English bishops and church courts had been forced to accept the *de facto* jurisdiction of the crown over all cases of advowson. By Bracton's time the crown and its courts were well prepared to cope, when they desired to do so, with any challenge to their exclusive jurisdiction over advowson. Royal reaction to ecclesiastical intervention, either direct or indirect, was most prompt and forceful when the rights of the crown itself were directly involved; but the several different judicial actions and procedures which enforced the king's jurisdiction were available to all suitors. Very early in the thirteenth century the royal courts had succeeded in vindicating the claim of the Constitutions of Clarendon by applying the prohibition *de advocatione* against ecclesiastical courts which attempted to assert the right of the church to cases of patronage. The crown's insistence on exclusive jurisdiction over advowson had already led to the development of additional prohibitory writs to curtail the church's role in deciding between contending presentees to the same benefice when there was any danger that the right to the patronage would be questioned or the decision of a royal court overturned. More important, however, than merely opposing the church in this area of law was the ingenuity of chancery and the king's courts in devising new common law actions, modeled after canonical precedents, which gave suitors useful and attractive alternatives to canonical justice. The possessory actions, *darrein presentment* and, especially, *quare impedit*, enhanced greatly the appeal of the king's courts for patrons and their presentees seeking justice in matters of

175. In the fifteenth century the writ, *praemunire facias*, was used against native ecclesiastical courts, even when they did not act by virtue of delegated authority. In 1449 the higher clergy of both provinces petitioned the king for assurance that the action would be restricted to cases which had been initiated abroad, Wilkins, III, 555–556; in 1462 a statute promised the church that the action would not lie against a native ecclesiastical judge who was merely exercising his lawful jurisdiction, *ibid.*, pp. 583–585.

176. *SR*, II, 84–86.

this kind. Despite the curtailment of the native ecclesiastical jurisdiction over the benefice, the bishops continued to exercise considerable influence over the disposition of clerical livings. The examination of clerical candidates and the admission and institution of presentees were aspects of the episcopal office with which the secular power seldom interfered, although it was recognized that the ex officio power of the diocesan could occasionally pose a threat to royal pretensions. Consequently, the writs *ut admittas* and *ne admittas,* coupled with the common law actions based upon *quare non admisit* and *quare incumbravit,* forced the bishops to exercise their spiritual duties with an eye to the expectations of royal justice. The enthusiasm of the royal jurisdiction for deciding all cases of advowson also prompted it to broaden its definition of patronage to include the disposition of such substantial parts of the benefice as a major portion of its revenues in tithes or the right to appoint to vicarages or chapels attached to it. Especially when the interests of the crown itself were involved, the royal courts resorted in the fourteenth century to the use of the lay inquest in ways which, though offensive to the bishops, enabled them to escape reliance upon the church for information concerning the status of a benefice. The multiplication of papal provisions to English benefices and the growing prominence and popularity of papal jurisdiction did not appreciably affect the course of jurisdictional conflict. The older methods for countering ecclesiastical jurisdiction over cases of advowson were as effective against the bearers of letters of papal provision or papal judges delegate as they had been against native church courts at an earlier date. The outcry against the Roman challenge to royal jurisdiction and even the antipapal legislation of the second half of the fourteenth century were possibly more the result of strong lay opposition than of royal efforts. To the end of the fourteenth century the native bishops continued to influence the disposition of ecclesiastical properties, but in an indirect and mainly administrative fashion. Sometimes episcopal authority assumed the form of sanctioning arrangements concerning a benefice disputed between two clerics. The bishop approved concords between rival presentees, authorized pensions in favor of one party, and in other extrajudicial ways exerted control over the possession or enjoyment of the revenues of an ecclesiastical living. After all, the essence of a benefice was the income which it provided. Consequently, the ability of the bishop as diocesan to approve agreements (especially those concerning tithes) affected in an important way the value of the benefice.[177] The bishop retained his authority over admissions and deprivations within the

177. Cheney, *From Becket to Langton,* pp. 114–116.

diocese, and the appointment of a clerk to religious office depended upon his concurrence. The freedom of the bishop in exercising this ex officio authority was sometimes limited, however, by the requirement expressed by the crown and its courts that the royal jurisdiction over advowson be kept inviolate. In the case of the ecclesiastical benefice as in other areas of jurisdictional rivalry between royal and ecclesiastical courts, the church was obliged to conduct itself on both the judicial and administrative levels in accordance with the expectations of the crown and the assumptions of the common law.

II. The Conflict over Frankalmoign and the Descent of Land

Unlike the French legists, who in the fourteenth century were still worrying about encroachments of the Courts Christian on real property and feudalities, the royal courts in England had succeeded in ousting the church from this area of law.[178] From about the middle of the thirteenth century it had become a well-established fact that the right to or possession of land was a question exclusively for the royal courts to decide. For the remainder of the middle ages the vast majority of such cases were tried according to common law actions initiated by royal writs in the courts of the king. The abolition of ecclesiastical jurisdiction over real property, very broadly defined, was the result of the progress of royal justice in the first half of the thirteenth century. The competition of the two courts in this respect points to some conclusions applicable to the jurisdictional conflict generally. First, it shows the limited nature of the conflict, which in this instance focused on a particular type of case—pleas of land held in free alms, *frankalmoign* so-called, in which one of the contending parties was a cleric. Second, it shows that the ability of the royal courts to push back the frontiers of ecclesiastical justice was due not only to successful opposition but also to successful innovation, which enabled the common lawyers to provide suitors with attractive alternatives to ecclesiastical justice. Third, the casual and impersonal nature of the conflict shows that it was not the result of a direct frontal assault by the crown on the church but, rather, the product of the efforts of a large number of little people to get the sort of justice they needed wherever it could be found. Finally, even after the ecclesiastical courts had lost jurisdictional competence over real property, they continued to exercise some influence on the descent of

178. Martin, *L'Assemblée de Vincennes*, pp. 159–160.

land by virtue of their purely moral authority over marriage and legitimacy—an influence which the king's courts eventually had to curtail in order to maintain control over the disposition and inheritance of landed estates.

The normal place for litigation concerning land was, with a brief lapse in Stephen's reign, always a secular court, and especially the king's court, although in the twelfth century the church courts tried a significant number of pleas concerning lands given to religious persons or monastic foundations in free alms. Such properties constituted the endowment of churches and monasteries, which owed purely spiritual services for them.[179] As "spiritualities," they were considered to fall within the scope of ecclesiastical jurisdiction.[180] It is likely that this jurisdictional competence was broadened during Stephen's reign to include a number of land cases, especially those disputed between clerics or a layman and a cleric, whether or not they conformed to the classification of frankalmoign. Generally speaking, church and state agreed in distinguishing lay fee from free alms, and the church courts in England did not lay claim to questions of feudal tenure or the estates of the laity, as they did in France by virtue of their jurisdiction over the feudal oath.[181]

Archbishop Becket specifically denounced the provision of the Constitutions of Clarendon which reserved to the king's courts the right to decide jurisdictional competence over a particular case. This was to be accomplished by means of the action known as *utrum*, which declared land to be lay fee (*laicum feodum*) or free alms (*elemosinam*) and, therefore, subject to either secular or ecclesiastical jurisdiction.[182] Doubtlessly, Becket was opposed to the pretensions of the crown to decide jurisdictional competence in this area and also to the proposed extension of royal justice

179. The term *free alms* is somewhat ambiguous, and contrary to what might be expected was not limited in its usage to lands held by the church for which no secular services were rendered: E. G. Kimball, "Tenure in Frank Almoign and Secular Services," *EHR*, XLIII (1928), 341–353. Often the church paid secular services for lands held in free alms, and it was necessary to distinguish between this kind of tenure and that "of pure and perpetual alms" for which only spiritual services such as prayer were paid. See Kimball, "The Judicial Aspects of Frank Almoign Tenure," *EHR*, XLVII (1932), 1–11.

180. F. W. Maitland, "Frankalmoign in the Twelfth and Thirteenth Centuries," *The Collected Papers of Frederic William Maitland*, ed. H. A. L. Fisher, 2 vols. (Cambridge, 1901), II, 215, 221; Pollock and Maitland, *History of English Law*, I, 240 ff.

181. See the first article of the petition composed by Philip Augustus and the French baronage in 1205–1206, *Recueil des Actes de Philippe Auguste*, ed. Delaborde, II, 489–491; early English examples of suit in Court Christian for breach of faith concerning a covenant for land are *CRR, 4 Henry III*, p. 171; *CRR, 5–6 Henry III*, p. 65.

182. *Select Charters*, pp. 165–166.

even further over the persons and properties of the clergy.[183] In his effort
to withstand royal pressure, Becket did not receive much help from the
papacy, which in the thirteenth century continued to place jurisdiction
over frankalmoign rather low on its list of priorities. During the early
thirteenth century the English church focused attention not on opposing
the challenge of *utrum* but, rather, on defending its jurisdiction over
frankalmoign against the common lawyers who were bringing most cases
concerning land and its appurtenances within their purview and who were
virtually abolishing frankalmoign as a legal category.

The conflict over the trial of land cases, which had been successfully
resolved in favor of the king's courts by the middle of the thirteenth
century, shows how the royal courts were able to impose their point of
view on the church. The assize utrum enabled the crown to draw the line
distinguishing spiritual from temporal pleas.[184] By Glanvill's time this
discretionary power had been reinforced by the invention of the prohibitory writ *de laico feodo*, which ordered the judge and the plaintiff in the
Court Christian to stop prosecuting a case which the defendant alleged to
belong to the royal courts as a plea of lay fee.[185] The evolution of the assize
utrum from a preliminary hearing to decide the question of jurisdiction
to a fully developed possessory action, whereby one party gained possession of the land as frankalmoign or the other as lay fee, broadened
considerably the jurisdictional competence of the royal courts. Utrum,
which became the "parson's writ of right," provided a useful alternative
to the actions available in the ecclesiastical courts.[186] In the early thirteenth century the jurisdictional competence of the church courts was
further narrowed by restricting the meaning of frankalmoign to include
only consecrated lands, churchyards, cemeteries, and the like.[187] During
this same period the meaning of "lay fee," as the term was used in writs
of prohibition, was extended to cover such items as houses, standing grain,
rights of pasturage, and services and customary obligations, as well as
land, marshes, and pastures.[188] The availability of royal prohibitions to
any suitor desiring them encouraged private persons to challenge ecclesiastical jurisdiction whenever it seemed to their advantage to do so.

183. Kimball, "Judicial Aspects of Frank Almoign Tenure," p. 10.
184. Pollock and Maitland, *History of English Law*, I, 250–251; S. E. Thorne, "Assize
Utrum and the Canon Law," *Columbia Law Review*, XXXIII (1933), 428–436.
185. Glanvill, XII, 21.
186. Pollock and Maitland, *History of English Law*, I, 250–251.
187. Kimball, "Judicial Aspects of Frank Almoign Tenure," p. 7; Bracton, IV, fol.
407.
188. Flahiff, "Writ of Prohibition (i)," p. 273.

This competition between the two court systems occurred in the first half of the thirteenth century, and it ended with the triumph of royal jurisdiction. Subsequently, in the second half of the thirteenth century and the whole of the fourteenth century the church courts seldom presumed to intrude into an area which had long before been surrendered to the common lawyers. Regrettably, only the methods and the results of this jurisdictional conflict are visible. Early records of the ecclesiastical courts are unavailable, unprinted, or unstudied. The citations of prohibited cases in the *Curia Regis* rolls are distressingly brief or are attenuated by endless postponements and delays and recurrent distraints and attachments. Only occasionally can we glimpse the impact of an aggressive royal jurisdiction on the church courts or the retreating action of the church in its hopeless struggle with the king's courts. The fairly considerable number of attachments on the prohibition *de laico feodo* reported in the first three or four decades of the thirteenth century indicate the popularity of this means for challenging ecclesiastical jurisdiction. Almost invariably the defendant in the church court, who was a layman, sought to prevent the plaintiff, a cleric, and the ecclesiastical judge from trying a case which was said to belong to the king's courts as a plea of lay fee.[189] The close association of the royal prohibition and the assize utrum, the active and passive instrumentalities of royal encroachment, respectively, is illustrated in cases from early in Henry III's reign, which may reveal the way in which many such disputes were resolved. In these instances a clerical suitor in the Court Christian was attached on a prohibition *de laico feodo* brought by a layman, who had been the defendant in the Court Christian. After both parties replied to the question of violating a royal prohibition, they agreed to put their case to the assize. A jury was convened to give testimony as to whether (utrum) the land in dispute were free alms, as claimed by the churchman, or lay fee, as claimed by his antagonist. In this way the separate questions of violation of a royal prohibition, jurisdictional competence, and ultimate possession of the property were combined into one, and that one determined by the royal court.[190] It would not seem that there was anything deliberately hostile in the actions and attitudes of the royal courts in these pleas of attachment on the prohibition. They were

189. The plaintiff on attachment on the prohibition *de laico feodo* was, so far as can be determined, invariably a layman, whereas the defendant, who had brought the original suit in the Court Christian, was a cleric. For some examples, see *CRR, 14–17 Henry III*, Nos. 88, 302, 651, 2104, 2331.

190. The culmination of suit on an attachment on the prohibition *de laico feodo* in the assize utrum is shown by the following cases, *CRR, 3–5 John*, p. 42; *CRR, 4 Henry III*, pp. 63, 118–119; *CRR, 14–17 Henry III*, No. 1372.

brought by private parties, not by the king. If the purchaser of the writ failed to prove his case, the church court was told to proceed to judgment and the false suitor was held for punishment.[191] In other instances, the ecclesiastical judge was able to avoid the penalty for being in contempt of the king's command by proving that he had obeyed the writ of prohibition. Apparently, however, such writs were issued generously and not too discriminatingly—a fault which the bishops always denounced. Occasionally it is evident that the church court had not been trying a case of lay fee but something quite different, such as defamation, tithes, a testamentary matter, or a matrimonial plea.[192]

There was an abrupt decline in the number of attachments on the prohibition *de laico feodo* reported in the royal court rolls of the second half of the thirteenth century.[193] The writ registers from Edward I's reign forward continue to offer examples of this kind of writ,[194] but there is no evidence whatsoever that the church was effectively defending its jurisdictional competence in respect to what it once claimed as frankalmoign. The complaint of the gravamina compiled in Bracton's time and the statements concerning royal encroachment on free alms contained in Boniface's legislation sound more like wishful thinking than a serious or easily remediable grievance.[195] The implications of the church's criticism of this situation were that it opposed the loss of jurisdiction over personal actions involving the clergy as much as the infringement of its authority over free alms. The church courts continued to decide cases in which both litigants were religious persons, and neither chose to purchase the royal prohibition, but these were relatively few. When one of the contending parties was a layman, it was more than probable that the case would finally go to a royal court, wherein the common lawyers were well prepared to handle it. This was the result of the virtual abolition of the rationale underlying the jurisdictional pretensions of the church court through the restriction of cases of frankalmoign to those concerning only consecrated soil, churchyards, and the like. The progress of the common law in the early thirteenth century had narrowed ecclesiastical jurisdiction

191. Action on attachment on the prohibition is quashed in *CRR, 4 Henry III*, pp. 338, 358, 383; *CRR, 9–10 Henry III*, No. 1318.

192. *CRR, 9–10 Henry III*, No. 1258; *CRR, 11–14 Henry III*, No. 2349; *CRR, 14–17 Henry III*, Nos. 575, 579, 665.

193. See Flahiff's chart, "Writ of Prohibition (i)," p. 310.

194. *Ibid.*, p. 273 n. 55.

195. Article 4 of the gravamina of 1280, rehearsed in 1309, in *Councils & Synods*, pp. 876–877; article 17 in *Documents Illustrative of English History in the Thirteenth and Fourteenth Centuries*, ed. H. Cole (London, 1844), p. 357.

over cases concerning land even more stringently than had been contemplated by Henry II in his famous constitutions.

For the remainder of the middle ages the church courts in England seldom presumed to try openly a case concerning real property. Pleas of attachment on the prohibition *de laico feodo* become rare in the records of the king's courts. The position of the crown and its courts was forcefully stated in the reign of Edward II by the proctors of certain English magnates in the course of a protracted dispute over the disposition of the estates of the Templars. By writs dated December 20, 1307, which ordered the sheriffs to arrest members of the order in England and to occupy their lands and properties, Edward II showed his reluctant compliance with the pope's decision to dissolve the society.[196] Subsequently, a number of English lords, the overlords of the Templars for certain estates, seized these lands and refused to surrender them to the Hospitallers at the demand of the Council of Vienne.[197] In order to force them to disgorge their illgotten gains Pope John XXII ordered the bishops to proceed against the most stubborn of the English magnates by canonical process.[198] When the lords were called to the Courts Christian to answer for their contumacy, they brought writs of prohibition *de laico feodo* which accused the church courts of encroaching upon royal jurisdiction over lay fee and lay chattels.[199] The English bishops repeated these arguments in a letter to the pope dated November 16, 1320, wherein they excused themselves for failing to execute the papal mandate on the grounds that the violation of the king's prohibition would make them liable to imprisonment and the forfeiture of their temporalities.[200] The bishops explained that they had

196. *CCR, 1307–13*, pp. 48–49.

197. *Calendar of Entries in the Papal Registers Relating to Great Britain and Ireland*, ed. W. H. Bliss and J. A. Twemlow, 14 vols. (London, 1893–1960), *Papal Letters, 1305–42*, p. 95; hereafter cited as *Calendar of Papal Letters*. For background, see A. M. Leys, "The Forfeiture of the Lands of the Templars in England," in *Oxford Essays presented to H. E. Salter*, ed. F. M. Powicke (Oxford, 1934), pp. 155–163; T. W. Parker, *The Knights Templars in England* (Tucson, 1963), pp. 98–104.

198. For the bull of November, 1320, see *Registrum Hamonis Hethe, Diocesis Roffensis, A.D. 1319–1352*, ed. C. Johnson, CYS, 2 vols. (London, 1948), I, 85–89.

199. Wilkins, II, 499–500.

200. *Registrum H. Hethe*, I, 77–78: "... nobis brevia regia prohibitoria per manus comitum et baronum quodammodo ab invito concessa, ne circa laica feuda de quibus agitur quicquam aliqualiter attemptemus, antequam possemus ad execucionis actum procedere in medio sunt porrecta," and later, "convictis facientibus contra eas ... convicte persone bona omnia mobilia et immobilia nostris ecclesiis annexa apud dominum regem forisfacta undique confiscantur, corpusque attachiatur carceris custodie detrudendum."

sought consultations on the prohibitions from the king in council, but that certain laymen and magnates, *murmurando replicationibus*, had persuaded Edward to reject their petition as contrary to established custom and the rights of the crown. Somewhat later, in 1321, the spokesmen for one of the guilty magnates, the earl of Lancaster, argued during the course of an appeal to the court of Canterbury that cases of lay fee were the exclusive concern of the royal courts and that the recent activities of the ecclesiastical courts in regard to the former properties of the Temple were clearly opposed to the laws and customs of the kingdom.[201]

Despite the abolition of ecclesiastical jurisdiction over landed estates of any kind, the church continued to exercise an indirect but important influence on their disposition and descent by virtue of its responsibility for deciding questions concerning matrimony and the intent and enforcement of testaments. In the reign of Edward I the growing interest of the king's courts in testamentary matters, coupled with the expansion of the activities of borough courts, raised the question of jurisdiction over devisable burgage tenements. Such properties were distinguished from the usual estate in land in that they were viewed as bequeathable. Ecclesiastical courts had probably been doing justice in cases concerning burgage tenements through the default of other courts and because of their interest in the enforcement of testaments. In Edward I's reign, however, the secular courts had been intervening in a sufficient number of cases to provoke the dismay of the higher clergy. In the royal response to the gravamina of 1280, which were rehearsed in 1309, the crown insisted that the municipal courts should have the authority to decide whether or not a burgage tenement could actually be bequeathed—an interesting application of the theory of the assize utrum.[202] It is quite probable that in this instance as previously the assize had the effect of determining the issue

201. *Ibid.*, pp. 91–94. The arguments are worth repeating: "de consuetudine in Anglia a tempore cujus non exstat memoria notorie optenta ac pacifice observata omnis cognicio ac omnimoda juris discussio necnon quecumque execucio super quibuscumque bonis temporalibus, tam mobilibus quam immobilibus vel se moventibus, a quibuscumque personis eciam ecclesiasticis possessis sive qualitercumque occupatis, necnon super accionibus et juribus ad quecumque bona temporalia quibuscumque personis eciam ecclesiasticis vel contra eas qualitercumque competentibus in regno Anglie existentibus qualitercumque facienda, ad excellentissimum dominum nostrum dominum regem Anglie qui pro tempore fuerit jure suo regali pertinuisset ac pertineat in presenti, fuerintque toto tempore predicto et predicto excellentissimo domino nostro domino regi Anglie omnes et singuli hujusmodi persone, cujuscumque status vel condicionis existant, in premissis omnibus et singulis subdite et pleno jure subjecte" (pp. 91–92).

202. *Councils & Synods*, pp. 876–877; M. M. Sheehan, *The Will in Medieval England* (Toronto, 1963), pp. 264, 268, 274–278, 295.

of the lawful possession of such properties, thereby rejecting ecclesiastical jurisdiction.

The most famous conflict of common law and canon law in English history came to the forefront during discussions between Bishop Grosseteste and the barons at Merton in 1236.[203] It arose from the refusal of the English nobility to accept the canonical principle that the subsequent marriage of parents legitimatized their offspring. The crown and the common lawyers never disputed the purely spiritual nature of matrimony nor the right of the church courts to determine cases concerning the validity of the marriage contract and the legitimacy of children. Throughout the middle ages royal courts sent to the bishops for certification of the legitimacy or bastardy of suitors, and cases concerning the inheritance of land and of a number of other issues were decided in accordance with the findings of the church.[204] On the other hand, as early as 1208 the conflict of the canons with good English custom encouraged the king's courts in certain instances to employ a device for circumventing the church in order to enjoy the final word over the descent of real property.[205] Often in the late thirteenth and the fourteenth centuries the testimony of a jury of laymen was substituted for the bishop's certificate. The royal courts adopted the practice whereby the issue of bastardy was stated as a question of fact—"born before espousals, and therefore bastard," or "born after espousals, and therefore legitimate"—the truth or falsity of which could be put to a jury of laymen. By rephrasing the question which previously had been sent to the bishop for certification the royal courts had freed themselves from total reliance upon the bishop and the canon law and were able to avoid reference to the church when it suited their purpose. The old spirit of cooperation endured, however. There was no question of ousting the church courts entirely from this area of law, nor did the common lawyers intend to do so. Throughout the middle ages royal courts sent to the bishops for information on such matters, and royal judgments were based upon these returns. The king's courts restricted exceptions of "special" bastardy so-called, i.e., born before or after the parents'

203. See the invaluable study of Norma Adams, "Nullius Filius—A study of the Exception of Bastardy in the Law Courts of Mediaeval England," *University of Toronto Law Journal*, VI (1946), 361–384. R. Génestal, *Histoire de la Légitimation des Enfants Naturels en Droit Canonique* (Paris, 1905), explains the canonical position. For the Council of Merton, consult Powicke, *King Henry III and the Lord Edward*, I, 150–151, and *Thirteenth Century*, pp. 70–71; Pope Alexander's statement may be found in *Decretals*, IV, 17, 4. Bracton's view of the canon law on this point is well known, see Bracton, IV, fol. 417b.

204. Adams, "Nullius Filius," p. 364, and references to bishops' registers.

205. *Ibid.*, p. 369.

marriage, to possessory actions or as exceptions against the person demanding certain properties.[206] Action on the writ of right or an averment against the tenant required a plea of "general" bastardy, which only the bishop could decide.[207] In other words, the king's courts reserved to the bishop the right to certify the legitimacy or the bastardy of a person in those cases when such a decision would be most crucial or its effect most permanent.

In the fourteenth century the use of the lay jury was extended when the king's judges put the question of the legitimacy of the dead or of persons not party to the original plea to the sworn inquest.[208] The advantage of using lay juries in such instances led the king's courts to extend their use to cases concerning the validity of the marriage contract and of divorce.[209] The common law courts preserved a certain flexibility in the reception of such pleas, and held that the results of the inquest did not bar future exceptions of bastardy made by other persons against a suitor.[210] The bishop's certificate kept its permanent effect, however, and was considered to be conclusive in the one case and in all future actions where the writ to the bishop would be awarded.[211] The judgment of one case did not, however, bar another court from putting the exception of special bastardy against the same person to another jury.[212] The efforts of the commons in

206. This point is made quite strongly in a number of interesting cases from the Year Books. See the case of Chamber v. Chamber, Trinity, 5 Edward II, and editor's comments (Introduction, pp. xxi–xxiv) for a careful distinction between the pleas of special and general bastardy; *YB 5 Edward II [1312]*, ed. W. C. Bolland, SS (London, 1916), pp. 161–169; also *YB 11–12 Edward III*, ed. A. J. Horwood, RS (London, 1883), pp. 351–353; *YB 14 Edward III*, ed. L. O. Pike, RS (London, 1888), pp. 49–63; *YB 6–7 Edward II [1313]*, ed. W. C. Bolland, SS (London, 1918), pp. 95–105; *YB 6–7 Edward II [Eyre of Kent: 1313–14]*, ed. W. C. Bolland, SS, 3 vols. (London, 1910–13), III, 92–93; also the comments of Adams, "Nullius Filius," p. 376.

207. See *YB 17–18 Edward III*, ed. L. O. Pike, RS (London, 1903), pp. 259–261; *YB 11–12 Edward III*, p. 163; *YB 6–7 Edward II [1313]*, pp. 158–162.

208. Since a deceased person could not be canonically examined, his case was put to a lay jury: *YB 5 Edward II [1311]*, p. 258; *YB 1–2 Edward II [1307–1309]*, ed. F. W. Maitland, SS (London, 1903), pp. 95–96. An instance of the trial of the bastardy of one not party to the original plea is contained in *YB 11 Edward III [1317–18]*, ed. J. P. Collas and W. S. Holdsworth, SS (London, 1942), p. 149.

209. *YB 5 Edward II [1311–12]*, ed. W. C. Bolland, SS (London, 1915), pp. 38–42, and Introduction, pp. xvi–xvii.

210. *YB 2–3 Edward II [1308–1309 and 1309–10]*, ed. F. W. Maitland, SS (London, 1904), p. 110; *YB 13 Richard II [1389–90]*, ed. T. F. T. Plucknett, AF (London, 1929), pp. 143–148.

211. *YB 18–19 Edward III*, ed. L. O. Pike, RS (London, 1905), pp. 39–41.

212. *YB 11–12 Edward III*, pp. 231–233.

1347 to annul the conclusiveness of this act of certification failed, and the result of the bishop's inquest remained a matter of record.[213]

As in the case of all communications from the church courts to royal courts, care was taken to establish the validity and authenticity of such documents.[214] Whenever the ecclesiastical judge, who would customarily have had jurisdiction over the plea, was himself a party to the original case, the request for certification of legitimacy was sent to the metropolitan.[215] Further, it was said that only the royal courts had the authority to require such certification. A plea begun in a manorial or borough court was sent to chancery and thence to the King's Bench for further action.[216] Although the king's courts respected the right of the bishops to certify concerning such matters, they were careful to distinguish between the bishop's certificate and the actual judgment rendered by the royal court.[217] It was said that the king's courts should act only on those findings which they had specifically sent to the bishop for certification. A case which came to the attention of the king in parliament during Edward I's reign made this point quite clearly. William Paynel and Margaret, his wife, brought a petition asking for Margaret's dowry from a previous marriage. To counter the objection that they had been denounced by an ecclesiastical judge for adultery, they produced the bishop's certificate of purgation. While disclaiming any interest in such matters, the king's answer to the petition carefully stated the conditions under which the royal courts were willing to receive and act upon ecclesiastical judgments: "Nec super testimonio episcoporum sunt judicia in curia Regis facienda, licet littere episcoporum in curia Regis fuerint porrecte, nisi iidem episcopi ad mandatum regium ipsi Regi rescriberent."[218]

The dispute over the trial of cases of frankalmoign was ended by the virtual elimination of this type of case as an important area of canonical jurisdiction. In the later middle ages the bishop as diocesan occasionally decided pleas concerning consecrated soil or glebe lands and sanctioned agreements concerning the possession of properties disputed between

213. *Rot. Parl.*, II, 171. A petition of the Commons, designed to avoid reference to the Court Christian when the issue of bastardy was raised between brothers, likewise failed to win acceptance: *ibid.*, p. 10.

214. *YB 12–13 Edward III*, p. 203; *YB 32–33 Edward I*, p. 30.

215. *Rot. Parl.*, I, 198.

216. *YB 13–14 Edward III*, ed. L. O. Pike, RS (London, 1886), p. 323; *YB 14 Edward III*, p. 88.

217. See Willóughby's statement in Michaelmas term, 18 Edward III, *YB 18–19 Edward III*, p. 39.

218. *Rot. Parl.*, I, 147.

churchmen. This jurisdictional competence seldom evoked the criticism of the royal courts or the crown; and, of course, the jurisdictional conflict in this area as in most others was primarily the result of challenges posed by private persons. The jurisdiction of the church over matrimony continued to impose the more liberal and humane canon law of legitimacy upon the king's courts, which were encouraged to resort to the use of the jury so as to free themselves from total reliance upon a law that was patently contrary to English custom. Such procedures were justified as necessary for preserving the jurisdictional competence of the crown over feudalities and the descent of real property. During much of the thirteenth and fourteenth centuries the royal and church courts shared competence over pleas of bastardy, when the inheritance of land was at issue. But such cooperation was always on terms laid down by the king's courts, which decided when the bishops' certificates would be accepted and carefully distinguished between the findings of the church and their own solemn judgments.

III. EXCOMMUNICATION AND CAPTION

A dramatic illustration of the ability of the two powers to cooperate is provided by the crown's willingness to arrest and imprison excommunicates and to enforce the church's spiritual censures. During the thirteenth and fourteenth centuries the bishops and a few other prominent English clerics sought the assistance of the secular power to force unrepentant persons, who had been excommunicated for forty days or more, to submit to ecclesiastical justice. Such cooperation was based upon both secular and canonical precedents and upon the assumption that the Christian prince should apply his coercive power to the enforcement of the legitimate jurisdiction of the church.[219] The assistance of kings was very useful and was often requested. Excommunication was the customary method for forcing individual persons to submit to the corrective authority of the clergy and for obliging sinners to come to the ecclesiastical courts for judgment. The frequency and familiarity of sentences of excommunication launched by the church in the later middle ages tended, however, to dissipate the effect of this form of constraint and to diminish the anxiety

219. William I recognized the crown's responsibility to coerce excommunicates: *Die Gesetze der Angelsachsen*, ed. F. Liebermann, 3 vols. (Halle, 1898–1916), I, 485. I investigate the principles, both legal and theological, underlying church-state relations in "The Two Laws in England: the Later Middle Ages," *A Journal of Church and State*, XI (1969), 111–131.

which it evoked in its victims.[220] English kings reinforced these censures by allowing certain prelates to petition for the arrest and imprisonment of particular persons who had displayed their unwillingness to abide by the judgments of the church. Between the ages of Glanvill and Bracton a regular method for doing this was made available in the royal writ called *significavit* or *de excommunicato capiendo*.[221] This writ issued from chancery upon certification by the bishops and archbishops, together with certain privileged abbots and archdeacons and the chancellors of Oxford and Cambridge. It ordered the sheriffs to arrest and detain in royal custody persons who had been excommunicated for forty days or more and who were obviously avoiding reconciliation with the church.[222] A few exempt jurisdictions had the right to apply directly to chancery for the writ of· caption.[223] Most ecclesiastical judges inferior in rank to the bishop were obliged to obtain its issuance through their diocesan. The delay which this caused may have led to its use only as a final resort.[224] To expedite this process, perhaps, the archbishop of York was granted the privilege in 1267 of applying directly to the sheriff for the arrest and imprisonment of excommunicates who had been under the ban for forty days or more,[225] and he evidently made use of this power.[226] The more usual method of applying to the king for the issuance of the writ of caption was followed until events in the reign of Richard II encouraged the government to speed up the procedure for apprehending persons in order to cope more effectively with a particularly troublesome kind of criminal.[227]

The theory of the cooperation of church and state as represented by the writ of caption was never challenged during the middle ages.

220. R. Hill, "The Theory and Practice of Excommunication," *History*, XLII (1957), 9–10.

221. The writ is not in Glanvill, but see Bracton, IV, fols. 408b–409.

222. For an authoritative discussion of caption, see F. D. Logan, *Excommunication and the Secular Arm in Medieval England* (Toronto, 1968); also I. J. Churchill, *Canterbury Administration*, I, 521–523.

223. The grant to the chancellor of Oxford is cited in *CPR, 1358–61*, p. 193; and those to the archdeacon of Richmond and the abbot of St. Edmund's in *CPR, 1350–54*, pp. 182, 470. The archbishop of York obtains the king's permission that his vicar-general shall be able to impetrate the writ while the archbishop is absent from the country, *CPR, 1281–92*, p. 129.

224. Woodcock, *Medieval Ecclesiastical Courts*, p. 97.

225. *Register of W. Giffard*, p. 103; for an example, see *ibid.*, p. 109.

226. Logan, *Excommunication and the Secular Arm*, p. 101. Canterbury seems not to have been given similar authority.

227. H. G. Richardson, "Heresy and the Lay Power under Richard II," *EHR*, LI (1936), 8 ff.

Individual English prelates often enlisted the aid of the crown in enforcing spiritual sanctions declared by themselves or the lesser clergy. Nevertheless, controversy did erupt. What the church viewed as an absolute responsibility, the secular power saw as a special privilege dependent on royal grace. The crown insisted on its right to grant or to withhold its help according to its convictions in the particular instance. The debate over the mutual responsibilities of the two powers in this respect shows that the jurisdictional conflict was as much the result of problems of procedure and enforcement as it was the product of competing laws. Although the crown was prepared to recognize the censures of the church by disqualifying excommunicates who sought to plead in its courts and by coercing impenitent sinners in accordance with the writ of caption, it defended its right to decide when to give such recognition and assistance. Louis IX of France likewise insisted on possessing this discretionary authority and argued against the notion of a blind obedience by the state to the judgments of the church.[228] The English crown and its courts were especially adamant on the issue of the independence of the secular power when royal rights or the immunity of its own servants were involved. Whenever it seemed that the cause of law and order would be better served or the maintenance of royal justice better guaranteed, the crown could act or refuse to act in accordance with what it saw as right and just. Jurisdictional conflict focused on this discretionary authority whereby the crown respected or ignored spiritual sanctions declared against particular persons or places, arrested excommunicates or released them from imprisonment, and occasionally forced prelates to defend their action in the presence of laymen.

It would be a mistake to exaggerate the extent of the controversy which this issue provoked. The large number of "significations," or requests for caption sent to chancery by bishops during the thirteenth and fourteenth centuries and preserved in the Public Record Office, testify to the considerable cooperation which prevailed between the two jurisdictions.[229] In the majority of instances the secular power accepted its responsibilities and complied with the expectations of the church. Long before the innovations of Richard II's reign, undertaken to cope with the extraordinary problem posed by the outbreak of the Lollard heresy, there were compelling precedents for the cooperation of church and state in the enforcement of the legitimate jurisdiction of the clergy. In many instances

228. Jean, Sire de Joinville, *Histoire de Saint Louis*, ed. N. de Wailly (Paris, 1874), pp. 368, 370.

229. The PRO classification of requests for caption is Chancery Significations [C.85].

the efficacy of canonical authority depended upon the coercive power of kings—a fact which was generally admitted by both sides; and in a large number of particular cases this assistance was forthcoming, although not in the peremptory and mechanical fashion that some bishops seemed to expect. Without questioning the theory of cooperation and while enforcing it frequently, nevertheless, the royal and ecclesiastical jurisdictions could squabble over their respective rights and responsibilities in individual instances.

Occasionally the crown argued for the exemption of privileged persons or places from excommunication. William I, according to Eadmer's report, reserved to himself a voice in the trial or excommunication of tenants-in-chief and his ministers;[230] and Henry II demanded in the Constitutions of Clarendon that he or his justiciar consent to the excommunication of such persons before the sentences were published.[231] On the basis of these claims the magnates of a later day argued that tenants-in-chief of the crown should not be made to answer to ecclesiastical citations outside of their native parishes.[232] In response to the bishops' complaint, however, the statute of 1316 renounced this exemption.[233] The only serious and successful attempt to exempt persons or places from the effects of ecclesiastical justice concerned the king's household, clerical servants, and royal officials.[234]

During the thirteenth century the crown repeatedly insisted upon the freedom of its clerical ministers from the ordinary jurisdiction of the bishop and said that this immunity encompassed their exemption from the canonical regulations concerning residency, against holding a plurality of benefices, of complying with the rules of age and professional advancement, and of being cited by church courts or excommunicated by the higher clergy.[235] Although the kings denied that they wished to free their clerks entirely from episcopal authority, they often came to their assistance against the bishops and the ecclesiastical courts, and defended these actions as necessary for the preservation of royal rights and the operation

230. *Historia Novorum*, ed. M. Rule, RS (London, 1884), p. 10.
231. *Select Charters*, p. 100.
232. Article 5 of the grievances of 1309, in *Councils & Synods*, p. 1272.
233. *SR*, I, 173.
234. For examples of the king's protection extended to such persons, see *CCR, 1302–1307*, p. 90; *CCR, 1354–60*, p. 530.
235. Henry III obtained papal bulls in 1247 and 1252 permitting his clerks not to reside in their benefices: *Foedera*, vol. I, part 1, pp. 268, 285. In 1289 Edward I obtained indults from Pope Nicholas IV allowing thirty of his clerks to enjoy exemption from residence and from the necessity of proceeding to higher orders: *Calendar of Papal Letters, 1198–1342*, pp. 503, 505, 507.

of royal government.[236] Chancery and Exchequer clerks jealously defended, often in the face of episcopal opposition, their right not to answer in personal actions outside of these great offices. In Edward I's reign the bishops denounced, with little success, the jurisdictional immunity of the clerks of the Exchequer.[237] In the fourteenth century the chancery clerks claimed the privilege of being judged on civil pleas within chancery.[238] In the reign of Edward I, again, the archdeacon of Exeter was accused of contempt for excommunicating two royal clerks (*secretarii clerici*);[239] and the king wrote to the pope on behalf of the archdeacon of York, his chancellor, against a citation outside the kingdom.[240] In the fourteenth century other monarchs complained against the citation of their officials outside the realm, saying that this had the unfortunate effect of depriving the crown of valued servants and expert advisors.[241] The crown insisted that this immunity from ecclesiastical intimidation or coercion extended to the king's household as well as to the great offices of state and to all who served the crown or were resident at court. In 1293 a clerk petitioned Parliament in the king's name against a process against him in the Court of Arches, claiming that only the steward and marshal had the right to cite persons within the king's household or palace.[242] In 1315 the council heard the king's attorney request the amercement of the archdeacon of Norfolk and his official in the amount of £20,000 for citing a person who was resident at the court at Westminster.[243]

    This freedom from ecclesiastical persecution extended to secular

236. *SR*, I, 172. For interesting references to the exemption of the royal clerks, see *Registrum R. Winchelsey*, II, 811–812; *Registrum Thome de Cantilupo, Episcopi Herefordensis, A.D. MCCLXXV–MCCLXXXII*, ed. R. G. Griffiths, CYS (London, 1907), pp. 169–170; *Registrum Ade de Orleton, Episcopi Herefordensis, A.D. MCCCXVII–MCCCXXVII*, ed. A. T. Bannister, CYS (London, 1908), p. 196. Clerks in the service of the higher clergy were also exempted: *Registrum R. Winchelsey*, I, 411–412.

237. Article 10 of the gravamina of 1280, in *Councils & Synods*, pp. 879–880.

238. *CCR, 1374–77*, p. 2; *CCR, 1389–92*, pp. 219–220; *Foedera*, vol. III, part 1, p. 13; *Rot. Parl.*, II, 154–155; and W. A. Morris, Introduction, in *The English Government at Work, 1327–1336*, ed. J. F. Willard and W. A. Morris, 3 vols. (Cambridge, Mass., 1940–50), I, 61.

239. Cited in the Exchequer memoranda from Edward I's reign printed in *Les Reports des Cases argue et adjudge en le Temps del Roy Edward le Second . . .* (London, 1678), pp. 38–39.

240. *CCR, 1296–1302*, pp. 309–310.

241. *Diplomatic Correspondence of Richard II*, ed. Perroy, pp. 152–157; *Calendar of Papal Letters, 1342–62*, pp. 304–305, 625, 627.

242. *Rot. Parl.*, I, 97.

243. *Select Cases before the King's Council, 1243–1482*, ed. I. S. Leadam and J. F. Baldwin, SS (Cambridge, Mass., 1918), pp. 27–32.

officials of the crown—to sheriffs, justices, royal bailiffs, and other ministers engaged in official business. In 1231 Henry III obtained Pope Gregory IX's assurance that his officials should be immune from excommunication while on the king's service.[244] But this privilege did not completely eliminate problems of this kind. At the middle of the century the king had to come to the aid of the sheriff of Rutland who had been excommunicated by the bishop of Lincoln for failing to execute a writ of caption—an affront to the royal dignity which prompted Henry to seek a renewal of the papal promise exempting his servants from the effects of spiritual censures while they were performing their duties.[245] Not only the permanent servants of the crown, clerks and laymen alike, but any person temporarily engaged on royal business might argue his exemption from excommunication or other forms of ecclesiastical coercion, and the king was expected to come to his aid.

A famous case, discussed in the Easter Parliament of *21 Edward I* (1293) and involving the bishop of Durham and the archbishop of York, illustrates this point.[246] Archbishop John Romeyn had excommunicated the bailiffs of Anthony Bek, the bishop of Durham, for arresting certain of the archbishops' messengers (*nuncios*). Since the bishop had been abroad on the king's business when this had happened, he was given the king's special protection. The archbishop was cited to answer *coram rege* for violating the king's protection and for encroaching upon the royal jurisdiction over jail delivery. The archbishop's attempt to question the jurisdiction of a royal court over a case of excommunication and his exception to the effect that Anthony Bek was subject to him as metropolitan did not prove sufficient. He was judged guilty of violating the king's special protection and of intruding into an area of royal justice. The court awarded damages to Bek and a fine to the king in the amount of 4,000 marks.

In another parliamentary plea discussed in the Hilary term of *18 Edward I* (1290) the unruly and powerful clerk, Bogo de Clare, who had conspired with the prior of the Holy Trinity, London, to cite the earl of Cornwall to appear before the archbishop of Canterbury, was attached, together with the prior, to answer *coram rege* for the contempt. It was said

244. *Registres de Grégoire IX* [*1227–41*], ed. L. Auvray *et al.*, 4 vols. (École Française de Rome, 1896–1955), No. 688; *Councils & Synods*, p. 283 n. 1.
245. Discussed in *Councils & Synods*, p. 472 n. 1.
246. *Placita Parliamentaria*, ed. W. Riley (London, 1661), pp. 135–141; *CCR, 1288–96*, pp. 330–334; and *Rot. Parl.*, I, 102–105; discussed by C. M. Fraser, *A History of Antony Bek, Bishop of Durham* (Oxford, 1957), pp. 94–96; R. Brentano, *York Metropolitan Jurisdiction*, pp. 167–174.

that the earl had been troubled while on his way to parliament.[247] Both
Bogo and the prior were found guilty and threatened with ruinous fines.
That the clergy both great and small needed the protection of the crown
against the church courts is revealed by the appeal to the king of the abbot
of Osney against a suit in a church court being prosecuted by a rector
whom the abbot had been pressing to contribute to a clerical subsidy for
the monarch.[248] The crown took a particularly dim view of actions,
citations, or censures by church courts which seemed to intrude into an
area of law and justice claimed for the king's courts. The court *coram rege*
in 1248 amerced the bishop of Worcester 10,000 marks, plus damages, for
excommunicating the bailiffs of William de Valence during the course of
a dispute, so it was said, which properly belonged to the jurisdiction of
the crown.[249] In 1302 the king wrote to the archbishop of Canterbury
ordering him to revoke the sentence of excommunication declared against
the warden and constable of Dover castle, who had arrested the abbot of
Faversham, because the king's ministers should not be made to answer in
the Court Christian for an act performed in the exercise of their office or
in the execution of a judgment of the royal courts.[250] Whenever it appeared
that spiritual sanctions were being employed to usurp royal jurisdiction, the
crown and its officials could be expected to react and to react vigorously.

Except in these particular cases, when the excommunication of individual persons seemed to jeopardize royal prestige and dignity and the
operation of government or the administration of justice, the secular
power in England, respected, recognized, and, so far as it was physically
able, enforced the censures of the church courts. The symbol of this
cooperation was the writ *de excommunicato capiendo*, which commanded the
king's sheriffs to arrest and imprison unrepentant sinners. Yet the gravamina of the higher clergy from the reigns of Henry III and Edward I
indicate that the church was never wholly convinced that the crown and
its officials were living up to their responsibilities or the expectation of the
church.[251] The complaints of the bishops were probably based upon

247. *Placita Parliamentaria*, pp. 6–7. Both Bogo and the prior were sent to the Tower;
the prior had to await the judgment of chancery.

248. See above n. 239.

249. *Select Cases in the Court of King's Bench under Edward I*, III, 1–3; *Select Cases before the
Council*, pp. 5–8.

250. *CCR, 1296–1302*, pp. 124, 582. For another example, see *Registrum Simonis de
Sudbira, Diocesis Londoniensis, A.D. 1362–1375*, ed. R. C. Fowler, CYS, 2 vols. (Oxford,
1927–38), I, 56–58.

251. Grievances from 1253, 1280, 1285, 1295, 1300/1301, 1309, 1316, and 1327 may
be found in *Councils & Synods*, pp. 472, 879, 883–884, 957–958, 1139, 1143–1144, 1147,
1213, 1272; *SR*, I, 172; and *Rot. Parl. Inediti*, pp. 108–109. See also the four articles later
incorporated into the new grievances of 1309 preserved in *Register of J. Halton*, p. 172.

abuses arising from the general limitations of medieval law-enforcement and official communication. The indifference, incompetence, or easy corruptibility of bailiffs and sheriffs, the inadequacy of medieval jails, and the exasperating dilatoriness of medieval justice were some of the causes of the church's discontent. Edward I admitted the laxity of his ministers, who *prece vel petio, amore vel favore, corrupti,* had not performed their duties with the care and discretion expected by king and clergy alike.[252] Those who replied on the king's behalf to these particular grievances mentioned a recent example of official incompetence perpetrated by a sheriff at the expense of the king's justice, which implied some sympathy on the other side for the bishops' plight. "Unde non mirentur prelati de factis vel negligentiis vicecomitum."[253] On several occasions in the reigns of Henry III and Edward I the church complained that writs of caption were being denied them; that sheriffs and other royal officials failed to keep persons once arrested in close confinement; that the crown ordered the release of arrested persons before they had satisfied the church; and that royal officials forced good Christians to consort with notorious sinners. Both Archbishop Boniface and Archbishop Pecham tried to make these faults a major issue between church and state by including within their legislation of 1258, 1261, 1279, and 1281 the excommunication *ipso facto* of royal officials who failed to execute the writ *de excommunicato capiendo.*[254] Although the debate over caption disappears in the gravamina and statutes of Edward III's and Richard II's reigns, canonists and prelates remained unconvinced that the secular power was doing all it could to improve the system.[255] Archbishop Stratford devoted a constitution to explaining the crown's responsibility in this regard;[256] and the fifteenth-century canonist William Lyndwood was disappointed by the lack of total cooperation on the part of the royal jurisdiction.[257]

In all of this, the crown refused to view its duties as absolute and peremptory. Henry III had stressed the point that the sheriffs executed

252. Article 17 of the grievances of 1280 in *Councils & Synods,* p. 883.

253. *Ibid.,* p. 884. The king's reply continues, "Et rex, cum querelas huiusmodi audierit prelatorum, comperta veritate proponit vicecomites corripere et ut tenetur castigare."

254. *Ibid.,* pp. 576–577, 676–677, 849, 907; Douie, *Archbishop Pecham,* pp. 121–122.

255. The *Articuli cleri* of 1316 (*SR,* I, 172) promised that letters for the release of persons seized on the writ of caption should no longer be issued unless the king's liberties were prejudiced. The answers to the petition of 1327 (*Rot. Parl. Inediti,* pp. 108–109) promised that arrested excommunicates would not be released if the bishops certified chancery of legitimate reasons for their excommunication and detention and that the sheriffs would not be permitted to allow such persons, once arrested, to roam at large.

256. Wilkins, II, 708.

257. See Lyndwood's *Provinciale* (Oxford, 1679), pp. 264–266, commenting on Stratford's *Saeculi principes.*

the bishops' requests *de gratia speciali*.[258] Edward II promised that he would order the release of those arrested on a writ of caption *only if his royal rights were threatened*.[259] The secular power was quite willing to admit the right of the church courts to excommunicate persons who refused to submit to ecclesiastical justice and in most instances it was willing to assist in bringing such people to justice. On the other hand, the crown could and did reserve the right to refuse to comply with the requests of the bishop, to discuss and decide the validity of individual requests, and even to interpose itself between the church and its target when it appeared that there was the likelihood that the king's rights or the integrity of royal justice would be infringed or that the issuance of the royal writ would result in the violation of due process of law.[260]

To the end of the middle ages the church always insisted that caption should be automatic upon certification by the bishops and other authorized persons and that deliberations concerning the legitimacy of particular sentences of excommunication should be heard in ecclesiastical courts.[261] It denounced, accordingly, the custom of the royal courts of ignoring spiritual censures against individual suitors on the basis of their allegation that they had appealed to a higher spiritual court or the refusal of chancery to grant the writ against persons who had appealed to Canterbury, York, or Rome.[262] Similarly, the higher clergy opposed the royal practice, which made its appearance in Bracton's time, of releasing arrested excommunicates before they had made their peace with the church.[263] This was accomplished by the royal writ, *de caucione admittenda*, which instructed the sheriff to command the judge ordinary to accept a pledge or bail for the prisoner's appearance in the church court and then to release him from royal custody.[264] If the excommunicate had been surrendered to the bishop,

258. Article 9 of the gravamina of ca. 1261 in *Councils & Synods*, p. 689.

259. Chapter 7 of the Articles of the Clergy, *SR*, I, 172.

260. In a case in Michaelmas, 1330, before the King's Bench, quoted in *Select Cases in the Court of King's Bench Under Edward III*, ed. G. O. Sayles, SS (London, 1965), pp. 51–52, it is said that the king has often (sicut pluries), in accordance with customs (secundum consuetudinem), caused excommunicates to be imprisoned until they had satisfied the church for their sins, and such he had commanded in the case of the three men denounced by the bishop of Coventry and Lichfield. Upon learning that two of the men are not subject to the bishop's jurisdiction, however, the crown commanded their release and ordered the bishop to come to chancery to answer to the stay of caption.

261. This was Lyndwood's view, *Provinciale*, pp. 351–352, s.v. "dari debet."

262. *Councils & Synods*, pp. 957 (seventh article from 1285), 1272 (third article of 1309).

263. *Ibid.*, pp. 472, 576.

264. Bracton, IV, fols. 408b–409; for an example, see *CCR, 1296–1302*, p. 522.

the judge ordinary was himself commanded to receive the pledge or else answer in chancery for his unwillingness to comply with the king's order.[265] The offer of *caucio*, the ecclesiastical form of what the common lawyers called *mainprise*, was acceptable to the church when it was allowed by the church courts themselves or when an ecclesiastical judge authorized the sheriff to accept it.[266] The higher clergy denied, however, the competence of laymen to decide the appropriateness of *caucio* in a particular instance, since, they argued, such discretionary power resided only with those who had jurisdiction over the original plea. Although ecclesiastical courts were willing to release imprisoned excommunicates in order to allow them to prosecute a legitimate appeal to a higher ecclesiastical tribunal,[267] they refused to admit the right of laymen to determine the validity of such appeals. From the secular point of view, admittance to *caucio* was directed against the obvious abuse which resulted from the lengthy and unwarranted imprisonment of people who had expressed their willingness to be judged by the church by offering assurances for their appearance at a future date. Chancery was quite willing, it appears, to entertain petitions of this kind,[268] and on some occasions it was possible even to appeal directly to the crown for the revocation of a sentence of excommunication. In response to a private petition in parliament in 1334, for example, the council decided that the king should write to the bishop of Lincoln urging him to revoke a sentence of excommunication.[269] The crown permitted anyone opposing the release to argue his case in chancery,[270] and a pledge for the prosecution of the appeal could also be demanded.[271] The church, of course, denounced practices which allowed laymen to decide the validity of appeals to spiritual tribunals and the legitimacy of sentences of excommunication and which let excommunicates go free before they had satisfied the church.

The king's courts were usually willing to accept the legal disqualification of suitors who were proven excommunicates.[272] Such persons were

265. *CCR, 1339–41*, p. 125; *CCR, 1327–30*, p. 716; and W. A. Morris in his Introduction to *English Government at Work*, ed. Willard and Morris, I, 58.

266. *Registrum R. Winchelsey*, I, 432–433, provides an example.

267. For instance, see *Register of Bishop Godfrey Giffard, 1268–1301*, ed. J. W. Willis-Bund, Worcestershire Historical Society, 2 vols. (Oxford, 1902), II, 196.

268. For examples of petitions to chancery to release a person from prison in order to prosecute an appeal, see *CCR, 1302–1307*, pp. 99, 216–217, 254–255, 356, 453–454.

269. *Rot. Parl.*, II, 73.

270. Richardson, "Heresy and the Lay Power," p. 8.

271. *CCR, 1343–46*, pp. 339–340.

272. In Easter term, 1340, the justices sent to the metropolitan to determine whether or not the plaintiff had been absolved of all sentences of excommunication pronounced

beyond the Christian pale both morally and legally. Good Christians were expected to avoid their company; and they were prohibited from receiving justice from any source until they had been absolved of the censures imposed upon them. Proof that a plaintiff in a royal court was excommunicate was accepted as a valid exception against his suit, and this was the way whereby the defendant could defeat his action. On the other hand, when it was obvious that the judge ordinary or other ecclesiastical person, who had proclaimed the sentence of excommunication, was himself a party to the plea in the royal court, even when there were other plaintiffs, the king's justices could reject such a disqualification.[273] Even if the excommunication of a party were proved and there were no signs of collusion or personal motivation, the royal courts were careful to demand sufficient proof of its validity and authenticity.[274] Only a letter from a bishop was acceptable in order to disqualify a plaintiff.[275] If such a certificate were based simply upon the report of a lesser ecclesiastical official, without having been enrolled in the royal court as a matter of record, the king's judges could refuse to accept it.[276] Similarly, if the judge ordinary who certified the excommunication of a suitor had died, his certificate could be disallowed if it had not been made a matter of record during the judge ordinary's lifetime.[277] In such ways the common lawyers were able to draw a distinction between the judgments of ecclesiastical courts and the decisions of the royal tribunals.

The most significant innovation in respect to excommunication and caption occurred in Richard II's reign and was the direct result of the appearance of the Lollard heresy. History, popular conviction, and official opinion dictated that the church might expect the support of the crown in repressing false belief. Long ago Maitland made the point that the spiritual law and custom of England was, in respect to the treatment of heretics, identical with that of the church universal.[278] Centuries before

---

against him: *YB 14 Edward III*, p. 159; and Archbishop Chichele notified the chancellor and royal judges of the excommunication of certain suitors: *Register of Henry Chichele, 1414–1443*, ed. E. F. Jacob, CYS, 4 vols. (Oxford, 1937–57), IV, 146–147.

273. For examples, see *YB 18–19 Edward III*, pp. 355–357; *YB 3 Edward II [1309–10]*, ed. F. W. Maitland, SS (London, 1905), p. 134.

274. *YB 30–31 Edward I*, ed. A. J. Horwood, RS (London, 1863), p. 43; *YB 32–33 Edward I*, p. 30. It was said that the exception of excommunication was insufficient in a case of attachment on the royal prohibition: *YB 12–13 Edward III*, p. 142.

275. *YB 20 Edward III [Part I]*, pp. 378, 382.

276. *YB 14 Edward III*, p. 70.   277. *Ibid.*, pp. 226–228.

278. This is one of the major arguments of *Roman Canon Law in the Church of England* (London, 1898); but see Gray's critique of the Stubbs-Maitland controversy in *Studies in Church History*, ed. Cuming, III, 48–68.

heresy became a serious problem confronting English kings and their people there were unimpeachable precedents for the exclusive jurisdiction of the church over such matters as heresy, apostasy, and sorcery and for the responsibility of the Christian magistrate to assist the clergy in the defense of the faith.[279]

In accordance with this spirit of perfect cooperation, the English government in Richard II's reign went beyond the requests of the bishops in giving its assistance to the common struggle against the Lollards.[280] In 1382 royal commissions empowered the sheriffs to arrest heretics at the request of the bishops without the necessity of certifying chancery in individual cases as had been previously required. Similar commissions in 1384 and 1391 extended the new procedure to the northern province and to Ireland.[281] These new procedures were designed to cope with the problem posed by Lollard preachers who flitted from shire to shire and whose apprehension called for quicker, more efficient measures. Afterwards both the new commissions and the old writs of caption were employed against the heretics.[282] Although a commons' petition complained against these commissions as prejudicial to the rights of the laity, and although the king assented to their repeal, they were kept as an alternative method for dealing with England's first great heresy.[283] The crown imposed few limitations upon its cooperativeness. In 1391 the right of lesser ecclesiastical officials to apply directly to chancery for the arrest of suspected heretics, who had been excommunicated, was revoked; but this was done at the request of the bishops.[284] In the latter part of Richard II's reign and in that of Henry IV the king authorized the bishops themselves to arrest and imprison suspected heretics.[285] Persons who had been seized by the sheriffs were either surrendered to the bishop in whose diocese they had originally been cited, or were brought before chancery

279. Richardson has surveyed the evidence prior to the outbreak of Lollardy in "Heresy and the Lay Power," pp. 1–4; see also Pollock and Maitland, *History of English Law*, II, 547–555.

280. Richardson, "Heresy and the Lay Power," p. 8. See also *Rot. Parl.*, III, 124–125; *Register of Thomas de Brantyngham, Bishop of Exeter*, ed. F. C. Hingeston-Randolph, Episcopal Registers of the Diocese of Exeter, 2 parts (London, 1901–1906), I, 466–467.

281. The commission to the Archbishop of York and his suffragans (dated December 8, 1384) is cited in *CPR, 1381–85*, p. 487; and that to Ireland (dated July 16, 1391) in *CPR, 1388–92*, p. 462.

282. Richardson, "Heresy and the Lay Power," p. 14.

283. *Rot. Parl.*, III, 141.

284. *CPR, 1388–92*, p. 415, discussed by H. E. Salter, *Snappe's Formulary and other Records*, Oxford Historical Society, LXXX (Oxford, 1924), 24.

285. *CCR, 1396–99*, p. 158; *CPR, 1413–16*, p. 34.

or the council. As was previously the case in respect to the writ of caption, the accused party was able to plead his case and, perhaps, escape imprisonment and punishment. To read into this practice any notion of competition between the two jurisdictions, however, is to ignore the long history of their cooperation.[286] High ranking prelates attended the sessions of both chancery and the council. Archbishop Thomas Arundel, who was the chancellor, was the first English primate since Pecham to enact constitutions against heresy.[287] Accused persons were always examined according to canonical forms and the final sentence would have been declared by the church.

Those differences of opinion which occasionally arose between the two jurisdictions touched only minor procedural details such as the disposition of the movable properties of convicted heretics or the efforts of the popes to introduce novel and extraordinary judicial processes into the realm. In the reign of Edward II, for instance, the arrival in England of two papal inquisitors raised momentarily the possibility of a conflict of laws.[288] The hostility of some Englishmen to "ecclesiastical law," which permitted the use of torture and the secret deposition, was reflected in the complaint that such methods were contrary to good English custom and in the pope's request that the Templars be removed to the king's lands in Poitou where such squeamishness did not exist.[289] Although there is evidence to suggest that neither Edward II nor his ministers were pleased at this blow struck against an ancient and respected order, the king was not one to engage in a vigorous battle of wills.[290] His submission to the pope's demand for the application of inquisitorial methods against the Templars marked the premature conclusion of what might have been a serious (and interesting) conflict of canon law and common law.[291]

Another minor procedural matter relative to the disposition of cases of heresy concerned the confiscation of the properties of convicted heretics. There was no question, of course, but that the lands and tenements of convicted heretics would revert, according to English feudal custom, either

286. Richardson, "Heresy and the Lay Power," p. 8; for persons answering in chancery and council, see CCR, 1389–92, pp. 453–454; CCR, 1385–89, p. 519.

287. Wilkins, III, 314 ff.

288. Regestum Clementis Papae V, 7 vols. (Rome, 1885–88), VI, 85–86.

289. Ibid., V, 455–457.

290. See Edward's letter to the kings of Portugal, Castille, Aragon, and Sicily in Foedera, vol. II, part 1, p. 19.

291. Ibid., p. 115: "Et eosdem permittatis de corporibus praedictorum Templariorum facere id quod eis, secundum legem ecclesisaticam, videbitur faciendum." See also M. McKisack, The Fourteenth Century, 1307–1399 (Oxford, 1959), p. 292 n. 2.

to the crown or to the immediate suzerain. This was the point that the earl of Lancaster and other English magnates sought to make against the efforts of the pope to transfer these properties to the Hospitallers. Prior custom seemed to dictate, although there were few precedents available, that the goods and chattels of convicted heretics would be confiscate to the crown. According to Innocent IV's decree a threefold division of the convicted heretic's chattels was to be made: one portion to go to the judge ordinary, one to the king, and the third to the municipality where the trial occurred.[292] As early as the reign of Henry III the crown was quietly insisting on the right to the forfeiture of the chattels of convicted heretics.[293] In the Hilary parliament of 1397 the bishops of both provinces asked for a statute declaring the death penalty and forfeiture as the punishment for impenitent heretics.[294] Without such legislative authorization, however, the crown was having its way. Such a minor matter was no cause for controversy or even considerable discussion, since both church and state were more interested in the defense of the faith than in the profits of justice. On the other hand, when the canonist William Lyndwood commented on this matter in the middle of the fifteenth century he is obliged to admit that once again English custom does not coincide with the law of the church universal.[295] In 1401, for instance, the king ordered the bishops to certify chancery concerning any fines imposed by their courts in order that they might be levied from the heretic's chattels "*auctoritate Regis ad opus suum.*"[296] Since the early Lollards were either clerks or poor men the issue of confiscated chattels did not possess great material significance.

292. *Decretals*, V, 7, 10. For the legislation of the Fourth Lateran Council in 1215 concerning confiscation by the laity, see Hefele and Leclercq, *Histoire des Conciles*, vol. V, part 2, p. 1329.

293. Richardson has collected, "Heresy and the Lay Power," p. 2, evidence which suggests that the crown was confiscating the chattels of convicted heretics in the thirteenth century. See also T. F. T. Plucknett, "The Case of the Miscreant Cardinal," *American Historical Review*, XXX (1924), 1–15. For a survey of the struggle on the continent, see H. C. Lea, "Confiscation for Heresy in the Middle Ages," *EHR*, II (1887), 235–259. See also the interesting case cited in *Foedera*, vol. II, part 1, p. 213.

294. The petition of the clergy at the Hilary Parliament, 1397, printed by H. G. Richardson and G. O. Sayles, "Parliamentary Documents from Formularies," *Bulletin of the Institute of Historical Research*, XI (1934), 154, implies a recognition by the church of the right of the secular power to impose fines on convicted heretics after judgment in an ecclesiastical court: "quant ascuns sont condempnez par l'eglise de crime de heresie ils sont tantost liverez a seculer iuggement pour estre mys a mort et leur biens temporales confiskez."

295. Lyndwood, *Provinciale*, p. 293, s.v. "occupentur."

296. *SR*, II, 127.

After the rebellion of Sir John Oldcastle, the considerable number of prosperous laymen who were caught up in the persecution greatly increased the financial awards which could accrue to the crown. The nature of the Lollard problem and the character of the legal issue at stake had been drastically changed in the early fifteenth century. The political ambitions of the Lollard movement during Henry V's reign and the fact that conspirators were tried for treason in Parliament or the king's courts before being handed over to the church for trial for their spiritual crimes, made forfeiture of their chattels to the crown a foregone conclusion.[297] It was this alteration of the original character of the Lollard problem, a change marked by the statute of 1414, which Lyndwood failed to appreciate.[298] When he criticized English practice as being contrary to his doctrine that the disposition of the chattels of convicted heretics should be the responsibility of the same authority which had pronounced judgment on him, in other words the church, he was thinking of Lollardy as it had been in pre-Oldcastle days—and as a canonist would still think of it—a matter of faith rather than of politics.[299]

The principle of cooperation underlying the crown's respect for ecclesiastical censures, its enforcement of caption, and its defense of the true faith was never questioned or denied in later medieval England. When controversy sometimes arose it focused on peripheral or secondary issues such as the release of arrested excommunicates, the occasional denial of caption, or the exemption of certain persons. The persistent but not necessarily irreconcilable opposition of the crown and the bishops on these issues was most intense during the reigns of Henry III, Edward I, and Edward II. But such disagreements never constituted a stumbling block to the continuing cooperation of the two powers; and it would seem that for the remainder of the fourteenth century the church accepted the definition of their mutual rights and responsibilities expressed by the state at an earlier period. This agreement on first principles, the limitation

297. See the record of the trial of Sir John in Parliament, *Rot. Parl.*, IV, 107–110. He was convicted of rebellion by the secular power and was pronounced an incorrigible heretic by the clergy. This dual judgment is attested by the writ to the sheriff of Kent, which ordered his execution: *CCR, 1413–19*, pp. 106–107. Although his goods and lands were confiscate to the king, the lands were returned to his son in 1417, according to *ibid.*, p. 396. For background, see K. B. McFarlane, *John Wycliffe and the Beginnings of English Nonconformity* (London, 1952), pp. 160 ff.; and J. A. F. Thompson, *The Later Lollards, 1414–1520* (Oxford, 1965), pp. 220–236.

298. *SR*, II, 182.

299. Lyndwood, *Provinciale*, p. 293, s.v. "confiscata"; and the indictment in *CPR, 1413–16*, p. 175.

of conflict to matters of procedural details, and the actual cooperation
which characterized relations between the two jurisdictions is nowhere
more clearly nor more dramatically exhibited than in their combination
to defeat the threat to Christian orthodoxy posed by Lollardy.

IV. TITHES AND PENSIONS

During the thirteenth and fourteenth centuries the church often denounced the intrusion of the royal courts into tithes cases. The king's courts
seldom presumed to try tithes cases as such, that is, when the issue was
explicitly that of the possession by the clergy of these customary religious
payments. But the common lawyer's and the crown exercised considerable
influence over the disposition of tithes by deciding questions of advowson,
debt and contract, trespass, or the interpretation of royal charters. In
other words, the jurisdiction of the royal courts was concealed behind
their claim to try purely secular pleas, which, from a different point of
view, might also concern the right to tithes. Like several other topics of
jurisdictional controversy, the conflict over tithes did not extend very far
into the past. During the twelfth century both jurisdictions cooperated in
deciding cases of this kind. Clerics sued in the royal courts for the recovery
of lands, churches, and tithes as if such were natural and normal.[300] The
Third Lateran Council had, however, denied the right of laymen to
possess or to confer such revenues upon other laymen, and the growth of
the canon law in the later twelfth and early thirteenth centuries tended to
bring tithes more and more within the scope of ecclesiastical jurisdiction.[301]
By the middle of the thirteenth century the canonists were well prepared
to do justice to clerics claiming tithes.[302] On the other hand, the royal
courts and chancery had come to realize the extent to which this expanding
spiritual jurisdiction was threatening royal jurisdiction over purely secular
matters like advowson and lay chattels. At least two royal prohibitions
were available to cope with the problem. During the course of these two
centuries the common law expanded its jurisdictional claims to include a
variety of tithes cases which seemed to concern questions more secular
than spiritual in nature. Although the conflict over tithes sometimes

---

300. Van Caenegem, *Royal Writs*, Nos. 9, 22, 40, 41, 44, 64, 80, etc.

301. *Decretals*, III, 37, 4; Hefele and Leclercq, *Histoire des Conciles*, vol. V, part 2,
p. 1099.

302. Adams, "Judicial Conflict over Tithes," pp. 2–4, and sources cited in notes.
Cheney, *Hubert Walter*, p. 72, mentions cases of tithes and pensions among the archbishop's records.

became rather intense, it was not the product of a frontal assault by one jurisdiction on the other. Rather, it was the result of the efforts of individual suitors to exploit the ambiguous nature of certain kinds of cases concerning movable properties and chattels in order to get the justice they demanded.

The king's courts recognized the fact that the advowson of an ecclesiastical benefice might be seriously affected by decisions as to the disposition of tithes. In some instances the total value of the benefice derived from tithes and oblations.[303] Judgments by the church concerning the possession of such revenues, despite their ostensibly spiritual nature, could very well diminish or abolish the actual right of patronage. Long before the second Statute of Westminster in Edward I's reign recognized the close relationship between the right to bestow tithes and the advowson itself by creating the common law action for the advowson of tithes, chancery and the king's courts had equated the two in the course of dispensing justice to suitors. Early in John's reign plaintiffs were permitted to sue for the recovery of tithes on the basis of the common law action for asserting the patron's possession of the advowson—*darrein presentment*.[304] The royal prohibition against trying a plea of patronage in a church court proved very useful in protecting royal jurisdiction over advowson. By the middle of Henry III's reign the majority of attachments on the prohibition *de advocatione* brought by laymen and clerics did not concern advowson as such, but were aimed at preventing trial in a church court of a plea of tithes.[305] If the defendant in a case of attachment on the prohibition of advowson (or lay fee or chattels) could prove that the case in the Court Christian actually concerned tithes, then the prohibition was quashed.[306] But the availability of these writs doubtlessly attracted many people, especially laymen, to use them to defeat actions against themselves in the church courts.

The attack on ecclesiastical jurisdiction over tithes was sufficiently severe in the reigns of Henry III and Edward I to provoke a series of complaints from the higher clergy.[307] Of the twenty-nine articles of grievance compiled for presentation to the king in 1239, four of these

303. See *CRR, 7–9 Henry III*, No. 2666, where it was said that only tithes constituted the chapel of Lewes; in *CRR, 14–17 Henry III*, No. 1336, it was noted that the loss of tithes was equivalent to the loss of advowson.

304. *CRR, 3–5 John*, pp. 157, 163.

305. Flahiff, "Writ of Prohibition (i)," pp. 275–276.

306. For examples, *CRR, 9–10 Henry III*, Nos. 948, 1258, 1318.

307. *Councils & Synods*, pp. 280–281, 687–688, 874–875, 970, 1208, 1210–1211.

explicitly mentioned tithes as a subject of jurisdictional controversy.[308] The bishops denounced royal intrusion into tithes cases under the guise of protecting advowson, and insisted that such issues were purely spiritual in nature, especially when both suitors were clerics. Not only were the royal courts meddling with spiritualities, but they were encroaching on the church's jurisdiction over personal actions involving members of the clergy.[309] By Bracton's time the king's courts were using the royal prohibition called *indicavit* to establish their jurisdiction over tithes cases involving a significant portion of the total value of the benefice.[310] Although one quarter of the goods of the living was finally established as the amount which would allow the case to be challenged by a royal prohibition, the church courts were sometimes losing jurisdiction when less of the worth of the benefice was disputed.[311] Boniface's legislation denounced this jurisdictional loss by declaring censures against persons responsible for defrauding church courts of their legitimate jurisdiction over tithes.[312] Well before the end of the thirteenth century, however, the church had been forced to accept the royal point of view in this matter. During Edward I's reign the second Statute of Westminster attempted to assist the clerk who had been prevented from suing in a church court for the recovery of his tithes by the royal prohibition.[313] It created the means whereby his patron could bring the common law action, *praecipe quod reddat*, for the right of advowson of tithes. But the church complained against this innovation, saying that it forced poor clerks to resort to two law suits to get their rights and made it virtually impossible for them to recover tithes in small amounts.[314]

Another means of royal intrusion was to view tithes as lay chattels and to argue for their recovery in a secular court by an action of debt. The crown insisted throughout the thirteenth and fourteenth centuries that debt and lay chattels were not for the church courts to try. This assumption, coupled with the common law doctrine that tithes were transformed into

308. Articles 5, 9, 10, 11, in *ibid.*, p. 281.

309. *Ibid.*, p. 281 (article 2); pp. 688–689 (articles 5, 6); p. 885 (article 19).

310. Bracton, IV, fol. 402b; Flahiff, "Writ of Prohibition (i)," pp. 275–276. The writ, *indicavit*, for advowson appears in Glanvill, IV, 13. See also the arguments in a case in Michaelmas, 1342, *YB 16 Edward III* [*Part II*], RS, ed. L. O. Pike (London, 1900), pp. 277–285.

311. Established by *Circumspecte agatis* (1285) and *Articuli cleri* (1316): Graves, "Circumspecte Agatis," pp. 15–16; *SR*, I, 171–174.

312. *Councils & Synods*, pp. 573, 579, 671, 678.

313. *SR*, I, 77.

314. Article 9, *Councils & Synods*, p. 965; and for the royal reply, *ibid.*, p. 967.

temporalities by sale or lease, enabled some litigants both to challenge the jurisdiction of the church and to seek justice in the first place in royal courts.[315] A claimant for a sum of money due from a contract based upon tithes might choose to sue a writ of debt at common law.[316] The Articles of the Clergy in 1316 promised that tithes collected remained a spiritual thing even though lengthy detention made it necessary to commute their worth for a sum of money;[317] on the other hand, there was a tendency for the king's courts to assume that the severance of tithes affected their nature, especially if one of the claimants were a layman or proof of a contractual obligation could be produced in court.[318]

The ingenuity of the royal courts and chancery in encroaching on ecclesiastical jurisdiction over tithes is revealed by the evolution and popularization of the two common law actions, trespass and annuity, whereby suitors of all conditions could obtain justice in the king's courts on pleas which otherwise might have fallen to the church to decide. Both of these actions appeared in the latter part of the thirteenth century and became more familiar in the fourteenth. Both, moreover, represented an intrusion upon ecclesiastical jurisdiction over customary religious payments such as tithes and pensions based on tithes.[319] In the first instance, some claimants to tithes were encouraged to sue on the royal writ, *de bonis asportatis*, if their rival had simply seized their properties. The royal courts claimed jurisdiction by virtue of the tort or trespass which had been committed.[320] The popularity of this action is shown by the statute of *1 Richard II* (1377), which promised that the church court would not be ousted from a tithes case on the general grounds that a trespass had occurred unless the plaintiff possessed a deed or some sort of written proof of his right.[321] If such proof were unavailable then the church court was competent to decide the case, and the prohibition would not be issued or,

315. Flahiff, "Writ of Prohibition (i)," pp. 277–278; Adams, "Judicial Conflict over Tithes," pp. 7–11; Bracton, IV, fol. 412.

316. For this argument in actual cases, see *YB 32–33 Edward I*, pp. 409–411; *YB 13 Richard II* [*1389–90*], pp. 84–88; if the case were actually found to concern only tithes the king could grant a consultation: *Register of William Wickwane, Lord Archbishop of York, 1279–1285*, ed. W. Brown, Surtees Society (Durham, 1907), p. 43; *CCR, 1302–1307*, p. 539.

317. *SR*, I, 171.

318. Adams, "Judicial Conflict over Tithes," pp. 8–9.

319. *Ibid.*, pp. 8–9, 13–14.

320. In Trinity term, 1 Edward I, trespass issued against a parson: *YB 1–2 Edward II* [*1307–1309*], p. 36. See a similar case in *YB Henry VI* [*1422*], ed. C. H. Williams, AF (London, 1933), pp. 76–80.

321. *SR*, II, 5.

as was more likely, a consultation would be granted to return the case to the ecclesiastical court. On several occasions during the second half of the fourteenth century the church complained that consultations were not forthcoming or were inordinately delayed. Consequently, such a promise would not have eliminated all of the difficulties the church courts were encountering.

The second means of competition was the writ of annuity, which also appeared in Edward I's reign. The church's claim to try cases involving chattels and monies became increasingly tenuous in the last half of the thirteenth century. *Circumspecte agatis* in 1285 and the Articles of the Clergy in 1316 gave cases concerning pensions, oblations, obventions, mortuaries, and tithes of less than a quarter of the value of the benefice to the ecclesiastical courts. Cases concerning such obviously spiritual matters as oblations and obventions, which were pious gifts customarily rendered to churches, and mortuaries, the traditional death duty which medieval parishioners paid, were almost never challenged as belonging properly to the church courts.[322] Contested pensions were, however, another matter. Often they arose from agreements concerning disputed claims to the advowson of benefices, to their possession by rival presentees, or to the enjoyment of tithes. Sometimes they were the result of episcopal arbitration; and the bishop sanctioned and authenticated them.[323] At other times they were the result of litigation in secular courts,[324] and some persons took the precaution of enrolling them in chancery or obtaining proof in the form of a royal deed or letter. Since pensions frequently had a spiritual origin in agreements concerning tithes, they were claimed for the church courts. On the other hand, they also could seem to be temporal things, much like any other secular debt or contract. During the course of Edward I's reign the common law action based on the writ of annuity made its appearance.[325] The dual nature of annuity, poised as it was between real property and contract, and allowing proof either by prior seisin or a deed, worked to the disadvantage of the church. A litigant could claim an annuity in the king's courts on the basis of proof of seisin or by producing a bond or deed. Even when both suitors were clerics, they were not denied justice in the royal courts. In Trinity term, 1345, the bishop of Winchester brought a writ of annuity against the archdeacon of

322. Adams, "Judicial Conflict over Tithes," p. 1.

323. For an example of a pension in favor of one claimant to a contested benefice, see *Rotuli R. Gravesend*, pp. 139–141.

324. Pensions are mentioned in cases cited, *CRR, 3–5 John*, pp. 1, 85.

325. For annuity, see W. Holdsworth, *History of English Law*, 7th ed. rev.; 14 vols. (London, 1956), III, 151–152.

Surrey.[326] To Robert Thorpe's exception on behalf of the defendant that both parties were clerics and the plaintiff did not have written proof of his claim, Justice John Stonore replied that title by prescription was sufficient under the circumstances. The availability of the common law action based on the writ of annuity doubtlessly drew other churchmen to the king's courts, and, like the action of trespass, deprived the church of jurisdiction in an appreciable number of pension cases.[327]

The practice of enrolling agreements in chancery also encouraged royal competition with the church in this area. Sometimes such concords were purely private;[328] at other times they represented royal grants of tithes of demesne land or of lands in royal wardship. The king always claimed the right to dispose of such properties, including their tithes, and to have jurisdiction over disputed cases since they brought into question the validity or interpretation of royal charters.[329] In 1344 a statute promised that writs of *scire facias* would not henceforth be issued to compel clerics to answer in chancery for their tithes.[330] The reason for the church's objection to this practice is shown by a case which occurred about a decade before the enactment of the statute.[331] In 1333 the king forbade the official of the court of Canterbury to proceed in a tithes suit initiated by Hervey of Staunton against the prior of Lewes because the binding effect of certain royal charters was in doubt. According to the prior, the tithes in question had been granted to him and his successors by their lawful lay owner, the earl of Surrey. This grant had been authenticated by the earl's charters, confirmed by the king. Claiming to be despoiled of the income from his parish church, Hervey had begun suit in the court of Canterbury. A royal prohibition brought by the prior halted the case, but the official was told to proceed after a consultation was granted to Hervey, who had appealed to chancery. At a later date additional information brought to chancery led to the reopening of the case. Both the prior and Hervey were summoned to appear there, and, upon the latter's default, the original prohibition was confirmed. But how exasperating this must have been for the poor official of Canterbury!

326. *YB 19 Edward III*, p. 291; *YB 18 Edward III*, ed. L. O. Pike, RS (London, 1904), pp. 351–355. See also Adams, "Judicial Conflict over Tithes," pp. 13–14, and sources cited in notes.

327. Greater and lesser clergy alike were among the offenders. See *Register W. Giffard*, p. 109.

328. It was usual to register private loans in chancery, according to W. A. Morris in his Introduction to *English Government at Work*, ed. Willard and Morris, I, 55.

329. Adams, "Judicial Conflict over Tithes," pp. 14–18.

330. *SR*, I, 303.   331. *CCR, 1333–37*, p. 180.

During the thirteenth and fourteenth centuries the crown insisted that local custom, the opinion of the community, and, if no precedent existed, the royal courts should decide whether a particular tithe should be paid.[332] The final decision as to what kinds of things gave a yearly increase and, therefore, owed a tithe to the church rested with the secular power. Although there was general agreement concerning the tithing of lands and livestock, English custom and the canons differed as to tithes of minerals, new mills, certain kinds of wood, and rights of pasturage, i.e., agistments.[333] Both Edward I and Edward II agreed to the church's request that the ecclesiastical courts be permitted to enforce the payment of tithes of new mills by canonical processes.[334] The clergy continued to encounter difficulties in attempting to collect tithes of agistments, quarried stone, and older trees.[335] In the fourteenth century the debate over tithes was intensified by the efforts of the parish clergy to increase the incomes of their churches, perhaps, as a result of serious problems created by the Black Death.[336] This controversy tended to focus on the clergy's effort to broaden the tithe of wood to include types of trees which previously had not owed the tenth. The church claimed tithes of certain trees because they gave an annual increase and, therefore, fell within the class of tithable wood known as *sylva cedua.* The laity frequently petitioned the king in parliament against these efforts to tithe *sylva cedua,*[337] and after 1344 the demand for a restriction of the term to young trees and underwood (*subbois*) was added to their request for a precise definition. This petition was doubtlessly the

332. See the declaration by the country as to the legality of tithes, *CRR, 14–17 Henry III,* No. 117; Adams, "Judicial Conflict over Tithes," pp. 17–21.

333. Although the debate on the tithing of certain items continued into the early modern period in England, it was generally agreed during the later middle ages that corn, hay, wood, fish, and bees, together with lesser agricultural products, owed tithes, and that certain professions and crafts giving a yearly increase owed personal tithes. For the history of tithing, W. Easterby, *History of the Law of Tithes in England* (Cambridge, 1888); G. Constable, "Resistance to Tithes in the Middle Ages," *JEH,* XIII (1962), 172–185, describes the continuing opposition to their payment. The canonical position in respect to tithes is explained by P. Viard, *Histoire de la Dîme Ecclésiastique, principalement en France, jusqu'au Décret de Gratien* (Dijon, 1909), and *Histoire de la Dîme Ecclésiastique dans le Royaume de France aux XIIe et XIIIe Siècles, 1150–1313* (Paris, 1912). A. G. Little has an interesting note on an obscure aspect of the history of tithes: "Personal Tithes," *EHR,* LX (1945), 67–88.

334. Article 5 of the gravamina of 1280, in *Councils & Synods,* p. 877; *SR,* I, 172.

335. *Rot. Parl.,* III, 540. See also the petition concerning agistments of new lands, *ibid.,* p. 474.

336. Adams, "Judicial Conflict over Tithes," p. 20 and n. 6, citing *Rot. Parl.,* III, 65.

337. *Rot. Parl.,* II, 149, 170, 241, 301, 305; *ibid.,* III, 43, 116, 201, 281, 295, 307, 318, 470; *ibid.,* IV, 21, 382, 451.

result of Archbishop Stratford's legislation extending the term to cover all kinds of wood that grew from the roots of trees that had once been cut.[338] The complaints of the laity prompted the enactment of the statute of 1376, which rejected Stratford's definition by exempting trees of twenty years or more of age from the category of tithable items.[339] The dispute remained a live one even in the fifteenth century, and there was ample opportunity for abuse and deception on both sides.[340] The important thing to notice in this respect, however, is the recognition generally that the crown possessed ultimate authority for deciding questions of tithing and that chancery and the king's courts were able to enforce this prerogative in England.

To summarize, tithes cases sometimes fell within the scope of royal prohibitions against the trial of cases of lay chattels, debt, or even lay fee in a church court.[341] During the second half of the thirteenth century, and especially in the reign of Edward I, it seemed that the royal courts were making a deliberate attempt to confine ecclesiastical jurisdiction over the chattels of laymen to cases involving matrimonial and testamentary matters alone. Sometimes the spiritual nature of tithes seemed to have been altered by their sale, lease, severance, or long detention. The common lawyers insisted that tithes which had been sold or which had become the object of a contract were no longer tithes, but were purely secular things within the scope of the common law of debt or contract. Both clerics and laymen were encouraged to make use of the king's courts for the recovery of such revenues, especially when they could produce a written deed or an enrolled charter, and the prohibition of lay chattels was available to them to frustrate a counter action in an ecclesiastical court. In 1285 it would appear that the crown was deliberately attacking ecclesiastical jurisdiction over chattels in the possession of laymen, but *Circumspecte agatis* brought this systematic attack to an end. Subsequently in the thirteenth and fourteenth centuries royal encroachment followed the older, slower, and more individualistic approach of selling prohibitions *de catallis et debitis* to defendants in the church courts, or else by providing them with alternatives to canonical justice. The gravamina and statutes of the reigns of Edward III and Richard II indicate that the jurisdictional

338. Wilkins, II, 704–705.

339. *SR*, I, 393.

340. See the admonitions of the prelates in Wilkins, III, 90, 113; and Lyndwood's statements, *Provinciale*, p. 190, s.v. "renascitur."

341. For examples of the use of prohibitions *de laico feodo, de advocatione,* and *de catallis et debitis*, when tithes were at issue, see *CRR, 4 Henry III*, p. 304; *CRR, 7–9 Henry III*, Nos. 268, 2307, 2666; *CRR, 9–10 Henry III*, Nos. 948, 1258, 1318; *CRR, 14–17 Henry III*, Nos. 1858, 2252.

controversy over cases concerning tithes and pensions was a major issue between church and state at this time. Evidently, prohibitions were granted too freely and consultations on them were either delayed or refused.[342] The result was that, at the very time when the clergy were attempting to use the church courts to augment their tithes, they were encountering serious and effective opposition from the laity and the crown —the one opposing them for financial, the other, for jurisdictional reasons.

V. Debt and Breach of Faith

Jurisdictional conflict over petty debt reveals how the two courts could presume to try the same case under different names and also how the greater versatility of the canon law enabled it to enjoy a considerable popularity in an area of law and justice which was officially claimed for the secular courts. Despite the existence of the common law action for debt and of competition from borough courts, manorial courts, hundred courts, and chancery, the church continued to enjoy a considerable jurisdiction over debt cases by virtue of its corrective authority over faith and morals. This jurisdictional competence can be ascribed to the fact that the ecclesiastical courts were satisfying real economic and legal needs.

The king's courts tried a large number of debt cases during the middle ages, but there is no evidence that the crown aspired to a monopoly of this type of litigation. The common law actions on the writs of debt and contract required the plaintiff to produce proof of the obligation in the form of a written deed or agreement or at least a quid pro quo. If such were unavailable, the king's courts were of little help.[343] Suitors on verbal contracts frequently went elsewhere for justice. During the thirteenth and fourteenth centuries the borough and manorial courts exercised a wide competence in cases of petty debt based upon oral agreements, since they were willing to force the execution of contracts not recognized as binding by the common lawyers.[344] The hundred and county courts continued to

342. For the clergy's complaints in respect to tithes and pensions, see *Rot. Parl.*, II, 357, 373; III, 26–27; Wilkins, III, 241, 244.

343. Pollock and Maitland, *History of English Law*, II, 198–199; T. F. T. Plucknett, *Concise History of the Common Law*, 5th ed. (London, 1956), pp. 633–635.

344. For the manorial courts see *The Court Baron*, ed. F. W. Maitland and W. P. Baildon, SS (London, 1891), pp. 47, 84, 131; and for the borough courts, *Borough Customs*, ed. M. Bateson, SS, 2 vols. (London, 1904–1906), I, 109, 186–195, 206–207.

try debt cases even after the evolution of royal jurisdiction.[345] Some persons recognized the advantage of enrolling obligations in the chancery rolls and of using chancery jurisdiction to force their payment.[346] Throughout the middle ages a large number of people brought cases of petty debt to the church courts, especially the archdeacons' courts, by virtue of the willingness of the canonists to enforce verbal agreements.[347] Canon law stressed the binding effect of the oath or pledge of faith and accepted and tried debt cases under the guise of punishing breach of faith (*fidei laesio*).[348] Not only did the judge ordinary punish the sin committed, but he also compelled restitution, thereby forcing the execution of the original obligation. The popularity of the church courts and the other rivals to the king's courts can be ascribed to their greater attractiveness to suitors and their willingness to do justice in cases which were ignored by the common law. Despite the existence of the prohibition of lay chattels which denied the right of ecclesiastical courts to try cases involving properties of this kind, the king's courts could never seriously expect to oust the Courts Christian from this area of law. It is unlikely that such was ever contemplated, since the crown showed little interest in enhancing the rather impoverished common law of debt.[349] The legislation of Edward I which established the statute merchant was aimed at helping foreign merchants by facilitating the collection of debts owed by natives.[350] It did not diminish the number or affect the type of cases coming to the church courts.[351] Not until the creation of *assumpsit* in the sixteenth century did the king's courts pose a serious challenge to their several rivals in this area of law and justice.

This ecclesiastical jurisdiction over debt was not, however, universally

345. Lady Stenton remarks on the importance of the shire courts for the collection of small debts even after the development of royal jurisdiction in *English Justice*, p. 79. For debt in the county and hundred courts, see *Brevia Placitata*, ed. G. J. Turner and T. F. T. Plucknett, SS (London, 1951), p. xli.

346. W. T. Barbour, *History of Contract in Early English Equity* (Oxford, 1914), pp. 160 ff. It would appear that chancery jurisdiction was not universally popular: *Rot. Parl.*, III, 267; IV, 84.

347. See F. Spies, *De l'Observation des Simples Conventions en Droit Canonique* (Paris, 1928), pp. 40 ff.; and Esmein's paper, "Le serment promissoire dans le droit canonique," *Nouvelle Révue Historique de Droit Française et Étranger*, XII (1888), 248–277; 311–352.

348. Lyndwood, *Provinciale*, p. 315, s.v. "perjurio."

349. Plucknett, *Concise History*, p. 636.

350. Plucknett, *Legislation of Edward I* (Oxford, 1949), pp. 139 ff.

351. Woodcock, *Medieval Ecclesiastical Courts*, pp. 89–91; debt cases are numerous in the court records printed in *Acts of the Chapter of SS. Peter and Wilfrid*, ed. Fowler, p. vii. See also C. Morris's observation in "A Consistory Court," p. 157 n. 4. Cheney noted debt cases among the records of *Hubert Walter*, p. 73.

popular. There existed the royal prohibition of debt and lay chattels whereby defendants in the church courts could halt actions of this kind either temporarily or permanently;[352] and this was rather frequently used during the thirteenth and fourteenth centuries.[353] In 1239 the bishops complained that certain laymen of London were causing the imprisonment of persons suing in local ecclesiastical courts for perjury, breach of faith, usury, simony, and defamation, unless such pleas were explicitly concerned with testamentary and matrimonial matters.[354] In the reign of Edward I some important people of Cornwall prevailed upon the government to appoint a special commission to investigate the judicial activities of the bishop of Exeter in respect to debt and lay chattels.[355] The laity and especially townsmen may have been annoyed by the citations of the ecclesiastical courts; and these complaints continued in the fourteenth century. In 1373 a petition of the commons complained of ecclesiastical jurisdiction over lay contracts and also criticized the recent efforts of some ecclesiastical judges in attempting to determine cases concerning the Statute of Laborers. Further, it would appear that some judge ordinaries had been granting blank letters of citation to creditors, whereby they could draw their defaulting debtors to judgment in a church court.[356] These occasional expressions of dissent were probably the exception to the prevailing rule of the popularity of ecclesiastical justice among suitors in cases of petty debt. Generally speaking, the crown showed a willingness to share responsibility for doing justice in debt cases with the several competing jurisdictions.

During the reigns of Henry III and Edward I the church believed itself to be under severe attack insofar as its jurisdiction over breach of

352. Flahiff, "Writ of Prohibition (i)," pp. 277–279; Glanvill, X, 12; Bracton, IV, fols. 407–407b.

353. The Common Plea rolls from 1 and 2 Edward III contain in excess of two dozen cases of attachment on the prohibition of lay chattels and debt: interesting examples are the case of Robert Lascy v. Master John Grandisson, Archdeacon of Nottingham, and Master John de la Launde in PRO, CP 40/268, 3; CP 40/271, 7; CP 40/272, 117; CP 40/273, 90d; CP 40/274, 94d, 187d, 192; and also the case of Simon Carpenter v. Master Thomas Hereward and others in CP 40/275, 12; CP 40/274, 53d; CP 40/275, 301d. These cases are directed against plaintiffs and judges, and sometimes both are cited. For the thirteenth century, see examples in *CRR, 9–10 Henry III*, Nos. 502, 608, 637, 884, 1142, 1323, 1514, 2044, 2282, 2447.

354. *Councils & Synods*, p. 283 (article 28).

355. *CPR, 1272–79*, p. 293.

356. *Rot. Parl.*, II, 319. See also a similar petition from 1410, *ibid.*, III, 645–646. In 1414 a statute ordered ecclesiastical judges to supply copies of the libel, the basis for acquiring a writ of prohibition, to any defendant in the Court Christian who requested it: *SR*, II, 176.

faith was concerned. The frequency of clerical complaints against the use of royal prohibitions, and the wording of the writs themselves, suggest that the crown was undertaking to limit ecclesiastical jurisdiction over the chattels of the laity to matrimonial and testamentary cases alone.[357] But the bishops felt pressure in other areas as well. Grosseteste, Boniface, Pecham, and Winchelsey had all defended the exemption of the clergy from trial in secular courts on personal actions.[358] The gravamina of the thirteenth century denounced the practice of the royal courts of forcing clerics to answer there in cases of debt and contract, especially when such had been recognized and authenticated before their bishops or in the church courts.[359] It would seem that the existence of the royal writs of prohibition placed the church courts on unsure ground whenever they attempted to try a case involving monies or chattels, especially when one of the parties was a layman. This interference even extended to the restriction of the right of ecclesiastical judges to impose pecuniary, as distinguished from corporeal penances.[360] The crown always permitted the church courts to commute for a cash payment a judgment which originally called for corporal punishment.[361] On the other hand, when a fine was imposed in the first instance, and the church court tried to enforce its payment by canonical process, there was always the danger that a royal prohibition would be acquired by the defendant. It is important to note, of course, that this attack on ecclesiastical jurisdiction was the result of the activities of individual purchasers of prohibitions. With the exception of the general investigation of ecclesiastical justice launched by Edward I in 1285, the curtailment of ecclesiastical jurisdiction over the chattels of clergy and laity alike was the result of individual challenges. Toward the end of Edward I's reign the higher clergy plaintively remarked that many cases which had previously been tried in the church courts were now denied

357. See *Councils & Synods*, pp. 470 (article 7 of 1253); 537 (article 4 of 1257); 544 (article 27 of 1257); 573 (canon 1 of 1258); 671–672 (canon 1 of 1261); 958 (article 9 of 1285, which included the royal reply: "Curia intendit quod prelati bene sciunt cognoscere que placita sunt de testamento et que de matrimonio, et super aliis non cognoscant."). See editors' remarks, *ibid.*, p. 419 n. 3.

358. *Ibid.*, pp. 280–281 (article 2 of 1237); 538 (fifth proposal of 1257); 885 (article 10 of 1280).

359. *Ibid.*, pp. 542–543 (article 21 of 1257); 972 (article 16 of 1285); 1143 (article 33 of 1295); 1214 (article 21 of 1300/1301). See also the fifth and sixth articles of the grievances of 1261, *ibid.*, pp. 688–689.

360. *Ibid.*, pp. 544 (article 27 of 1257); 874–875 (article 2 of 1280).

361. See the royal response to the article of the gravamina of 1280, *ibid.*, p. 875; and chapter 3 of the *Articuli cleri*, in *SR*, I, 172.

them.[362] They had certainly lost their struggle for the total exemption of the clergy from secular jurisdiction, civil as well as criminal. It is unlikely that the bishops had the support of the lesser clergy in these efforts, since churchmen were themselves purchasers of royal prohibitions.[363] After the reigns of Henry III and Edward I pressures against ecclesiastical jurisdiction probably were relaxed. Ecclesiastical jurisdiction over debt was not prominent in the gravamina of the fourteenth century, and, apparently, church and state had arrived at something like an understanding in respect to this topic of controversy.[364] Through the inaction of the common law a fairly broad jurisdictional area was left to the church, although the existence of the royal prohibition of debt and lay chattels enabled individual suitors to challenge this competence at any time.

VI. TESTAMENTARY DEBT

Prior to Edward I's reign there had been no conflict over the execution of the English will. Through indifference or self-restraint the royal courts and chancery had abandoned the testament to the ecclesiastical jurisdiction, which had devised machinery for authenticating it, ensuring its enforcement, and satisfying various claims against the testator's chattels. The agent of this procedure was the testamentary executor, aided and superintended by the bishops and the church courts. Some aspects of this extensive jurisdiction of the church were seldom if ever challenged by the laity or the king's courts. The validation and interpretation of the will, the payment of legacies, and the acquittance of the executor were recognized to pertain to the church.[365] Until the time of Edward I the common law, stressing the role of the heir over that of the executor, had been relatively indifferent to the executor. The evolution of royal concern for the English will entailed the adoption of the executor by the king's courts and the creation by statute and judicial precedent of a large body of law to assist him in the performance of his task. The tacit agreement, which had allowed the ecclesiastical courts in England to decide all testamentary pleas, was now qualified to enable the royal courts to compete with the church courts in cases of testamentary debt. On the other hand, the inadequacy of the common law of debt and the ingenuity of the canonists

362. *Councils & Synods*, p. 969 (article 3 of the grievances of July, 1285). See also the thirty-third article of the gravamina of 1295, in *ibid.*, p. 1143.
363. Flahiff, "Use of Prohibitions by Clerics," pp. 101 ff.
364. Plucknett, *Concise History*, p. 636.
365. Sheehan, *The Will in Medieval England*, pp. 163–176.

allowed the church courts to continue to exercise considerable influence in this area during the later middle ages.

The church's right to grant probate of the will, to supervise the inventory of chattels, and to authorize the acquittance of executors was well received by crown and laity in England during the middle ages.The decision as to the legality or meaning of the will was left to the bishop or his delegate.[366] The royal courts usually sent to the church for information as to its intent and contents; and cases in the king's courts were decided in accordance with the bishop's certificate.[367] In the towns, where the borough courts exercised a rival testamentary jurisdiction, burgesses sometimes took the precaution of obtaining probate of their wills by the bishop prior to registering them with municipal authorities.[368] This ex officio jurisdiction of the church was considered to be useful, and the criticism of the laity usually confined itself to denouncing the high cost of probate and acquittance. On several occasions during the fourteenth century petitions were brought into Parliament requesting the king to force the prelates to exact only customary or reasonable charges for these services and to create judicial commissions to investigate alleged abuses.[369] At other times ecclesiastical authorities were accused of extortion for enforcing the payment of these fees.[370] In spite of the legislation of Archbishop Stratford, who tried to establish an equitable scale of charges, the costs of probate and acquittance continued to depend more on local custom and the initiative of individual officials than on standards approved by the canonists.[371] Yet the right of the church to grant probate and to require the acquittance of executors was never challenged, but, rather, was viewed as necessary for the lawful implementation of the testament.

The judicial competence of the church over the English testament was broad. Cases of disputed legacies were decided in the church courts.[372] The collection of debts owed the deceased or the payment of them were performed under the supervision of ecclesiastical authorities, who were prepared to use canonical procedures to remedy situations which stood in

366. This is Glanvill's opinion, VII, 8.

367. *YB 33 [Michaelmas] and 34–35 Edward I*, p. 71; *YB 20–21 Edward I*, ed. A. J. Horwood, RS (London, 1866), pp. 375–377.

368. *Borough Customs*, II, 195 n. 5.

369. For Commons' petitions from 1347 to the end of the century, see *Rot. Parl.*, II, 171, 230, 305, 313, 335–336; III, 25, 43; IV, 8–9, 19, 84.

370. *Ibid.*, II, 130.

371. Wilkins, II, 698.

372. Glanvill, VII, 8.

the way of the enforcement of the testator's wishes. The extension of
ecclesiastical jurisdiction over the will was concurrent with the evolution of
the office of testamentary executor as the legal representative of the deceased.
This office which may have had Germanic precedents was almost wholly
the creation of the canonists, who made him entirely responsible for
collecting and safeguarding the chattels of the testator from which legacies
would be paid and for implementing the provisions of the will itself.[373]

In contrast to the church courts which showed considerable interest
in and sympathy for the predicaments and problems of the executor, the
royal courts, preoccupied with the heir, virtually ignored him until late
in the thirteenth century.[374] In the era extending from Glanvill to Bracton
the role of the testamentary executor grew concurre.itly with the evolution
of the jurisdiction of the church over the will. Bracton, for instance,
recognized his growing importance by offering him the assistance of the
common law in certain instances. The royal courts and laymen had always
shown an interest in the apportionment of the testator's chattels and the
payment of legacies, but they had looked principally to the heir for the
performance of these duties. Bracton, however, is obliged to make room
for the executor within the scope of the still impoverished common law of
testament. Accordingly, he said that the royal courts and the church
courts should share responsibility for assuring the collection of monies
owed the deceased; and both jurisdictions recognized the importance of
the executor. Bracton stated that the executor might sue in a church
court for debts due the testator which had been formally recognized
during the latter's lifetime and should be considered as constituting part
of his chattels. A debt not so recognized would, however, have to be sought
by the heir in a royal court.[375] He did not want to place the debtors of
deceased persons at a disadvantage by making them submit to ecclesiastical jurisdiction in a case which would have been tried in a royal court
had the testator been alive.

In reality it would appear that before and after Bracton's time
executors were suing and being sued in the church courts whether or not

373. For a survey of the canon law, see H. Auffroy, *Evolution du Testament en France des
Origines au XIIIe Siècle* (Paris, 1899), pp. 384–398, 441–448; Sheehan, *The Will in Medieval
England*, pp. 148–162.

374. Glanvill, VII, 6–8. See article 4 of the Assize of Northampton in *Select Charters*,
p. 179.

375. Bracton, II, fols. 61–61b; IV, 407b. This point is made in cases preserved in
"Bracton's Note Book" so-called: *A Collection of Cases Decided in the King's Courts during the
Reign of Henry III, Annotated by a Lawyer of that Time . . .*, ed. F. W. Maitland, 3 vols.
(London, 1887), Nos. 162, 550, 810.

these obligations had been recognized during the testator's lifetime. The need to fulfill the testator's last wishes must have encouraged the bishops to lend their help to executors trying to enforce the payment of debts and the collection of the chattels of the deceased. It was probably a simple thing for the bishop to cross the line dividing the administrative from the judicial aspects of his office in order to decide the validity of debts owed to or by the deceased.[376] Canon law cared very little for deeds and contracts as a requirement of proof; the oath or sworn agreement was the thing. Consequently, the Courts Christian enforced verbal agreements as testamentary debts. The royal courts were in no position to compete effectively with this ecclesiastical jurisdiction. As regards the payment of the testator's debts the common law usually looked to the heir for this. Although the heir could be sued in a secular court, already by Bracton's day the difficulty of suing the heir when the executors actually had possession of the chattels was clearly evident.[377] Accordingly, creditors of deceased persons, especially when there was no written proof of indebtedness, probably came to the church court to get justice from the executor.

Growth of ecclesiastical jurisdiction over the will provoked no opposition from the crown. It is likely that the royal courts voluntarily withdrew from this area of law, abandoning it to the church until the end of the thirteenth century. When the gravamina from Henry III's reign mentioned testamentary matters, they confined themselves to complaining against the seizure of the chattels of prelates and others who had died in the king's debt or other forms of secular interference with the enforcement of the will.[378] This haste in occupying the lands and chattels of deceased debtors, especially royal debtors, led some people to take the precaution of obtaining the king's promise, enrolled in chancery, that their executors should have free disposition of their movable properties.[379]

376. This procedure is described in a fourteenth-century document from the *Register of Diocese of Worcester, Sede Vacante*, ed. J. W. Willis Bund, Worcester Historical Society (Oxford, 1897), p. 313. Creditors were cited to prove their claims before the bishop's delegate as shown in the *Register of W. Greenfield*, IV, 33. In 1287 the archbishop of York attempts to protect executors from vexatious litigation by citing creditors to appear before his commissary who would, supposedly, mediate their claims: *The Register of John le Romeyn, Lord Archbishop of York, 1286–1296*, ed. W. Brown, Surtees Society, 2 vols. (Durham, 1913–16), I, 76–77.

377. "Bracton's Note Book," No. 52, where Gilbert of Clare claims ignorance of the debt since, he says, his father appointed executors, who have knowledge of the testament.

378. *Councils & Synods*, pp. 281 (article 4 of 1239); 534 (proposal 8 of 1257); 543 (articles 23, 24 of 1257).

379. The chancery rolls contain numerous examples of this custom. Some interesting ones are found in *CPR, 1348–50*, p. 562, where the king grants the Black Prince free

Sometimes the king agreed to accept pledges for the satisfaction of debts due him.[380] Sometimes he promised free administration, saying that he would look to the heir for compensation.[381] The royal power knew few limits, however, and whenever it seemed that the treasury would suffer from the immediate execution of a testament, the king protected himself by seizing the chattels of a debtor and even by appointing executors of his own choosing. With the development of the Court of Exchequer this meddling sometimes took the form of prohibiting litigation in the church court against executors until they had paid debts due the king and others.[382] The prelates condemned such practices, which obstructed the fulfillment of testaments and which fell under those general censures published against impeding the execution of wills.[383] This growing attention to the role of the executor was a sign of the times, and revealed the crown's recognition of his importance.

Ecclesiastical domination of the will was challenged only in the last quarter of the thirteenth century when first the crown's financial agency and then its courts began to show greater attention to the testament by multiplying the actions available to the executor. This first major departure in the growth of royal attention to testamentary law came in Edward I's reign—a quiet change of attitude "as momentous," so Maitland said, "as any that a statute could make." [384] The growing interest of the royal courts in the problems of testamentary law and the office of the testamentary executor was followed by legislation in the form of the second Statute of Westminster (1285) which gave the executor the writ of account.[385] The common law treatises called *Britton* and *Fleta* were conscious of this transformation, whereby the executor was permitted to

administration of his estate by his executors; and *CCR, 1302–1307*, p. 304, where Edward I rewards the loyal service of a sheriff by granting free execution of his will by his executors. See also *CCR, 1341–43*, p. 462; *CPR, 1313–17*, pp. 290–291; *CPR, 1345–1348*, p. 122; and *CPR, 1396–1399*, p. 318.

380. *CCR, 1360–64*, pp. 348–349; *CCR, 1272–79*, p. 29.

381. *CPR, 1272–79*, p. 354; *CCR, 1381–85*, p. 327.

382. In 1295 Edward I on two occasions orders the bishop of Carlisle to distrain clerks of his diocese that they should appear at the Exchequer to answer executors suing them for debts: *Register of J. Halton*, I, 36–37, 53.

383. The bishops enforced the legislation of Boniface, Ottobono, Mepham, and Stratford by pronouncing general sentences of excommunication against persons within their diocese guilty of impeding the execution of wills: *Councils & Synods*, pp. 33, 76, 134, 151, 192, 231, 333, 356, 442, 466, 495, 618, 682, 717, 820, 1045–1046, 1047–1048, 1143. This was considered one of those types of cases reserved to the bishop.

384. Pollock and Maitland, *History of English Law*, II, 347.

385. *SR*, I, 83.

sue for debts in the king's courts.[386] Of course, the limitations of the common law of debt, which long remained indifferent to the verbal contract, meant that the church courts would continue to exercise wide competence in this area. Nevertheless, the second Statute of Westminster had inaugurated the process whereby testamentary debt and the executor would be drawn more and more within the orbit of royal justice. The royal prohibition of debt and lay chattels had always excluded explicitly matrimonial or testamentary cases from the effects of the royal prohibition.[387] Now such writs were turned to defend the expanding jurisdiction of the king's courts.[388]

The gravamina from Edward I's reign indicate the nature and effect of the new pressures on ecclesiastical jurisdiction. In 1285 in reply to the request that the church courts be permitted to have cognizance of cases concerning the debts of deceased persons, the crown replied that this kind of plea was not conceded to belong to the Courts Christian.[389] Executors, in short, should be sued in the royal courts to force them to satisfy the obligations of their testators. The church condemned this division of jurisdictional competence which, it claimed, interfered with the execution of wills. The king's courts were also claiming debts owed to the deceased. In 1295 the petition of the higher clergy defended the unity of ecclesiastical jurisdiction over the testament, including responsibility for its probate and the acquittance of the executor and also the collection of debts owed the deceased.[390] To counter the common law argument, at least as old as Bracton, that the debtor of the deceased person should not be in a more disadvantageous position than the debtor of a living one, the clergy insisted that such was often unavoidably the case. Further, the church's jurisdiction was necessary in order to ensure the fulfillment of the

386. *Fleta*, ed. H. G. Richardson and G. O. Sayles, SS, 2 vols. (London, 1955), II, 194; *Britton*, I, 174–175.

387. Flahiff, "Writ of Prohibition (ii)," p. 267; *Introduction to the Curia Regis Rolls, 1199–1230 A.D.*, ed. C. T. Flower, SS (London, 1944), p. 110, and references in n. 4. See also *CPR, 1332–47*, p. 31, which cites a writ to the justices in Ireland ordering the restriction of the church courts to pleas of testament and matrimony. The same point is made in 1247 in writs to the sheriffs, *CCR, 1242–47*, p. 543, and Mathew Paris, *Chronica Majora*, IV, 580, which are discussed by Powicke, *Thirteenth Century*, p. 455 and n. 1.

388. There are numerous examples of executors suing and being sued in pleas of testamentary debt in the Year Books of Edward I's reign. For early instances of executors suing for debts due the testator, see *Northumbrian Pleas from De Banco Rolls 1–19 [1–5 Edward I]*, ed. A. Hamilton Thompson, Surtees Society (Durham, 1950), pp. 35–36, 53, 67, 74.

389. *Councils & Synods*, p. 958 (article 9 of 1285). See also, *ibid.*, pp. 961, 963.

390. *Ibid.*, p. 1141 (article 18 of 1295). See also article 19.

testator's last wishes. The higher clergy were still defending the old *de facto* competence which they had exercised over all aspects of testamentary law since the beginning of the thirteenth century, but this was becoming a less and less defensible position as a result of the growth of royal law and the popularity of royal prohibitions.

Subsequently, royal interest in the office of the testamentary executor and in testamentary debt grew by formal legislation as well as the activities of the king's courts. The Statute of Westminster II, which gave the executor the writ of account, spoke of his liability for the debts of testators as if such had always been the case.[391] In 1307 at Carlisle the petition of the community of the realm condemned the practice of papal collectors of claiming chattels which had not been specifically bequeathed to legatees. It was stated that executors should be held responsible in the royal courts for paying the debts of their testators and that the activities of Master William Testa and his associates in forcing their payment by canonical processes entailed an encroachment on royal jurisdiction.[392] At a later date the king demanded satisfaction for suing a plea of testamentary debt at Rome in contempt of the crown.[393] In the reigns of Edward II and Edward III the interest of the king's courts in testamentary cases and the number of actions available to and against the executor continue to grow. A statute extended the action originally granted the victims of the Despensers to the whole realm when in 1330 the executors of executors were given the action of trespass committed on the testator's chattels.[394] In order to avoid delay in dispensing justice all executors were made responsible on a judgment rendered against any one of them.[395] Still later, the commons petitioned that the executor be given the writ of account against his coexecutor.[396] Early in the reign of Edward III it was already possible to say that the executor was the perfect representative of the deceased.[397] In this same reign the Commons petitioned the crown to force the bishops to grant administration only to responsible people, who could be drawn into the king's courts to acquit the testators' debts.[398] Further, it would appear that in the course of trials in the king's courts the executors were giving an explanation of their activities which amounted

391. *SR*, I, 82.
393. *CPR, 1345–48*, pp. 423–424.
395. *Ibid.*, I, 271.
397. *SR*, I, 271.
392. *Rot. Parl.*, I, 219–220.
394. *SR*, I, 252–253, 263.
396. *Rot. Parl.*, III, 497.

398. PRO, Parliament and Chancery Proceedings (Chancery), C. 49/33/22: "Item qe nul administracioun seit baille par ordinere as executours que ne pount estre justicez par lei ne menez en court a respondre as creauncers pur le qe un des executours est tiel qil nad terre ne tenement par qei estre justicez."

to a rendering of account—a practice against which the bishops complained.[399] In Edward III's reign the popularity of this action was revealed by a petition which requested the writ of account against the executors of deceased baliffs, thus indicating its value for suitors in the king's courts.[400]

Not only was royal jurisdiction expanding as a result of legislation, often in response to popular demand, but the king's courts were themselves contributing toward this process of growth by creating precedents which broadened the role of the testamentary executor as a litigant, which identified him more closely with the testator, and which attracted suitors to themselves in increasing numbers. Despite this growth the church courts retained a considerable competence in testamentary debt because of their willingness to enforce verbal contracts. In this they were in contrast to the king's courts which required written proof of indebtedness.[401] The growth of the equitable jurisdiction of chancery and the existence of the jurisdictional alternatives to the church courts did not significantly diminish the number of cases of testamentary debt brought by or against executors in the church courts of the later middle ages. Although the church had not succeeded in maintaining the exclusive competence over the English will which it enjoyed during the twelfth and thirteenth centuries, it did remain a popular and, apparently, a useful source of justice for many people.[402]

The resourcefulness that led the canonists to create the office of testamentary executor and the English church courts to expand their jurisdictional competence in this area of law and justice also resulted in the evolution of the office of the administrator and of the canon law of intestacy. The motivation was the same in both instances—the use of a portion of the deceased's chattels for pious purposes. In the development of an orderly procedure for dealing with the movable properties of in-

399. *Councils & Synods*, p. 1272 (article 6 of 1309); see also *YB 12–13 Edward III*, pp. 83–85.

400. C. 49/8/22.

401. Plucknett, *Concise History*, pp. 635, 741; *YB 20 Edward III [Part I]*, p. 320; *YB 17–18 Edward III*, pp. 6–12.

402. Woodcock, *Medieval Ecclesiastical Courts*, p. 85; a Ripon Minster source containing commissary court records of the fifteenth and sixteenth centuries identifies testamentary matters as constituting the major plea of this court (140 cases out of a total of 555): *Acts of Chapter of SS. Peter and Wilfrid*, ed. Fowler, p. vii; M. D. Slater, "Records of the Court of Arches," p. 146, noted the importance of testamentary jurisdiction in this instance. Of a total of 418 pleas tried by the court of the archdeacon of Huntingdon from 1590 to 1596, the largest number (121) concerned probate and other testamentary matters: Emmison, "Act Book of the Archdeacon of Huntingdon's Court," p. 28.

testates the church had to combat the English feudal custom of seizing the chattels of such people.[403] A chapter of Magna Carta represented a small victory for the ecclesiastical point of view by reserving the intestate's chattels to his kin and friends for distribution under the supervision of the church.[404] The bishops wanted to satisfy the debts of the intestate, collect his goods, and use a portion of them for his spiritual welfare. Shortly after Bracton wrote, the office of the administrator appears, and like his counterpart, the executor, he is the creation of the canon lawyers.[405] It was some time, however, before the administrator of the chattels of the intestate became that perfect representative of the deceased that the executor was becoming in Edward I's time. And this development was the result of the efforts of the church. The Statute of Westminster II focused attention on the bishop by making him responsible in the king's courts for satisfying the debts of the intestate, although he was explicitly excluded from suing in them for the recovery of property or money owed the deceased.[406] Only the church courts were available to him for this purpose. The royal courts continued to look to the bishop as the agent and representative of the intestate. As late as 1343 an answer to a Commons' petition shows that the bishop remained the person primarily responsible for paying the debts of the intestate and the one to be sued by creditors in the royal courts.[407] It was not until 1357 that the administrator was drawn within the orbit of the common law by a statute which gave him all of the actions available to the deceased himself had he survived, thereby making him what the testamentary executor had long been—the perfect legal representative of the deceased.[408] The ingenuity of the ecclesiastical courts had again succeeded in creating a legal personage which the common lawyers gradually accepted as necessary for the enforcement of the legal rights and responsibilities of the dead.

403. *Councils & Synods*, pp. 543 (article 25 of 1257); 681 (canon 19 of 1261); 878 (article 7 of 1280); article 21 of the gravamina of 1399, in Wilkins, III, 241. See also C. Gross, "The Mediaeval Law of Intestacy," *Select Essays in Anglo-American Legal History*, 3 vols. (Boston, 1907–1909), III, 730–735; *Memoranda de Parliamento*, ed. F. W. Maitland, RS (London, 1893), pp. 73–74, No. 121.

404. *Select Charters*, p. 296. The twenty-seventh article of the version of 1215 is dropped in later redactions (p. 338).

405. See the synodal statutes of Bishop Walter Cantilupe for the diocese of Worcester in 1240, *Councils & Synods*, p. 317.

406. *SR*, I, 82; *YB 6–7 Edward II [1313–14]*, p. 56.

407. *Rot. Parl.*, II, 142.

408. *SR*, I, 351. An action of debt against a bishop as administrator was abated where an administrator had been appointed and had performed these duties: *YB 12 Richard II [1388–89]*, ed. G. F. Deiser, AF (Cambridge, Mass., 1914), pp. 91–95.

The history of the relations of the two jurisdictions in respect to the will shows the effect of the energy and the ingenuity of both judicial systems. The virtual monopoly of the English will by the church courts was only challenged from the end of the thirteenth century forward by the belated growth of a common law of testament. This growth entailed the adoption of the testamentary executor as a familiar figure in the royal courts. Regardless of the resourcefulness of royal judges and parliamentary legislators, however, the church courts continued to the end of the middle ages to exercise an important and highly useful jurisdiction over one aspect of testamentary litigation wherein the common law remained backward and inadequate. That was the area of testamentary debt, which, as in the case of debt in general, was drawn to the courts of the bishops and archdeacons because of the flexibility and liberality of canonical methods of proof.

VII. BENEFIT OF CLERGY AND SANCTUARY

At few other points where the two jurisdictions touched was the spirit of compromise, cooperation, and mutual respect, which usually characterized their relations in the later middle ages, so visible as it was in regard to the treatment of criminous clerks. The exemption of clerics from criminal trial and punishment in English secular courts was the most important and permanent accomplishment of Thomas Becket. During the thirteenth and fourteenth centuries church and state agreed that clerics arrested and charged with crimes in the king's courts should be surrendered upon demand to their bishops, who would try and punish them according to canon law. Further, laymen showed their willingness to abide by the principle for which Becket had died and which Alexander III had declared as the law of the church—that clerks convicted of crimes and punished in the ecclesiastical courts should not suffer further at the hands of laymen. Becket not only kept English clerics from the gallows, he succeeded in forcing the crown and the laity to respect and accept the decisions of the church courts. Notwithstanding the fact that the gravamina of the church in these two centuries almost invariably contain a complaint against the violation of benefit of clergy, one never gets the impression that the crown seriously contemplated a general attack on the privilege (much less its abolition), nor that the English church was ever in real danger of losing Becket's victory. Despite several restrictions, qualifications, and limitations imposed upon the privilege during this period, the theory and practice of clerical immunity from the criminal jurisdiction of the crown was taken for granted. It is surely noteworthy that benefit of clergy was seldom the subject of legislation, and that the few royal statutes that refer to it display no signs of hostility or opposition. The most significant attempt during the later middle ages to legislate concerning the privilege—the statute *pro Clero* in 1352—aimed merely at clarifying relations between the jurisdictions worked out in practice long before. The records of chancery, the royal courts, and the bishops' registers convey an impression of co-operation, of the avoidance of controversy, and of a willingness to make the system work. The repeated complaints of the bishops that benefit of clergy was being violated must be read against the backdrop of the mass of evidence showing that in the majority of documented cases the crown and its courts were willing to recognize and enforce the privilege.

From early in the thirteenth century the procedure, which is described as follows, normally applied in the case of English clerics suspected of having committed murder, rape, arson, theft, or crimes of similar magnitude.[409] The accused cleric, after arrest, remained subject to royal jurisdiction, although not necessarily in royal custody, until a preliminary "hearing" or "indictment" or "arraignment" had been completed in the king's court. This preliminary hearing, which was based upon evidence drawn from a confession or the testimony of a jury, proceeded to the point just before sentence was pronounced. It could declare the accused innocent of the crimes alleged against him, in which case the king's court was expected to release him. If the judgment were adverse or if the accused confessed his crimes, then he might escape further trial in the royal court and the punishment which it could impose on laymen by "pleading his clergy." At this point the bishop could request that the accused be surrendered to him as a "convict clerk" either by sending a qualified representative to the royal court or by requesting his release from the keeper of a local jail. In some instances the cleric was surrendered to the church prior to his indictment by the inquest on the understanding that he would be returned to the king's court for the hearing. After the "delivery" of the clerk to the church, he was tried in the bishop's court according to canonical procedure. If he were found to be guiltless, then he was set free; if the church court declared him to be guilty of the alleged crimes then he could be punished by penance, imprisonment, or degradation to the status of a layman.[410] During the whole of the period

409. For a discussion of procedure, see L. Gabel, *Benefit of Clergy in England in the Later Middle Ages*, Smith College Studies in History, XIV (Northampton, Mass., 1928), pp. 30 ff. For the privilege in France, R. Génestal, *Le Privilegium Fori en France du Décret de Gratien à la Fin du XIVᵉ Siècle*, 2 vols. (Paris, 1921–24).

410. C. R. Cheney, "The Punishment of Felonious Clerks," *EHR*, LI (1936), 222–223.

after his delivery to the church, the crown occupied the goods and chattels of the convict clerk. Depending on the decision of the church court, the crown by "special grace" could restore the properties of innocent persons or else confiscate the chattels of those judged guilty of crimes.

This procedure did not remain absolutely fixed and invariable over these two centuries. In response to royal pressure and urging, it was tightened in the direction of strengthening the claims of the royal jurisdiction to determine the fate of particularly notorious felons and to encourage the accused cleric to remain subject to the king's courts until the last possible moment at which he could escape secular punishment only by claiming the privilege of his profession.[411] Nevertheless, there was an evident willingness on both sides to work within the limits imposed by certain time-honored principles, which were: that no churchman should suffer the physical punishment which would normally be inflicted upon a layman guilty of the same crime; that the accused clerk might, if he proved his clergy and the church were willing to protect him, choose to be tried according to canon law rather than royal law; and, in accordance with Becket's victory, that the state had no claim to punish further a cleric adjudged guilty of a felony.

The controversy over benefit of clergy in the thirteenth and fourteenth centuries did not question these fundamental principles, but focused rather on certain procedural matters and problems of enforcement. The gravamina indicate that disagreement between the two jurisdictions, especially during the reigns of Henry III, Edward I, and Edward II, centered around such issues as the delay in the delivery of convict clerks to the church caused by the preliminary indictment in the royal court or the custom of delaying their surrender until all who wished to accuse them had come before the king's justices; the efforts of the church to broaden clerical immunity to cover civil as well as criminal matters; the confiscation of the chattels of clerics; the refusal of the king's courts to honor the credentials of ecclesiastical officials in some instances; and the outlawry of clerics who fled justice or the banishment of others who had taken sanctuary.[412] During the period extending from 1341 to the end of the

411. The Council of Vincennes in France declared, according to Martin, *L'Assemblée de Vincennes*, pp. 224–225 and 233, its belief that the privilege should not be extended to cover "unworthy persons."

412. *Councils & Synods*, pp. 471–472 (article 14 of 1253); 541–542 (articles 14, 15, 16, 17, 18 of 1257); 677 (canon 9 of 1261); 883 (article 15 of 1280); 957 (articles 5, 6 of 1285); 958 (article 11 of 1285); 1139–1140 (articles 9, 10, 11 of 1295); 1211–1212 (articles 10, 11, 12, 13 of 1300/1301); *Rot. Parl. Inediti*, p. 107 (article 11 of 1327).

century the two jurisdictions disputed over matters less central to the privilege itself—the arbitrary arrest and imprisonment of clerics, often when they were in churches or performing divine service; the amercement of clerks in the court of the marshal; or their punishment in royal courts, in contempt of clerical immunity, on the charge of being *depopulatores agrorum* and *insidiatores viarum*.[413]

The gravamina from the reigns of Henry III and Edward I, which reflected the interests and motives of the English church in the days of Grosseteste, Otto, Boniface, Pecham, and Winchelsey, repeatedly condemned the delay occasioned by the preliminary hearing in the royal court—a procedure which was at this very time becoming an established requirement of the common law. This hearing, which was actually very similar to the procedure defended by the Constitutions of Clarendon, made its appearance early in the thirteenth century. Although Bracton does not make explicit mention of it, it was being applied during the time that he lived.[414] Perhaps, his reluctance to approve the preliminary inquest in the king's court shows the canonist prevailing over the common lawyer in this particular instance. Nevertheless, it was becoming a usual procedure of the royal courts and had become firmly established in practice by the beginning of Edward I's reign. Its existence is surely implied by the chapter of the Provisions of Westminster (1259), repeated in the Statute of Marlborough (1267), which forbade royal judges to amerce mainpernors so called of a clerk, who, although appearing in the king's court, refused to plead to the charges against him because of his privilege.[415] Mainpernors were those persons who assumed the responsibility under oath to produce an accused person for trial in a secular court. It would seem that such innocent persons had been amerced by the king's courts because of the refusal of a clerk, claiming benefit of clergy, to answer to some sort of indictment, doubtlessly, the preliminary hearing against which the prelates were complaining. The Statute of Westminster in 1275, which ordered the bishops not to release, without having purged themselves, clerks accused "par solempne enqueste des prodes homes fete en la court le Roy," implies that the royal jurisdiction viewed it to be a necessary and unavoidable procedure.[416] This point of view is clearly evident in the remark of Justice Hervey of Staunton during an eyre of

413. *Rot. Parl.*, II, 244, 358, 373; III, 27.

414. Bracton, II, fol. 123b, but see fol. 124. Bracton quoted a version of a writ for the purgation of a clerk indicated before the king's justices.

415. *SR*, I, 11, 25. See *CCR, 1279–88*, p. 514, where mainpernors are instructed to return the accused to answer to additional charges.

416. *SR*, I, 28.

Kent in Edward II's reign, when he said: "You must say that he was delivered after having been found guilty in this court, for otherwise he would never have been delivered." [417] Long before the Statute *pro Clero* in 1352 mentioned, almost in passing, the crimes for which clerks, "qi seront desore convictz devant les justices seculers," should be delivered to the church, the preliminary inquest had become an established practice of the royal courts. [418]

The English bishops never conceded this right to the royal courts. The earliest gravamina denounced the delay in surrendering clerks to the church and the contempt of clerical immunity which the inquest seemed to imply. The fourteenth article of the grievances of 1253 complained that, since it was said that only the king and the royal judges could legally deliver convict clerks to the church, the bishops were obliged to await the infrequent appearance of the king's justices in their districts. [419] In 1257 the prelates said that sometimes they were forced to return clerks released into their custody five or six years before to the king's courts to answer to the royal inquest. [420] On every occasion between 1280 and 1301 the prelates criticized the delay in delivering clerks; and in each instance the crown repeated its argument that the preliminary hearing was necessary in order to know how the clerk was to be delivered to the bishop—*pro quali deliberetur*. [421] Even though the crown declared its willingness to release accused clerks to their ordinaries prior to their indictment in a royal court, nonetheless, it defended its procedure of formal arraignment. The royal point of view was that the king's jurisdiction over such persons continued to apply until the inquest had declared one way or the other.

The continuing jurisdiction of the crown over clerks formally delivered to the church was expressed both by the requirement that they not be admitted to purgation without royal approval and by the practice of amercing bishops for their escape. During Henry III's reign the sum of £100 became the customary penalty imposed for the escape of criminous clerks prior to purgation. The fine was levied on the bishops whether or not the clerk, who had been released into episcopal custody, had been

417. *YB 6–7 Edward II [Eyre of Kent: 1313–14]*, II, 106, quoted by Gabel, *Benefit of Clergy*, p. 40.

418. *SR*, I, 326.

419. *Councils & Synods*, pp. 471–472.

420. *Ibid.*, p. 542.

421. See citations in n. 412; this point is made in *CPR, 1340–43*, p. 344. The author of *Britton*, I, 27, thought the primary inquisition as a matter of form. The Year Books assume the necessity of it, as, *YB 12 Edward II [1319]*, ed. J. P. Collas, SS (London, 1964), pp. 122–123.

and was based upon the belief of a number of persons in the accused's good
character and truthfulness. As a means of proof it had obvious weaknesses, and the common law had long since abandoned compurgation for
a more dependable procedure—the sworn testimony of a jury. The
secular inquest adduced the testimony of a dozen neighbors of the
accused or witnesses to the event, and it was supposed to provide evidence
as to whether or not a particular person actually did the things alleged
against him. At least as early as Edward I's reign the church courts were
reinforcing compurgation with an inquisition similar to the jury employed
by the secular courts.[433] Admission to compurgation was allowed at the
discretion of the ecclesiastical judge, who also stipulated the number of
compurgators required, and it would seem that the decision as to whether
or not the accused clerk would be permitted to purge himself depended
upon the results of the inquisition as well as upon the appearance of persons opposing his purgation. During the same period when the inquisition was introduced as a check upon easy purgation, the trial in the
Court Christian was further tightened by the practice of announcing in
the neighboring district the date of an expected compurgation and in-
viting all who so wished to come into the church court to testify against
the admission of the defendant to his method of proof.

These safeguards may reflect royal pressure or simply the desire of the
church to prevent obvious criminals from going scot free. The leaders of
the English church during the thirteenth and fourteenth centuries were
aware of certain weaknesses of the criminal jurisdiction of the church and
sought to eliminate some of the worst abuses. Archbishop Boniface's
canons of 1261 ordered the bishops to build and maintain stout jails for
the imprisonment of criminous clerks.[434] Archbishop Pecham urged his
bishops not to admit notorious felons too easily nor too quickly to purgation.[435] The discussion between the church and the crown which
preceded the enactment of the statute *pro Clero* in 1352 is cited in the article
of the statute itself, which says that Archbishop Simon Islip had promised
the king to ordain effective measures for the safekeeping and punishment
of notorious petty traitors, murderers, and thieves "ensi qe nul clerc
emprendreit mes baudure de ensi meffaire per defaute de chastiement."[436]
The archbishop's efforts in this direction are more fully described in the
mandate to the bishop of London preserved in the archepiscopal register.

433. *Ibid.*, pp. 98–99.
434. *Councils & Synods*, p. 684 (canon 29).
435. *Ibid.*, p. 1122 (canon 6 of the supposed statutes of Pecham).
436. *Rot. Parl.*, II, 244; *SR*, I, 326.

In an effort to avoid scandal to the church arising from the abuses of clerical privilege, easy purgation, and inadequate punishment, the archbishop decreed with the advice and counsel of the prelates attending the recent parliament, that henceforth clerks delivered to the church should be strictly confined "secundum qualitatem personarum et scelerum quantitatem." [437] Clerks notoriously defamed of crimes should suffer perpetual imprisonment on the bread of sorrow and the water of anguish (de pane doloris et aqua angustie). The decision to admit a clerk to his purgation should be based upon the presumption of his guilt derived from his confession or public notoriety, and should consider the scandal and the disturbance of public peace which his liberation might entail.

Evidently the crown and its courts were unwilling to rely wholly on the discretion of the higher clergy, since during the thirteenth and fourteenth centuries clerks were sometimes delivered to the bishops with the stipulation that they not be admitted to purgation without the king's permission or, perhaps, that they not be admitted to purgation at any time (absque alia purgatione). [438] The latter requirement was equivalent to a sentence of perpetual imprisonment. Of course, this constituted a violation of the freedom of the bishops to try and punish felonious clerks, and in 1295 the gravamina complained against it as a novel and illegal custom. [439] The church failed to obtain its abolishment, and throughout the thirteenth and fourteenth centuries bishops were sometimes punished for releasing clerks after their purgation contrary to the king's command or the instructions of the royal judges. In 1290 the abbot of Westminster was indicted for receiving the purgation of two clerks prior to the date arranged by agreement with the king's judges, who had insisted that they be kept in custody until all who so desired should have had the opportunity to accuse them. [440] Although the abbot appealed successfully to Parliament, as late as 1352 a statute condemned this practice of the royal courts. [441] No limitation was ever imposed on the number of times a clerk could claim his privilege. It appears, however, that royal judges were sometimes bending the rules of delivery in order to make certain that they had complete information concerning the crimes of accused clerks.

In compliance with the expectations of the king's courts and out of the desire to prevent the escape of notorious felons, some bishops exercised

---

437. Quoted by Gabel, *Benefit of Clergy*, pp. 134–135.

438. For examples of this practice, see *Register of G. Giffard*, II, 410; *Rot. Parl.*, I, 40; *Placitorum Abbreviatio*, p. 299; *CPR, 1330–34*, pp. 181–182.

439. *Councils & Synods*, p. 1139 (article 10).

440. *Rot. Parl.*, I, 41–42.   441. *SR*, I, 326.

considerable caution in demanding clerks and in detaining them for trial. The church never intended to use benefit of clergy as an excuse for deluging the country with criminals, and, generally speaking, cooperated with the secular authorities to repress crime and disorder. Sometimes the bishop could simply refuse to demand a churchman claiming the privilege.[442] In such cases there was doubt whether or not the accused should enjoy benefit of clergy. During this period the examination of clerks became the responsibility of the royal judges, and some could be very strict. In the course of an eyre of Kent in Edward II's reign, Chief Justice William Bereford remarked that only a bishop or archbishop could lawfully demand clerks from the king's courts and refused to surrender them on this occasion because the judge ordinary's commission did not empower him to receive as well as demand them.[443] The higher clergy denounced the requirements of some royal judges, who seemed to be unreasonably strict in accepting the credentials of ecclesiastical officials coming to their courts to take custody of convict clerks. In 1295 the gravamina complained against those royal judges who required separate mandates for the delivery of individual clerks rathers than surrendering them in compliance with an episcopal commission couched in general terms.[444] At other times the bishops' delegates were told to go home and get fresh authorization. The pressures of the crown and the strictness of royal judges encouraged some bishops to be very cautious in obtaining the delivery of notorious felons.[445] In 1286 Bishop John Pontissara warned his emissary, the dean of Southwark, to be careful in demanding the surrender of a clerical prisoner in the Tower of London, who had been charged with a double homicide.[446] The constable of the Tower had demanded the king's specific permission to deliver him to the church, and the bishop had written requesting the king's compliance. But the bishop cautioned the dean not to press for release until he had received sufficient bond from several substantial persons "*ne ex hoc periculum immaneat in futurum.*" Those who assumed responsibility for bringing the accused clerk to justice at some future date bound themselves to pay the bishop £100, plus all their goods and chattels, in the event of his escape. This caution was also shown by Bishop William Montacute of Worcester, who warned his

442. Douie, *Archbishop Pecham*, p. 203.
443. *YB 6–7 Edward II [Eyre of Kent: 1313–14]*, I, 123.
444. *Councils & Synods*, p. 1141 (article 20).
445. *Ibid.*, pp. 1212–13 (article 16). See the commission for an inquiry concerning the status of one claiming the immunity in *Registrum Radulphi Baldock, Gilberti Segrave, Ricardi Newport, et Stephani Gravesend*, ed. R. C. Fowler, CYS (London, 1911), p. 8.
446. *Registrum J. Pontissara*, II, 459–461.

agents to be careful in demanding and receiving convict clerks because of the jeopardy in which he was placed.[447]

A variety of circumstances jeopardized the enjoyment of their privilege by individual clerics and sometimes seemed to constitute a denial of benefit of clergy itself. The high-handed acts of zealous royal bailiffs, judges, and sheriffs were loudly and repeatedly denounced by the bishops. On some occasions the admission of a clerk to his privilege was hampered by the conditions of his apprehension or his status. The rights of accused clerks who were traitors or bigamists or who had been outlawed, banished from the realm, or who had confessed crimes were occasionally the focus of controversy. Very often the gravamina, when they complain against violation of the privilege, are mainly concerned with infractions arising from these complicating circumstances.

For example, some doubt surrounded the status of a clerk accused of treason, especially when he was a prelate. During much of this period this did not constitute a serious problem. The extension of the definition of treason and the political events of the second half of the fourteenth century occasionally brought this issue to the forefront.[448] Early in Edward III's reign the bishop of Hereford, Adam Orleton, was convicted of treason for adhering to the king's enemies. His lands and chattels were declared forfeit, and he was surrendered to the metropolitan as a convict clerk.[449] There was some feeling that a prelate, even when accused of a particularly atrocious crime, deserved special consideration. In reply to a request from the archbishop of Dublin in 1339 for the arrest of the bishop of Ossory for sorcery, the council said that a bishop ought not to be arrested.[450] This never became, however, an established right for all prelates. The statute of 1352 reserved cases of treason involving clerks to the royal courts, when the crime was committed against the crown, but allowed cases of petty treason, i.e., against persons other than the king, to go to the church courts when the accused was a cleric.[451] This did not entail a serious curtailment of benefit of clergy, since treason remained a fairly infrequent offense; and the statute of 1352 appears to have satisfied

---

447. See Haines, *Administration of the Diocese of Worcester*, p. 182.

448. *SR*, I, 319–320; Pollock and Maitland, *History of English Law*, I, 446.

449. L. W. Vernon Harcourt, *His Grace the Steward and Trial by Peers* (London, 1907), pp. 209–210.

450. *CCR, 1339–41*, p. 222.

451. *SR*, I, 302. In Henry IV's reign the bishop of Carlisle, who was indicted before the justices of oyer and terminer, and Archbishop Scrope of York, who was tried by the constable and a special committee of peers, were both denied benefit of clergy, according to Vernon Harcourt, *His Grace the Steward*, pp. 371–376.

the church by preserving the right of petty traitors to claim benefit of clergy.

The actions of clerks accused of crimes, who simply refused to come to justice, and of royal officials who desired their punishment, whatever their theoretical rights might be, led to the violation of benefit of clergy in some instances.[452] The bishops denounced the arbitrary arrest, trial, and punishment of outlawed clerks or the practice of forcing others to abjure the realm under threat of forfeiture and outlawry. In 1316 a statute promised that clerks would not be forced to abjure the realm, in contempt of their privilege,[453] nor would benefit of clergy be denied confessors in the king's courts, as had sometimes been the case.[454] Evidently the status of sanctuary-seekers, outlaws, abjurers, and confessers was complicating the procedure of delivering clerks to the church and was causing violations of their privilege.

Both church and state agreed in denying immunity to bigamous clerks. The Council of Lyons in 1274 had declared that clerks who had married twice or who had married widows were to be considered bigamous and, therefore, no longer clerics and worthy of clerical privileges.[455] In the reign of Edward I a statute extended the effects of the canon law to include clerics who were bigamous before as well as after the Council of Lyons.[456] The royal courts proceeded to enforce the conciliar decree, which had already established a point of law, by phrasing the question of an accused person's marital status in terms which would allow it to be put to a jury as a matter of fact.[457] The bishops complained against this practice,[458] and in 1344 a statute assured the church that the charge of bigamy would not henceforth be tried in a royal court by means of the inquest.[459] Such issues would be sent to the bishops for their certification.[460] Although exceptions of bigamy were subsequently sent to the bishops for investigation and

452. *Councils & Synods*, pp. 542 (article 16 of 1267); 690 (article 12 of 1261). See also A. L. Poole, "Outlawry as a Punishment of Criminous Clerks," in *Historical Essays in Honour of James Tait* (Manchester, 1933), pp. 239–246.

453. *SR*, I, 173. There seems to have been some doubt concerning the abjuration of the realm by clerks in Edward I's time, since it was a topic for discussion at the king's council: *CCR, 1279–88*, p. 399.

454. *SR*, I, 174.

455. Sext, I, 12, 1.

456. *SR*, I, 43.

457. Plucknett, "Execrabilis in the Common Pleas," p. 63.

458. *Rot. Parl. Inediti*, p. 109. For the Commons' petition of 1334, *ibid.*, p. 234.

459. *SR*, I, 302.

460. *CPR, 1381–85*, p. 1, where the exception of bigamy is sent to the ordinary for certification.

certification, the royal courts continued to deny benefit of clergy to bigamous clerks. In 1376 and 1377 petitions were introduced into Parliament asking that bigamous clerks be allowed the privilege, but these were not enacted into law.[461] Despite such minor disagreements as that over the procedure for determining bigamy, however, both jurisdictions continued to deny benefit of clergy to bigamous clerks.

Neither in the thirteenth nor the fourteenth century was there a concerted attack on the principle of benefit of clergy. During the reigns of Henry III and Edward I controversy focused on such secondary and procedural issues as the preliminary inquest, the fining of bishops for the escape of clerks, or the seizure and confiscation of the chattels of convict clerks. During the reigns of Edward III and Richard II the conflict again concentrated on the edges of the question; and the gravamina denounced the arbitrary arrest of clerics within churches or while engaged in spiritual tasks, their outlawry, and their amercement by the special household court of the marshal. One episode during Edward III's reign might have provided both the reason and the opportunity for a deliberate attack on benefit of clergy. This was the political crisis of the years 1341 to 1343, which had a distinctly anticlerical bent and which made such anti-clericalism respectable.[462]

During this episode the government arrested many clerks, tried and punished a considerable number of ecclesiastical officials accused of extortion, and disgraced several prominent clerical ministers. This controversy raged about the person of Archbishop John Stratford, who had served as regent during Edward III's ill-fated French expedition and who was blamed for the collapse of the king's foreign military venture. Encouraged by Stratford's enemies at court, Edward struck out at those whom he thought to be responsible for the recent catastrophe. What began as a vindictive attack on Stratford and his colleagues grew into a purge of the whole administration. A large number of clerks and laymen were arrested and imprisoned.[463] The greater offices of the royal government and the courts were turned upside down. A large number of clerical ministers who staffed the royal administration, including the archbishop's

461. *Rot. Parl.*, II, 33; III, 22.

462. The definitive study of the political crisis of Edward III's reign is still that by G. Lapsley, "Archbishop Stratford and the Parliamentary Crisis of 1341," in *Crown, Community and Parliament in the Later Middle Ages: Studies in English Constitutional History*, ed. H. M. Cam and G. Barraclough (Oxford, 1951), pp. 231–272.

463. In March, 1341, Bishop John Grandisson of Exeter published sentences of excommunication which fell on all who arrested clerks "non confessos nec convictos," *Register of J. Grandisson*, II, 945–946.

brother, Robert Stratford, the chancellor, lost their posts. Lesser churchmen were arrested, imprisoned, and fined in ways that seemed to flout
the great charter of liberties; and there was even talk about the seizure of
some bishops for real or supposed crimes against the state. The anticlerical
motive of the king was noticed by contemporary observers, who quoted
him as saying that he wished to rid the government of clerks and to
replace them with ministers subject to his own jurisdiction. Archbishop
Stratford did not miss the point, and in apologetic letters and sermons
which he composed in his defense he contrasted the present attack on
clerical rights and the liberties of the church with that of Henry II's reign.
Memories of Becket's martyrdom were recalled, and Stratford seemed
quite willing to assume the role of saint and martyr in the face of official
anticlericalism. But the misconduct of clerks and the abuses of ecclesiastical
jurisdiction were only two issues among several. Ultimately, Stratford
made his stand on judgment by his peers; and the controversy tended to
focus on constitutional issues such as ministerial responsibility and the
rights of all Englishmen to trial and punishment in accordance with the
promises of Magna Carta. In this way the archbishop broadened the basis
of his appeal and converted a dispute between clerks and laymen into a
much grander struggle of royal despotism against parliamentary government and the rule of law. Ultimately the primate and the king were
reconciled and the concerted attack upon clerical misconduct and
ecclesiastical abuse was ended.

During the remainder of Edward III's reign and that of Richard II
the debate over clerical immunity continued, as it had before the crisis,
to turn around procedural and secondary issues such as the arbitrary
arrest and punishment of clerics, often while they were engaged in their
ministerial tasks and their punishment on general charges of lawlessness.
The second half of the fourteenth century witnessed the aggravation of the
usual medieval conditions of violence and disorder—circumstances which
may have led to many individual acts which seemed to jeopardize the
status of the clergy.[464] The crown showed its willingness to avoid illegal
or unwarranted practices which appeared to threaten the principle of
benefit of clergy. In 1376 the king promised that clerks would not be
arrested on the king's highway or in churches, although the problem was
still a real one at the end of the reign.[465] The vague confirmation of the
liberties of the church and clergy in the parliaments of Edward III's and

464. Wilkins, III, 244; McKissack, *Fourteenth Century*, pp. 203 ff.
465. *Rot. Parl.*, II, 358; Wilkins, III, 245. See also the petition of 1397, *Rot. Parl.*, III,
397; *SR*, II, 5.

Richard II's reigns never eliminated the misdeeds of royal and local officials.[466]

During the thirteenth century the bishops continued to argue, with no success whatsoever, for the total exemption of the clergy from trial in secular courts on civil and criminal matters alike.[467] The clergy themselves were never united in defense of the ideal of the absolute immunity of churchmen from secular jurisdiction. Although prelates occasionally forced the lesser clergy to withdraw suits against their colleagues from the royal courts, writs of prohibition could prevent them from taking certain kinds of cases to the Courts Christian. The ideal of total clerical immunity from secular law survived, however, to the end of the thirteenth century. Archbishop Winchelsey gravely quoted the canons to the effect that "clericus contra clericum in foro civili nequeat litigare."[468] In 1287 Bishop Peter Quivil of Exeter published a synodal constitution which expressly forbade clerks from forcing their brethren to come to secular courts on personal actions and decreed excommunication against those lay plaintiffs and judges who prosecuted civil cases involving the clergy.[469] Although Edward I's legislation on the statute merchant exempted clerks from arrest and imprisonment, this single exception to the rule of the submission of the clergy to the civil jurisdiction of the crown was only a meager concession to the ideal of Grosseteste, Boniface, and the Sext.[470] The growth of the common law during the later middle ages and its popularity for suitors of all kinds and conditions made it impossible and not especially desirable to exempt the clergy from the civil authority of the king's courts.

The right of sanctuary, like benefit of clergy, was a privilege which was never denied in principle and usually respected in practice. Since Otto-bono's day the violation of sanctuary was one of those crimes for which excommunication *ipso facto* was decreed. The crown was normally willing

466. *Rot. Parl.*, III, 26; Wilkins, III, 245.

467. Article 2 of the gravamina of 1239, in *Councils & Synods*, pp. 280–281; and article 19 of the grievances of 1280, in *ibid.*, p. 885. See also the complaint of papal legates against Philip IV in *Registrum J. Pontissara*, II, 548.

468. See Archbishop Winchelsey's mandate in *Registrum R. Winchelsey*, I, 365–366. The editor cites (p. 365 n. 1) *Sext*, II, 2, 2 and *Decreti Secunda Pars*, XI, 1, 46–47. See also *Registrum Epistolarum Fratris Iohannis Peckham, Archiepiscopi Cantuariensis*, ed. C. T. Martin, RS, 3 vols. (London, 1882–1885), I, 15–16.

469. *Councils & Synods*, pp. 1027–1028.

470. *SR*, I, 99. Bishop Baldock of London applied to Edward I on the basis of this provision for the release of an imprisoned clerk. See *Registrum R. Baldock, . . .*, pp. 13–14; and for a discussion of this exemption, *Select Cases concerning the Law Merchant, A.D. 1251–1779*, ed. C. Gross and H. Hall, SS, 3 vols. (London, 1908–32), III, xxxii–xxxiii.

to respect the church's right to grant protection to refugee felons and to allow the punishment of sacrilege by threat of excommunication.[471] Most of the charges of the violation of sanctuary, which are prominent in the gravamina of Edward I's reign, were probably the result of local officials, who placed sanctuary under such close guard that seekers were starved into submission or the churches defiled or who sometimes arbitrarily and illegally seized and executed those whom the coroners had delivered from sanctuary and who were traveling the king's highway.[472] The crown never defended such acts by its bailiffs and sheriffs and invariably declared its willingness to respect the right of sanctuary.[473] Violations were usually the result of aggravated or aggravating local situations, such as that which occurred in the summer of 1378 and involved one of the most important houses of the kingdom. For a long time churches and monastic houses had been used by debtors as havens of refuge or as places for storing chattels to keep them from the grasp of creditors.[474] In 1378 this custom caused a sacrilege to be committed in Westminster Abbey when soldiers rumored to be in the service of the duke of Lancaster arrested two knights and murdered one of them in the precincts of the abbey.[475] The case was discussed in Parliament itself and one of those who spoke on behalf of the soldiers was John Wycliffe, not yet the archheretic. After scrutinizing the charters of the abbey the crown decided to exclude debtors from claiming sanctuary as an absolute right, but out of deference to the fame and sanctity of the house declared that honest bankrupts and debtors might seek sanctuary there until they could acquit themselves of their debts. In respect to sanctuary as in the case of benefit of clergy the crown showed a willingness to recognize the church's legitimate rights and to promise

471. *Councils & Synods*, pp. 762–764. R. F. Hunnisett, *The Medieval Coroner* (Cambridge, 1961), p. 37, says that, because of the gravity of the crime, violation of sanctuary was rare. J. C. Cox, *The Sanctuaries and Sanctuary-Seekers of Mediaeval England* (London, 1911) is still helpful. A description of a sanctuary register is contained in I. D. Thornley, "The Sanctuary Register of Beverley," *EHR*, XXXIV (1919), 393–397; and the same author discusses the abolition of the right in an essay in *Tudor Studies presented . . . to Alfred Frederick Pollard* (London, 1924).

472. Article 22 from the petitions of 1257, in *Councils & Synods*, p. 543; article 18 of the grievances of 1280 (rehearsed in 1309), in *ibid.*, pp. 884–885; and article 44 of the grievances of 1295, in *ibid.*, p. 1146. Hunnisett, *The Coroner*, pp. 37–54, discusses the ritual of abjuration. The king can order the return of felons to sanctuary as witnessed by the *Register of J. Romeyn*, I, 57; and *CCR, 1313–18*, p. 21.

473. *Councils & Synods*, pp. 884–885 (article 18); *SR*, I, 171.

474. See *Select Charters*, p. 167.

475. *Rot. Parl.*, III, 37, 50–51. See also *ibid.*, IV, 39–40, for a petition from 1414 concerning this enactment.

cooperation. In particular instances, however, there was always the problem of forcing local officials to comply with the royal promises, and violations of sanctuary were never eliminated.

The debate over benefit of clergy and the right of sanctuary during the thirteenth and fourteenth centuries occurred on the edges of these issues rather than focusing on the principles of them. The two jurisdictions disagreed over relatively minor procedural matters such as the punishment of bishops for the escape of clerks, the confiscation of their chattels, the outlawry of churchmen, or the close confinement of sanctuary-seekers. There was no discussion of the church's right to enjoy sanctuary or the immunity of the clergy from criminal trial and punishment in the royal courts. Many of the violations against which the bishops complained were doubtlessly the result of local conditions or the acts of individual royal officials. There was no attack on the principle of benefit of clergy itself even when in the middle of the reign of Edward III the clash of politics, personalities, and passions seemed to create an opportunity for it. Both jurisdictions were content to abide by a compromise which had been arranged by statesmen and lawyers long before.

VIII. The Independence of the Ecclesiastical Courts: Some Procedural Issues

Often the jurisdictional conflict revolved around certain procedures or quasi-judicial practices of the two court systems. In such instances controversy was not the product of competing laws, but arose from efforts to assure the proper operation of a particular judicial system or the enforcement of its judgments. The issues underlying conflict over caption, benefit of clergy, and even the execution of many royal writs of admission to ecclesiastical benefices were of this nature. There were, however, other problems of a procedural kind, which were less prominent and dramatic but no less troublesome for the maintenance of good relations between the jurisdictions. For instance, the royal courts always presumed to exercise jurisdiction over the abuses of local government, which encompassed the operation of ecclesiastical justice. The crown did not view the church courts as entirely separate from the rest of society nor as independent, untouchable, and possessed of an absolute integrity of their own. Rather, royal judges were willing to entertain complaints against their spiritual counterparts and to hear and determine cases of corruption, oppression, or extortion. In other words, the relations between the two jurisdictions was a one-sided one, which allowed the royal courts to scrutinize and amend the church courts, while refusing themselves to submit to the correction of bishops and archdeacons.

Occasionally, as in the reigns of Edward I and Edward III, this power to investigate and punish alleged misdeeds by ecclesiastical judges could amount almost to a persecution. At other times, however, conflict arose as a result of particular practices adopted or applied. In Henry III's reign, for example, the crown complained of the use of the lay jury by the church courts and of the nature of the inquiry into public morals launched by Grosseteste and his admirers among the higher clergy. On the other hand, the custom of the ecclesiastical courts of commuting corporeal for pecuniary penance sometimes annoyed the royal courts and seemed to represent encroachment on an area of law claimed for the king. Similarly, the royal courts took a very dim view of the use of spiritual jurisdiction to interfere with the operation of secular justice. This was especially the case when private persons charged others with defamation in the Courts Christian in order to escape from or retaliate to accusations made against them in the king's courts. Finally, the problem of getting men to come to court or to comply with judgments was a difficulty confronting both jurisdictions. The church relied on the king to grant caption. On its side, the crown always looked to the bishops to execute a variety of writs, some of them of a judicial nature, against lesser clerics who, for one reason or another, were called to respond to the king or his courts. Yet the bishops resented being forced to behave like royal ministers, responsible, under threat of punishment themselves, for enforcing the king's commands on the diocesan clergy or their properties. Procedural issues of this kind were among the most frequent areas of conflict cited by the gravamina of the thirteenth and fourteenth centuries, and evidently were recurrent problems for the two jurisdictions in their efforts to live together peacefully.

In 1239 the gravamina complained against those royal bailiffs who arrested and imprisoned ecclesiastical officials seeking to correct their sins; but this interference was probably not condoned by the crown itself.[476] From Edward I's reign forward the justices in eyre were taking notice of abuses committed by ecclesiastical judges.[477] False citations, exorbitant fees for probate and acquittance, and encroachment on royal jurisdiction were the acts, according to the author of *Britton*, for which the judge

476. *Councils & Synods*, p. 283 (article 25).

477. Douie, *Archbishop Pecham*, p. 117 and n. 5, citing *Rotuli Hundredorum temp. Hen. III. et Edw. I.*, [ed. W. Illingworth], 2 vols. (London, 1812–1818), I, 352. There is, however, no article concerning the ecclesiastical courts in the lists printed by H. M. Cam, *Studies in the Hundred Rolls* (Oxford, 1921), pp. 92 ff.

ordinaries could be indicted.[478] In 1285 this attack on ecclesiastical justice became deliberate and concentrated. Royal justices were accused of sitting at sessions of the church courts in order to gather evidence for indictments, of entertaining accusations of wrongdoing committed since the beginning of the reign, and of arresting, trying, and punishing a large number of ecclesiastical officials on a variety of charges.[479]

This was a trying period for the church courts, but a crisis was averted when Edward abruptly retreated from that position in which his zealous judges had placed him. Hereafter, although individual persons continued to complain against particular ecclesiastical judges,[480] there was no concerted attack on ecclesiastical justice until the political crisis of 1341. In that year the royal justices commissioned to travel through the shires to investigate mismanagement of public affairs by secular officials, also received indictments of corrupt or oppressive ecclesiastical judges. The statute of 1341 did not eliminate the practice, which continued as a regular policy of the government until 1343. In February, 1343, the king ordered Richard Talbot and other royal judges, working under such a commission in Hereford, to cease taking inquisitions concerning the extortions of ecclesiastical officials in accordance with a promise made by the king to the prelates at a council in December.[481] This was followed by similar letters dispatched in June, 1343, to the justices of oyer and terminer in York, Lancaster, Norfolk, and Gloucester, ordering them to stop prosecuting ecclesiastical judges until the next Parliament.[482] Although the church was probably relieved when the Trinity Parliament of 1343 abolished these annoying commissions, the problem was not permanently solved.[483] The royal courts and the crown continued to act as though the activities of the church courts constituted a subject falling within the competence of the king's jurisdiction. In 1352, for instance, Edward III promised that an ecclesiastical judge would not be indicted in a royal court on the general charge of extortion unless his accuser could allege a

478. *Britton*, I, 82–83.

479. Douie, *Archbishop Pecham*, pp. 302 ff.

480. See the complaint of the clergy in 1300/1301, *Councils & Synods*, p. 1217 (article 33), which the royal reply ascribed to the acts of magnates.

481. *CCR, 1343–46*, p. 96.

482. *Ibid.*, pp. 223, 255. According to PRO KB 27/342, 49–49d, several monks of Westminster were indicted for various extortions—demanding exorbitant fees for probate, convening an archdeacon's court before dawn and then punishing defendants who failed to appear, and the like—the record of which fills two membranes of the King's Bench roll for Michaelmas, 1344. Discussed by H. G. Richardson, "Year Books and Plea Rolls as Sources of Historical Information," *TRHS*, Ser. 4, V (1922), 44–45.

483. *SR*, I, 303.

specific wrong committed by him.[484] Although the laity were still using the visits of the royal justices as an occasion for complaining about the conduct of ecclesiastical courts, the trying years of 1285 and 1341–1343 were past.

On and off during the thirteenth and fourteenth centuries there were complaints by the laity of extortions and abuses committed by the ecclesiastical courts. The high cost of probate and the infliction of pecuniary penances were the most usual targets of attack.[485] The royal courts entertained and sometimes punished ecclesiastical officials guilty of exacting inordinately high fees for the probate of testaments and the acquittance of executors. Not until Henry V's reign, however, did the state enact legislation designed to control the cost of ecclesiastical justice in respect to testaments.[486]

Although the church insisted on its right to commute corporeal for pecuniary penance, the crown declared that such punishments should not be imposed in the first instance.[487] Further, the prohibition of lay chattels was always available against the ecclesiastical judge who attempted to force the payment of sums of money. That some abuses did exist in regard to the penances imposed by the church courts is revealed by the church's efforts to reform the system.[488] The papal legates Otto and Ottobono enacted laws against lesser ecclesiastical officials who hindered peaceful solutions of cases, who made distant and false citations, or who fraudulently delayed justice.[489] Otto tried to prevent the farming of the profits of ecclesiastical justice;[490] and Ottobono restricted the right of the archdeacons to commute corporeal penance.[491] In 1261 Archbishop Boniface

484. *Ibid.*, p. 326.

485. See the complaint of the men of London in 1290: *Rot. Parl.*, I, 60; also see the petitions printed, *ibid.*, II, 142–143, 305, 313; *ibid.*, III, 25, 43, 163; *ibid.*, IV, 9. E. F. Jacob is quite complimentary about the testamentary jurisdiction of the church in the fifteenth century in his essay on the archbishop of Canterbury's testamentary jurisdiction, *Mediaeval Records of the Archbishop of Canterbury: the Lambeth Lectures* (London, 1962), pp. 48–49. For the history of penance, see O. D. Watkins, *A History of Penance* (London, 1920); R. Hill, "Public Penance: Some Problems of a Thirteenth Century Bishop," *History*, XXXVI (1951), 213–226; T. P. Oakley, "Mediaeval Penance and the Secular Law," *Speculum*, VII (1932), 515–525.

486. *SR*, II, 195–196; *ibid.*, I, 350, seems to have been a warning.

487. See *Circumspecte agatis* in Graves, "Circumpsecte Agatis," p. 16, line 3 of the writ; *SR*, I, 171.

488. For examples of efforts to hedge this privilege with qualifications and restrictions see *Councils & Synods*, pp. 409–410, 597, 616, 721, 994, 1028.

489. Constitutions 21, 26 of Otto, in *Councils & Synods*, pp. 254–255, 256–257; and constitutions of Ottobono, in *ibid.*, pp. 773–774.

490. *Ibid.*, p. 248 (Nos. 7, 8).   491. *Ibid.*, pp. 768–769 (No. 19).

contributed to these reforming efforts by condemning the excesses of apparitors and beadles and limiting their powers of excommunication.[492] In 1281 Archbishop Pecham denounced rural deans who sold letters of citation without informing accused persons.[493] In 1342 Archbishop Stratford tried to legislate for the improvement of his Court of Arches.[494] At the same time that he tried to eliminate abuses, however, Stratford condemned those persons who used these as an excuse to procure the indictment of ecclesiastical officials.[495]

There was, doubtlessly, some basis for criticizing the church for the costs of probate and acquittance and for redemption of penance. At least the laity were quite outspoken.[496] Although secular attitudes toward the church and the clergy in England during the later middle ages, especially as regards such matters as ecclesiastical justice, papal provisions, and the alien priories, have never been thoroughly investigated, it would appear that the laity were pressing the crown to take a more active role in reforming the church. An interesting Commons' petition from 1372 throws light on this matter.[497] It said that, since the practice of commuting corporeal penance for cash favored clerical incontinence, the justices of assize and of the peace should be commissioned to inquire concerning the morals of the clergy and to accept indictments at the instance of the king or private parties. If the accused cleric were found guilty of immoral conduct for which he had been absolved by paying a sum of money, then the clerk and the judge ordinary would be liable for amercement at twice the value of the redemption. Although some bishops like John Grandisson of Exeter may have favored corporeal penances, especially for the more serious crimes, the church defended its right to commute them.[498] During the later middle ages in England the church courts were imposing both kinds of punishment and were arguing their right to do so.[499]

492. *Ibid.*, p. 683 (No. 27).   493. *Ibid.*, p. 908 (No. 12).

494. Wilkins, II, 681–695.   495. *Ibid.*, pp. 707–708.

496. Chaucer's "Friar's Tale," lines 1299 ff., is a well-known jibe at the archdeacons: *The Complete Works of Geoffrey Chaucer*, ed. W. W. Skeat, 2nd ed.; 7 vols. (Oxford, 1897–1900), IV, 359. L. A. Haselmayer, "The Apparitor and Chaucer's Summoner," *Speculum*, XII (1937), 50–54, assesses the conduct of the lesser officialdom of the English church, and is in agreement with Pantin, *English Church*, pp. 101–102, as to their corruption and oppressiveness. T. Wright has published in *Political Songs of England, from the Reign of John to that of Edward II*, Camden Society, VI (London, 1839), pp. 155–159, the "Satyre on the Consistory Courts," from the reign of Edward II.

497. *Rot. Parl.*, II, 313–314.

498. See the article relative to the consistory court of Exeter, *Register of J. Grandisson*, II, 808.

499. Note the gravamina of 1280 and 1300–1301, in *Councils & Synods*, pp. 874, 1209.

During the reigns of Henry III and Edward I the practice of certain bishops and ecclesiastical courts of impaneling sworn juries of parishioners to testify concerning the moral faults of the laity became the focus both of secular criticism and royal opposition. These incidents were exceptional. For one thing, the controversy erupted in the reign of Henry III as a result of the reforming ardor and the extraordinary energy of Bishop Grosseteste of Lincoln. Grosseteste took very much to heart the injunctions of the Fourth Lateran Council of 1215 and of the reforming popes of the thirteenth century to use the right of episcopal visitation as a means for effecting the moral and spiritual regeneration of clergy and laity.[500] In England in 1237 the cardinal legate Otto had urged the prelates to visit their dioceses in order to strengthen and perfect the Christian faith.[501] In compliance with the legate's injunction Bishop Grosseteste undertook in 1238 or 1239 a detailed inquiry into the conduct of the clergy of his diocese and their performance of the Christian ministry.[502] Grosseteste viewed his diocese of Lincoln as a foreign missionary would have viewed a distant Asian or African charge. The result of his efforts was a thorough investigation into the lives and conduct of the parish clergy—an innovation against which the clergy complained.[503] It would appear that in some instances he broadened his inquiry to include an investigation of the lives and morals of the laity which was based upon information collected from a sworn jury of laymen—a procedure identical with the jury of accusation employed by the king's courts. According to Matthew Paris, the laity complained, and Henry III wrote in 1246 to the sheriff of Hertfordshire ordering him to forbid laymen to swear before the bishop of Lincoln on any matter except testament and matrimony.[504] Evidently, this did not discourage Grosseteste, since he was summoned by royal writ in 1249 to answer to the king for forcing laymen to take the forbidden oaths.[505] In 1252 the king explained to the bishop his reasons for opposing such procedures.[506] The bishop's custom of forcing some laymen to accuse others of moral and spiritual failures was an unwarranted novelty, which interfered with their labor and which promoted perjury and defamation.

---

500. See C. R. Cheney, *Episcopal Visitation of Monasteries in the Thirteenth Century* (Manchester, 1931), pp. 17 ff.; M. Gibbs and J. Lang, *Bishops and Reform, 1215–1272, with Special Reference to the Vatican Council of 1215* (London, 1934), p. 151; Callus (ed.), *Robert Grosseteste*, pp. 178 ff., 202.

501. *Councils & Synods*, p. 255 (canon 22).   502. *Ibid.*, p. 265.

503. *Ibid.*, p. 262, and notes. Paris, *Chronica Majora*, IV, 579–580.

504. *CCR, 1242–47*, p. 543.

505. *CCR, 1247–51*, pp. 221–222.

506. *CCR, 1251–53*, pp. 224, 226.

The king criticized both the method of such inquests and the topics of investigation.

Apparently, Grosseteste's enthusiasm was contagious, because his example was imitated in 1251 in an inquiry into the lives of the clergy and laity of the diocese of Coventry and Lichfield.[507] In 1253, the year of the bishop's death, the gravamina compiled at a provincial council of Canterbury meeting at London, condemned royal interference with the exercise by the prelates of their corrective jurisdiction over clergy and laity.[508] Subsequently, Archbishop Boniface's legislation repeated the church's denunciation.[509] That the crown continued in Edward I's reign to curtail the exercise of ecclesiastical jurisdiction over the laity and to interfere with the church's use of the inquest is revealed by an article of the gravamina of 1285, complaining against the restriction of the church to matrimonial and testamentary pleas and the inability of the ecclesiastical courts to decide explicitly spiritual matters such as parochial boundaries *sine fidedigno testimonio laycorum*.[510] After the crisis which produced *Circumspecte agatis* the state did not continue its policy of firm opposition to the use of the inquest of laymen.

More significant, perhaps, was the tendency of the bishops and archdeacons to concentrate during their visitations on the correction of religious houses and the reform of the parish clergy rather than on disciplining the laity. During the latter part of the thirteenth century and the fourteenth century bishops and archdeacons continued to visit their respective districts and to receive the testimony of sworn parishioners—*iurati, testes synodales*, or *fidedigni*.[511] But the fact that the parishes did not pay procurations and the difficulties connected with such inquiries certainly did not encourage prelates to imitate Grosseteste. It would appear that Bishop John Trefnant of Hereford's visitation of the clergy and laity of his diocese in 1397 and his extensive use of the jury to obtain evidence of moral and spiritual shortcomings were rather exceptional in England in the later middle ages.[512] At least, after 1285 there is no

507. Contained in the Annals of Burton, *Annales Monastici*, ed. H. R. Luard, RS, 5 vols. (London, 1864–69), I, 296–298.

508. *Councils & Synods*, p. 470 (article 8). See the articles of inquiry in Annals of Burton, *Annales Monastici*, I, 307–310.

509. *Councils & Synods*, pp. 580 (canon 12 of 1258); 678–679 (canon 14 of 1261).

510. *Ibid.*, p. 971 (article 11).

511. See the citations from episcopal registers in *ibid.*, p. 262, notes 5, 6.

512. A. T. Bannister, "Visitation Returns of the Diocese of Hereford in 1397," *EHR*, XLIV (1929), 279–289, 444–453; XLV (1930), 92–101, 444–463.

evidence that the church's use of the sworn inquest was still a bone of contention between the two jurisdictions.

Perjury in the courts was an annoying problem confronting both jurisdictions and one which impeded the rendering of both kinds of justice. The crown and the church shared responsibility for punishing false accusations and were prepared to cooperate to stamp out this particular crime. The second Statute of Westminster (1285) decreed a year's imprisonment as the punishment for appealing falsely against a person to the king's courts.[513] On the other hand, the crown admitted the spiritual nature of perjury and allowed the church to punish it by declaring the excommunication of perjurers.[514] As in the case of all major crimes, absolution was reserved to the bishop.[515] In such efforts the church had the full support of the state. In 1334, for example, Edward III wrote to the bishops asking them to pronounce sentences of excommunication against persons who perjured themselves or who made false accusations in the king's courts.[516] This letter had its origin in a petition of the Commons presented in the Parliament at York during Lent of 1334, which requested the king to enact further safeguards against the crime.[517] The king's justices, said the reply to the petition, were to receive the indictment of such persons. The mandates mentioned above were dispatched to the bishops for their action. In the battle against perjury as in the common struggle with heretics the royal and ecclesiastical jurisdictions assisted each other.

Whenever the church's jurisdiction over false swearing seemed, however, to threaten the integrity or the operation of royal justice the crown could be expected to intervene. This occasionally happened in the trial and punishment of defamation—a type of case which the church long claimed for itself.[518] A case at Canterbury from the end of the thirteenth century shows how private persons could use the plea of defamation to protect themselves against being accused of crimes in secular courts or retaliate against their accusers.[519] A certain rector brought a charge of

---

513. *SR*, I, 81.   514. *Councils & Synods*, pp. 133, 172, 356, 455, 1063, 1067.

515. *Ibid.*, pp. 33, 76–77, 133, 151, 172, 192–193, 214, 231, 442, 455, 630.

516. *Register of J. Grandisson*, I, 53–54.

517. *Rot. Parl. Inediti*, p. 234.

518. *SR*, I, 171; *Placita Parliamentaria*, p. 202. See also Van Vechten Veeder, "The History of the Law of Defamation," *Select Essays in Anglo-American Legal History*, III, 446–473. For examples of manorial jurisdiction, see under "Slander" in the indices to *The Court Baron*, ed. Maitland and Baildon, and *Select Pleas in Manorial and other Seignorial Courts*, ed. F. W. Maitland, SS (London, 1889).

519. Library of Dean and Chapter, Canterbury, *Sede Vacante* Scrapbook 3, fol. 184.

defamation against another man for accusing him of having committed homicide. Unjust accusation of another was a crime for which the defendant had suffered excommunication *ipso facto* according to the general sentences of excommunication that were periodically published.[520] Ultimately the false accuser was absolved by the archbishop's commissary. In such ways, of course, wrongdoers could use the church courts to escape from punishment in the king's courts, and the crown realized this danger. The effect of the misuse of the church's jurisdiction over defamation would have been to interfere with the functioning of royal courts and to place disabilities upon persons giving testimony there. In 1327 a statute gave a writ of prohibition against persons suing in ecclesiastical courts for the punishment of others who had procured their indictment for secular crimes in the royal courts.[521] This legislation was based upon a petition brought forward in the name of the sheriffs and other royal ministers, and obviously this problem had recently been a serious one.[522] The prohibition against trying a case of defamation in a church court, when the intent was punitive or when it was directed against persons testifying in royal courts, had existed since the latter part of Henry III's reign.[523] It was available to prevent this kind of abuse of ecclesiastical jurisdiction. In 1349, for instance, the bishop of Hereford was forbidden to hear a plea brought by the archdeacon of Shropshire against a certain parson, who had procured the archdeacon's indictment for homicide by exerting his influence with the coroner's jury.[524] It is likely that others both before and after saw the advantage of using ecclesiastical jurisdiction in this way.[525] Although the state abandoned defamation to the church until the sixteenth century,[526] it continued to take a dim view of the use of this competence to challenge or defeat criminal accusations in its courts.

Both jurisdictions were troubled by the maddening and insoluble problem of getting people to appear in court or, after their appearance, of

520. Constitution 49 of Stephen Langton, in *Councils & Synods*, p. 33; and the sentences of Pecham at Reading and Lambeth, in *ibid.*, pp. 849 (No. 3), 906 (No. 3).

521. *SR*, I, 256.

522. *Rot. Parl.*, II, 9, 11.

523. Flahiff, "Writ of Prohibition (i)," p. 281.

524. *Registrum Johannis de Trilleck, Episcopi Herefordensis, A.D. MCCCXLIV–MCCCLXI*, ed. J. H. Parry, CYS (London, 1912), pp. 323–324.

525. Woodcock, *Medieval Ecclesiastical Courts*, p. 89.

526. There are many examples of pleas of defamation in the printed ecclesiastical court records of the fifteenth and sixteenth centuries. See Slater, "Records of the Court of Arches," p. 150; Emmison noted the same point in his description of the "Act Book of the Archdeacon of Huntingdon's Court," p. 28.

forcing them to satisfy judgments against them. The church relied heavily on the state to make its spiritual sanctions more persuasive, whereas the crown tended to view the bishops as it would any other royal minister when it was attempting to force clerics to appear in its courts or collect monies from them. The royal plea rolls and Year Books cite the seemingly endless process of exacting pledges and of attaching and distraining laymen to appear before the king's justices. When the defendant was a cleric, with no lay fee to seize, then the crown looked to the bishop for the necessary assistance. The king ordered the bishop to levy a fine from the properties of a cleric who owed money to the crown or who had recognized a debt by registering it in chancery. The crown commanded the bishops to distrain clerks who had been amerced in the royal courts or to force them to appear there. The episcopal registers of the thirteenth and fourteenth centuries are filled with examples of such royal writs—*venire facias, levari facias, distringas,* and *fieri facias*—commanding the prelates to exact fines from their diocesan clergy, to force them to appear in a royal court, or to compel them to do any number of things at the behest of the king.[527] Failing to satisfy the king's command, the bishop himself could be distrained and cited to appear in the royal court.[528]

The state defended such procedures as customary and as required for the enforcement of law and justice.[529] In the reigns of Henry III and Edward I the bishops repeatedly denounced this practice of holding them responsible for their diocesan clergy.[530] The church was especially outraged when it was called to levy an amercement in a case that properly belonged to the church courts.[531] The bishops also complained about the requirement that they appear personally in the royal courts rather than by attorney, as they said was their privilege;[532] and they insisted upon their immunity from such forms of coercion.[533] Although the bishops defended their right to distrain the diocesan clergy when it suited their

527. See *Register of J. Romeyn,* I, 17–18, where there is the note: "Quod quidem mandatum statim officiali nostro direximus exequendum;" also Haines, *Administration of the Diocese of Worcester,* pp. 330–331; Churchill, *Canterbury Administration,* I, 520–521.

528. *Registrum Palatinum Dunelmense,* II, 858–859; *YB 13–14 Edward III,* p. 75; *YB 16 Edward III [Part I],* ed. L. O. Pike, RS (London, 1896), p. 99.

529. See the royal reply to the clerical grievances, in *Councils & Synods,* p. 689 (article 8 of the gravamina of 1261).

530. *Ibid.,* pp. 469–470 (article 2 of 1253); 470 (article 4 of 1253); 538 (article 8 of proposals of 1257); 541 (article 8 of grievances of 1257); 880–881 (article 12 of 1280); 972 (article 16 of 1285); 1214 (article 22 of 1300/1301), etc.

531. *Ibid.,* pp. 538 (article 9 of 1257); 689 (article 8 of grievances of 1261).

532. *Ibid.,* pp. 549 (article 39 of 1257); 582 (chapter 18 of canons of 1258).

533. *Ibid.,* pp. 579 (canon 10 of 1258); 677 (canon 10 of 1261).

own purposes or the needs of their own courts, they vehemently condemned being forced to do so by the state. In Edward I's reign it would seem that laymen were themselves seizing or sequestering the properties of clerics, sometimes with undue haste after an initial citation and sometimes with no attention as to whether they were occupying temporal or spiritual properties.[534] The bishops opposed such conduct by secular officials, and managed to obtain relief from obvious abuses. Both Edward I and Edward II promised that the goods of clerics would not be seized on the king's highways nor would the "ancient fees" or glebe-land of the church be distrained, but that sequestrations would be limited to recently acquired properties of the clergy.[535] The prelates did not succeed in freeing themselves from the responsibilities imposed upon them by the crown; and in the vast majority of cases the bishops satisfied the royal demands.[536] This is indicated by their request for security from the lesser clergy against the latter's default,[537] by inquiries into the execution of royal writs by their subordinates,[538] and by the punishment which they inflicted on negligent officials.[539]

IX. SOME CONCLUSIONS

Jurisdictional conflict in England was limited, specific, and pragmatic—a steady but gentle pressure by the king's courts on those of the church. Its

534. *Ibid.*, pp. 971 (article 12 of 1285); 1138 (article 1 of 1295); 1142 (article 23 of 1295); 1145 (article 40 of 1295).

535. *Ibid.*, pp. 1216–1217 (reply to article 31 of grievances of 1300/1301); *SR*, I, 172.

536. Bishop John Drokensford of Bath and Wells in 1323 asserted that this was the custom of the realm. See *Register of John de Drokensford, Bishop of Bath and Wells, A.D. 1309–1329*, ed. Bishop Hobhouse, Somerset Record Society (London, 1887), p. 226. A commission of 1321 specified the execution of royal writs in "omnia et singula que ... natura exigit:" *Register of Thomas de Cobham, Bishop of Worcester, 1317–1327*, ed. E. H. Pearce, Worcestershire Historical Society (London, 1930), p. 28.

537. Clerks were forced to swear to keep the bishop harmless in the event of their default: *Register of William de Geynesburgh, Bishop of Worcester, 1308–1313*, ed. R. A. Wilson, Worcestershire Historical Society (London, 1927), p. 219. Defaulting clerks could be cited before the bishops on charges of perjury, for which see *Registrum Simonis de Gandavo, Diocesis Saresbiriensis, A.D. 1297–1315*, ed. C. T. Flower and M. C. B. Dawes, CYS, 2 vols. (Oxford, 1914–33), I, 88–89.

538. Archbishop Thomas Corbridge of York ordered an inquiry concerning those deans who neglected to sequestrate the goods of clerics in accordance with royal writs "per quod archiepiscopus incurrit periculum aliquando." See *Register of Thomas Corbridge, Lord Archbishop of York, 1300–1304*, ed. A. Hamilton Thompson, Surtees Society, 2 parts (London, 1925), I, 100–101.

539. *Registrum Henry Woodlock, Diocesis Wintoniensis, 1305–1316*, ed. A. W. Goodman, CYS, 2 vols. (Oxford, 1938–40), I, 57–58. Bishop Woodlock of Winchester threatens on one occasion to levy the sum from the archdeacon's revenues.

instigators and participants were private persons, almost never motivated by ideological considerations. Self-interest and temporary advantage, rather than the claims of allegiance or profession, determined its course and character. Exceptions to the competence of one court or another were usual ways for avoiding an unwelcome judgment or defeating an action brought by another party. Clerks and laymen alike purchased the royal prohibitions which were the major instrument for opposing ecclesiastical justice. And there was very little theorizing on either side. The eccentric views of an Occam or a Wycliffe never constituted official policy of the crown.[540] On the other hand, after Grosseteste, Pecham, and Winchelsey, none of the leaders of the English clergy, with the possible exception of Stratford, argued the high church position with any eloquence or conviction. There were few crises and no great victories or defeats.

In spite of restrictive statutes, occasional quips from royal judges, and the grievances against which the clergy complained, the crown showed a great willingness to tolerate the activities of the church courts within areas defined by the king's justice. The spiritual nature of many pleas was readily admitted. The disciplinary authority of the bishops over the lesser clergy was challenged only when royal rights were jeopardized as in the case of the king's own servants. The jurisdiction of the church over the morals of the laity was criticized briefly on one occasion, but that was the result of the energy and enthusiasm of a small group of clerical reformers. Vast areas of justice never figured in the conflict and were by common consent reserved to one court or the other. But the attitude of the secular power often went beyond mere tolerance to open support and encouragement; and in several instances the crown sought the advice or assistance of the church or lent its coercive powers to the enforcement of ecclesiastical decisions.

The advantage always lay with the crown. Whenever it seemed that the activities of the church courts might defeat a judgment of the royal courts or contradict a belief of the common law, then the crown could be expected to intervene. Acting independently or at the request of a private person, the royal courts and chancery drew the lines separating the two jurisdictions. Grosseteste never succeeded in establishing in practice his principle of the superiority of spiritual justice to temporal or of the

540. For the views of Occam see *Opera Politica*, ed. J. G. Sikes *et al.*, 3 vols. (Manchester, 1940), I, 283–284, and *Monarchiae S. Romani Imperii, sive Tractatus de Jurisdictione Imperii Regia & Pontificia seu Sacerdotali . . .*, ed. M. Goldast, 3 vols. (Frankfurt, 1668), I, 14. For Wycliffe's views see *Tractatus de Officio Regis*, ed. A. W. Pollard and C. Sayle (London, 1887), pp. 20, 66, 119 ff., 166, 169, 204; also the comments of McFarlane, *John Wycliffe*, pp. 59–62, 92–95.

absolute independence of the church from secular interference. During most of the thirteenth and fourteenth centuries the higher clergy had to focus their efforts on preventing the abuse of this discretionary power by assuring that consultations would be available to quash unjust prohibitions or that the crown would exercise care in granting prohibitions in the first place. The limits of both conflict and cooperation in the jurisdictional sphere were determined by the attitudes and actions of the royal courts.

The several areas of jurisdictional rivalry reveal the nature of the conflict and the reasons for it. Sometimes it was the product of the doubt and uncertainty surrounding a particular type of case, which, depending on one's point of view, might seem to belong to one jurisdiction or the other. The same confusion of terms which led William Stubbs to speak of the jurisdiction of the ecclesiastical courts over secular pleas and of the jurisdiction of lay courts over spiritual ones also beset the medieval mind when it tried to draw a clear division between the two jurisdictions.[541] At other times controversy resulted from the greater attractiveness of one court system, which drew litigants to it despite the formal pretensions and claims of the rival. And, further, jurisdictional conflict sometimes resulted from procedural requirements which obliged the two powers to cooperate but often generated friction and resentment in the process.

One of the most important areas of jurisdictional conflict, both in terms of the legal innovations which were stimulated and its material significance for state and church, was that concerning the ecclesiastical benefice. The benefice was very early equated with real property in the minds of the common lawyers; and during the thirteenth and fourteenth centuries every effort was made to defend the exclusive competence of the king's courts over the right to or the possession of advowson. The success of these efforts resulted not only from the existence of royal prohibitions against trying cases of patronage in the church courts, but also from the ingenuity of the crown in devising and popularizing alternative actions available in its own courts. The effect of these innovations was to defeat the claim of the church to decide cases of patronage and also to restrict severely its right to judge cases between presentees to the same benefice and to force the bishops to exercise their powers of admission and in-stitution with an eye to the expectations of the king's courts. The ex-pansion of the common law touching advowson even intruded royal power into the administrative and entirely spiritual activities of the

541. W. Stubbs, *The Constitutional History of England in its Origin and Development*, 3 vols. (Oxford, 1875–78), III, 341.

church. The king's judges realized that the integrity of royal judgments on pleas of advowson depended on their ability to enforce such decisions on the bishops who were responsible for bestowing benefices on their holders. Consequently, chancery developed several administrative and judicial devices which aimed at forcing compliance with the judgments of the king's courts. Relations between the jurisdictions were aggravated by the growth of papal power, but the king's courts were prepared to cope with any challenge to their exclusive competence over advowson, when they were prompted to do so, whether it came from abroad or arose at home.

The success of the royal courts in forcing the church to withdraw from certain jurisdictional areas is shown by the firm establishment of royal competence over pleas of lay fee, including free alms. Rather early in the thirteenth century the resourcefulness of the common law and the royal writs of prohibition *de laico feodo* had abolished ecclesiastical jurisdiction over real property, even when such properties were considered to be "spiritualities" by canonical opinion. Lay fee was not, therefore, a prominent topic of controversy during most of the thirteenth and fourteenth centuries. The little influence which the church continued to exert in this direction was dependent upon its moral competence in cases of matrimony and testament. To counter this influence, which threatened to contravene sacred English custom, the king's courts devised a procedure to limit the necessity for relying on the ecclesiastical courts in those cases when the descent of real property would have been conditioned by the decisions of the church on pleas of bastardy. The use of the jury was a handy device available to the royal courts and one which was occasionally used in other aspects of the jurisdictional conflict to restrict the influence of canonical opinion on the English secular courts.

Ideology, good example, and common sense recommended the co-operation of the two jurisdictions in those areas where they touched or shared responsibility. Throughout the later middle ages in England the jurisdictions of church and state cooperated in certain time-honored ways in the realization of certain traditional goals and ideals. The best example of this spirit at work is provided by the history of excommunication and caption. In most cases the secular power was prepared to respect the spiritual sanctions declared by the clergy and to assist the church in enforcing these by arresting and imprisoning recalcitrant sinners. The crown and its agents withheld such assistance only in those cases when the rights of the king, the integrity of royal judgments, or the maintenance of law and order required it. Such reluctance never seemed called for in the case of the repression of heresy, wherein both powers combined to defend the faith. On a day-to-day level the royal courts displayed their willingness to recognize and respect the proper competence of ecclesiastical courts by sending to the bishops for the certification of testaments, marriage contracts, the qualifications of presentees to benefices, and, after some discussion, pleas of bastardy. Yet the royal judges always insisted on maintaining the independence of the king's justice from the decisions of the church and claimed the right both to scrutinize such information and to reject it if unsuited to their purposes or convictions.

The church courts were always on unsure grounds when they attempted to try cases involving chattels and movables, especially when laymen were the defendants. The prohibition of lay chattels and debt was available against them, and this remained a popular means for defending royal jurisdiction throughout this period. Occasionally it was used to intrude into areas ostensibly spiritual in nature, such as cases of tithes, pensions, testaments, breach of faith, and even the imposition of penance. On the other hand, the ecclesiastical courts continued to exercise a wide competence over chattels by virtue of the ingenuity of canon law and the attractiveness of its courts for a large number of suitors. The willingness of the church courts to enforce verbal contracts drew many suitors on cases of petty debt to the bishops and archdeacons even after the royal courts had made provisions for expanding their offerings by adding actions on trespass, annuity, and testamentary debt. The belated development of the common law enabling it to cope with the emergence of the testamentary executor as the principle agent of the English will did not entail the enlargement of its notion of debt, which would have been necessary if the king's courts were ever to oust the church courts from an area over which they had long held a monopoly.

Sometimes jurisdictional controversy was the result of competing laws or rival claims to try the same kind of case. Early in the thirteenth century both jurisdictions were still trying pleas of patronage, and the church courts, although they lost this contest, never formally admitted the king's right to exclusive competence in this area of law. On the other hand, the conflict was frequently of a procedural rather than a substantive nature. This fact is illustrated by the relations of the two jurisdictions in respect to the enforcement of caption, but more vividly, perhaps, in the treatment of criminous clerks. The king's courts never claimed the right to judge felonious clerks in the age following Becket nor did they attempt to inflict secular punishments on such criminals after their conviction by the church. Despite the cooperation and restraint which characterized the crown's attitude toward criminous clerks, the gravamina from the thirteenth and fourteenth centuries almost invariably complain of infractions of the principle of benefit of clergy. Very often such violations were merely the result of local acts of vengeance or vindictiveness. At other times, however, they were the product of procedural difficulties which neither power condoned or caused. The rights of particular criminals, such as traitors, bigamists, outlaws, or sanctuary-seekers, were often in doubt; and royal judges and bailiffs were sometimes imposing swift justice without attention to supposed rights. In the second half of the fourteenth century the needs of law enforcement were evidently leading to a rash of individual violations of benefit of clergy, although at no time during the thirteenth and fourteenth centuries did the secular power, even when it was prompted to do so, ever show the desire to renounce the responsibilities imposed on it.

The superiority of the crown in the jurisdictional conflict is clearly shown by its success in subjecting the church courts to scrutiny and correction. Whereas the king insisted on the absolute immunity of his judges and officials from ecclesiastical interference, he allowed his courts to accept charges of oppression, corruption, and wrongdoing made by private persons against ecclesiastical judges. At times, as in the reigns of Edward I and Edward III, this could amount almost to a persecution of the Courts Christian. The church was, in short, expected to comply with secular standards of propriety and right, and the church courts could be punished for not doing so.

Royal opposition to the jurisdictional pretensions of the church was fiercest when the king's rights themselves were involved and when the monarch was an especially able and energetic ruler. Consequently, the conflict of the two jurisdictions was most acute during the reigns of Henry III and Edward I. It was during this period that, as a result of the expansion and refinement of the common law and the activities of the king's courts, the frontier between the two jurisdictions was most clearly defined. This process of definition and distinction sometimes left a jurisdictional area to be shared between them; at other times the crown forced the church to retreat; and in some instances the common law acceded to the pretensions of the church courts. At the same time when the common lawyers and royal judges were expanding their ambitions and activities they were also enforcing definite restrictions on that one coherent body of law which could possibly pose a challenge to themselves. Despite the gravamina and occasional royal concessions the bishops were unable to withstand the advance of royal law or its intrusion, when it was willing or able, into the precincts of ecclesiastical justice. The fourteenth century witnessed the culmination of this process which followed paths marked out generations before, leaving to the English church courts of the pre-Reformation era a limited but still important sphere of authority now seldom challenged.

THE ENGLISH PREPARATIONS BEFORE THE TREATY OF ARRAS: A NEW INTERPRETATION OF SIR JOHN FASTOLF'S "REPORT," SEPTEMBER, 1435

Reginald Brill

Beaver College

THE ENGLISH PREPARATIONS BEFORE THE TREATY OF ARRAS: A NEW INTERPRETATION OF SIR JOHN FASTOLF'S "REPORT," SEPTEMBER, 1435*

At some time in early September, 1435, Sir John Fastolf, master of the household to John of Lancaster, duke of Bedford, submitted a lengthy and detailed staff memorandum to the French council of Henry VI, then sitting at Rouen, capital of English Normandy. In this well-known "Report upon the Management of the War upon the Conclusion of the Treaty of Arras,"[1] Fastolf summarized certain political, strategic, and tactical precepts and opinions. This paper was written in Sir John's official capacity as Bedford's senior military planner and consultant. Bedford's own position at the time was a viceregal one as lieutenant and governor of France and Normandy for the hapless King Henry of England. The document is therefore regarded by most historians to be at least a semiofficial statement by Bedford's government of its present position and future plans at a vital stage in the later Hundred Years' War. The document itself states that the negotiations of the French, English, and Burgundian plenipotentiaries at Arras had already reached that point at which the Valois had made his final offer, "to whyche peas fynalle and demandes the ambassyatours of the said Regent of France,[2] Johne, duc of Bedford, yn the behalf of England, yn no wise wold graunt or

* An abbreviated version of this article was presented in a paper at the Midwest Medieval History Conference at the University of Cincinnati in November, 1968.

1. The entire report by Sir John Fastolf is located in William of Worcester, *Collections Respecting the Wars of the English in France and Normandy*, ed. and published by Rev. J. Stevenson in his, *Letters and Papers Illustrative of the Wars of the English in France*, Rolls Series, 2 vols. (London, 1861–64), Vol. II, Part II, pp. 575–585; hereafter cited as Stevenson, *Letters and Papers.*

2. The title "Regent of France," used here for Bedford in 1435, is an odd and unexplained error on Fastolf's part, perhaps attributable to haste or habit of long standing. Bedford's regency of France had, of course, ended with Henry VI's coronation as "King Henry II" of France in Paris on December 16, 1431. Bedford's lieutenancy dated from his sovereign's coming of legal age in his French dominions in December, 1431.

condescend."[3] The fact that Fastolf's report was written *after* the English
rejection of the French terms serves as the most important piece of internal
evidence in dating this document.[4]

A political and diplomatic *démarche* was thus about to take place which
would at the very least deprive the English of their chief ally against the
Valois enemy and rob the dual monarchy of "Henry VI and II" of its
remaining practical significance. Without the Burgundian alliance, the
English king's claim to political supremacy over all of France would become mere pretense. The Fastolf report, written with these events and
considerations clearly in mind, is therefore generally accepted by scholars
as a most important contemporary source for this period. The report gives
a careful and informed estimate of the English military and political
situation in the now-certain event of the duke of Burgundy's return to the
Valois allegiance he had cast off by the Treaty of Troyes in 1420. The
report has often been utilized by modern students of this period,[5] especially
since there are so few contemporary English documents dealing with the
progress and future of the war. As the date and contents of the document
are directly related to the results of the congress, Fastolf's report has
previously been employed by historians as a source for evaluating the
political and diplomatic impact of the treaty upon the future English
position in France. These scholars have contended that the report was

3. Stevenson, *Letters and Papers*, Vol. II, 575.

4. On September 1, 1435, John Kemp, archbishop of York, acting in his capacity as
the chief spokesman for Henry VI, rejected the French offer. Kemp then announced that
the conference was at an end as far as the English were concerned, although Henry's
envoys did not leave Arras until September 6. Since the Fastolf report takes this rejection
into account, it must have been written at some point between September 1 and September
21, on which latter date the treaty was finally engrossed by Burgundy. See Sir J. H.
Ramsay, *Lancaster and York: A Century of English History (1399–1485)*, 2 vols. (Oxford,
1892), I, 471–474. The wording of the report, as quoted above, almost certainly places its
composition before September 14, 1435, on which date Bedford himself died, since he is
not called "late Regent." For Bedford's death, see *ibid.*, I, 474.

5. The Fastolf report is discussed by almost all of the main secondary sources per-
taining to the later period of the Hundred Years' War. See, e.g., E. F. Jacob, *The Fifteenth
Century: 1399–1485*, Oxford History of England, VI (Oxford, 1961), 263; E. Perroy, *The
Hundred Years War*, trans. by W. B. Wells (London, 1951), p. 295; Sir C. W. C. Oman, *The
History of England from the Accession of Richard II to the Death of Richard III*, Vol. IV of the
Political History of England in Twelve Volumes, ed. W. Hunt and R. L. Poole (London, 1910),
p. 323; Ramsay, *Lancaster and York*, I, 471 and n. 4; G. du Fresne de Beaucourt, *Histoire
de Charles VII*, Vol. II of 6 vols. (Paris, 1882), pp. 55–56 and notes; E. C. Williams, *My
Lord of Bedford, 1389–1435* (Oxford, 1964), p. 251; J. R. Lander, *The Wars of the Roses*
(London, 1965), pp. 36–37; G. A. Holmes, *The Later Middle Ages, 1272–1485* (London,
1962), p. 207.

written as a direct reaction to the treaty negotiations. They have used Fastolf's military proposals as evidence of panic and an unrealistic refusal on the part of the English government to face the overwhelming disaster which had overtaken them.[6]

Although Fastolf's report is itself primarily a military document, it has heretofore been used as evidence for political and diplomatic hypotheses. It is the purpose of the present study to investigate the report's precepts and opinions from its intended military viewpoint as opposed to previous political and diplomatic interpretations. This military frame of reference and the use of the report as evidence for certain strategical hypotheses will thus form the basis of a reinterpretation of this document. It is also hoped that this new approach to the Fastolf report will serve as a useful contribution to the larger study of the over-all English position at the time of the Burgundian withdrawal. The basic framework of this paper, however, will remain within the spheres of military and military-institutional history and will concern itself with the English military and financial preparations *before* the Treaty of Arras.

Such a study, while interesting in its own right, may also be of some value in considering one of the primary historical problems of this period in later medieval history: the failure of the Valois state of 1435 and the years immediately succeeding to muster sufficient political, financial, and therefore military strength to become the master of its own territory once again. Despite the very costly political and diplomatic victory of Arras, fifteen years elapsed before the kingdom of France was able to complete the conquest of the hard-core, English-occupied territories which had been lost by the Valois during the terrible years of princely strife and central weakness. Normandy and its surrounding territories remained English until 1449–1450. Nor was the government of Charles VII able to make more than a minimal impression on the English duchy of Guienne, a Plantagenet holding since 1154, until after the final fall of Normandy. The issue in the south remained undecided until 1453. It can therefore be stated that the Treaty of Arras generated almost no immediate military impact.

France's failure to drive the English from her soil immediately after Arras did have consequences, however, which were vitally important to the future of French history and indeed to that of early modern western Europe. France was unable to reconquer Normandy and the vital Seine

6. See, among others using the report in this manner, Ramsay, *Lancaster and York*, I, 471 and n. 4; Lander, *The Wars of the Roses*, p. 37; Jacob, *The Fifteenth Century*, p. 263; Perroy, *The Hundred Years War*, p. 295.

basin which splits that province without a major shift in her military and financial structure. She was therefore forced to undergo certain decisive changes from 1439 onwards. Among these steps were to be numbered the adoption of direct royal payment of regular army forces, the famous *gens d'Ordonnances* and the lesser formations which supported them, and the institution of permanent taxes, such as the taille, which would enable the French king to maintain an army without the approval of the various estates and without regard to noble and princely opposition. These forces and monies, along with a purely royal force of guns and gunners under the brothers Bureau and others, were to be the final, decisive weight in clearing the English from Normandy and Guienne. The genesis of these forces, with all of the consequences for France and Europe which lay in their creation, had its roots in the glaringly apparent military inadequacy of the Valois state following the Treaty of Arras.

The English were able to prevent a complete French victory because they had already taken stock of their own strong points and anticipated the Valois weaknesses in every important respect.[7] The results of this analysis can be seen in the Fastolf report, which will be studied here as a carefully drawn position or status paper setting forth strategic and tactical concepts long under consideration. It will also be seen that these plans and precepts had already been subjected to the ultimate—and successful—test of field operations. It is proposed, therefore, that the Fastolf report be interpreted as the single military document which permits us to understand the English preparations before Arras. The adoption of a new English strategy, in turn, would eventually result in the French military failure of the years immediately following the treaty. This English foresightedness was therefore the underlying cause of the drastic institutional and political changes described above.

A detailed examination of the Fastolf report immediately makes clear Fastolf's first objective in composing the paper. Since it was written after the final French offer at the Congress of Arras already had been rejected, the report had to justify that grave political decision from the viewpoint of the English government and Bedford's French council at Rouen. The early sections of the report, therefore, consist of a detailed explanation or rationalization of that decision. This portion of the report is of secondary concern to the present study, however, and can only be summarized briefly here.

In the first of his substantive paragraphs, Fastolf sets forth the official English position on Henry VI's claim to the French throne. How can the

7. See below, pp. 220–222.

an unacceptable future of very heavy losses, arising from battle itself, as well as from disease and desertion.[16]

Since these three factors were the primary causes of manpower attrition in medieval warfare and since the proper utilization of the field forces was the pivotal point of the new strategic and tactical proposals that Sir John was about to make, the causes of these losses must be eliminated at once. Before advancing a solution to the problem Sir John makes clear his opinion of what can be expected if his suggestions are not implemented. Continued offensive and siege warfare could only end in a slow, painful, and completely pointless sapping of England's power to maintain her armies in northern France. The final result of playing into the hands of the enemy by conducting these types of operations, says Fastolf, can be nothing but defeat, an ultimate victory for the Valois through English attrition and exhaustion. Taking note of the smaller manpower reserves available for the English army and of the fact that the fighting must take place in France, at a distance from England's base and in the presence of an unfriendly native population, Sir John concludes that the heavy losses of a siege-oriented strategy can only be made good by a continuous new supply of short-term and thus inefficient soldiers from England. Since these troops will in turn be depleted in a short time, this strategy will only result in the English army sinking ever more deeply into a bottomless pit of loss and final defeat because of the superior military resources available to the enemy.[17]

Rather than accept this obsolete strategy and its tactical implications, Sir John now proposes a totally different method of operation. His avowed purpose is to reverse the impact of this attrition and to bring the weight of military and financial exhaustion down upon the still-shaky governmental structure headed by Charles VII of France. It is in the realm of the available French military strength, reflecting as it did the total capabilities of the Valois regime, that Fastolf finds tangible weaknesses of royal power and controlling authority. If the English battle plan can be shaped to take advantage of those weaknesses, the true objective of continuing the war can be gained. Normandy and the heart of the English-occupied territories in northern France can be held, says Fastolf, because France is not strong enough to reconquer them. To force this military standoff, Sir John now proposes a carefully considered and practicable military scheme. At its heart lie two primary concepts, both of which are of the utmost importance to the present study. First, he advises the adoption of a basically defensive strategy, its objective the total retention of the

16. *Ibid.*   17. *Ibid.*

English possessions in the north. From a tactical viewpoint, the proposed strategy must depend on mobility, shock, timing, and the maximum use of the successful counterattack. Secondly, Fastolf points out the necessity of a new and highly efficient, long-service professional army. The paragraphs which follow are therefore the core of the report and the proposals contained therein form the basis of this document's importance in the larger spheres of late medieval and European history.[18]

Beginning with his basic premise of a defensive strategy, Fastolf makes it clear that he proposes to wear out the French army and the state which supports it by forcing the Valois armies into a series of abortive thrusts against a well-defined English frontier perimeter. The delineation of this geographical borderland, along with the tactical scheme designed to protect it from French conquest, forms the first portion of Fastolf's detailed military proposal. No longer must the English army attempt to protect each and every territorial foothold still in their control after the shock of Joan of Arc's campaigns. Such holdings would be defended only if their retention served the over-all purpose of protecting Normandy and its neighboring districts.

For this reason, Sir John at once specifies by name these border zones which must be dominated and controlled if the ring of protection was indeed to be formed and if it was to become a viable defensive area. From the northern boundary of Normandy, where the waters of the Somme and its estuary marked the dividing line with Burgundian Picardy, around through the territories lying between Normandy and the Isle de France to the southern frontier of the duchy in Maine and the Breton marches, a rough bloc of primary defensive areas is set forth by the report. These areas form, in sum, a zone which Sir John feels must be dominated at all times by the English army. These districts, moving in a clockwise direction from the Somme around to the frontier with the duchy of Brittany, are Picardy, Artois, Vermandois, Lannoy, Valois, and those areas of ducal Burgundy which lay dangerously close to Paris and the Seine Valley, the Isle de France itself, Maine, and the Breton marches. Since the English army was far too small to occupy any such vast area in force, Sir John immediately makes it clear that he merely has in mind the simpler and more feasible task of denying the Valois the use of these districts as staging and supply areas for a major offensive against Normandy. Without trying to hold these provinces in permanent subjection, the English army would simply sweep them clear of anything which might be useful to an enemy trying to base his own operations within these specified frontier zones.

18. *Ibid.*, pp. 579–580.

For this reason, Sir John continues, the treatment of these areas must be extremely harsh, but the grounds of this policy were clear military and strategic necessity, not purposeless and vengeful terror or aimless destructiveness. English forces were to sweep through these areas, according to Fastolf's proposal, "brennyng and destruynge alle the lande as thei pas, bothe hous, corne, veignes, and alle treis that beren fryte for mannys sustenaunce, and alle bestaile that may not be dryven, to be destroiede; and that that may welle be dryven and spared . . . to be dryven into Normandie, to Paris, and to other places of the kingis obeissaunce. . . ."[19] "For it is thoughte," Sir John's justification pursues, "that the traitours and rebellis must nedis have anothere manere of werre. . . ."[20] No longer would these areas support French troops for operations of a sustained nature. Furthermore, Fastolf implies, the careful spoliation of these areas would, in effect, make the Norman heartland and its immediate environs safe from all major attacks. The French state was too weak from both the military and financial-political standpoints to mount a major offensive against Normandy if it was deprived of nearby supply and staging points.

The specific tactical implementation of Sir John's proposal required the constant availability of two highly professional columns of English cavalry—men-at-arms and mounted archers—each of them under the command of a picked, veteran "captain," or field commander. The two mounted columns would each be made up of troopers contracted to serve on a year-round, permanent basis rather than for the campaign-duration or short-term service then customary in both the English and French armies.[21] Seven hundred fifty picked "spears," the mounted and armored men-at-arms who would make up the core of each column, would be reinforced by at least an equal number of mounted archers and the captain of each force would be a man well trained to make the most effective use of such balance and power.[22] Each column would go into the field from either of the main English bases in the northern sector, Calais in the marches of Flanders or Le Crotoy on the Somme, sweep toward the east and south in the indicated clockwise direction and be available for instant action in any portion of the frontier zone set forth by Sir John. In addition, either column could quickly and easily reinforce the other in the case of a large-scale attack by the Valois armies. Both columns were to remain in action and on the move without regard for the seasons or the weather, a reversal of the usual medieval tactical doctrine which planned

19. *Ibid.*, p. 580.   20. *Ibid.*
21. *Ibid.*, p. 581.   22. *Ibid.*

for campaigning only in the few months of dry ground and summer weather.[23]

The mobile columns would also be well suited, according to Sir John, for another mission of vitally important politico-military persuasion. In this case, the object of the English cavalry's attentions would be to overawe the ever-vacillating dukes of Brittany. These magnates had long played a dangerous, often skillful, waiting and watching game from their centers of power around Rennes and Hennebont, and thus maintained their small principality as an independent makeweight in the larger duel between Valois and Plantagenet. England could not afford to have an active Breton enemy in play across the southern marches of Normandy. Since Britain's archfoe, Arthur of Brittany, count of Richemont and constable of France for Charles of Valois, was himself of the ducal house of Rennes, such a shift to active belligerency was always a dangerous possibility and the events at Arras, in great measure Richemont's own work, unquestionably heightened this risk. The constant threat of a heavy, destructive attack by one of the English mobile columns would therefore be the surest means of persuading the dukes of Brittany that a watchful neutrality was a safer form of ducal diplomacy than a costly flirtation with the French.[24]

The foregoing military analysis of the Fastolf report would indicate that the "disaster" or "desperation" evaluation of this document requires further examination. Far from admitting that the war was lost at Arras, it seems that Fastolf has given his superiors and fellow captains a careful and entirely feasible plan for preserving the heart of Henry V's conquests. He has set forth a program of offensive-defensive warfare skillfully calculated to take advantage of the known weaknesses of the Valois army and state. His program is one which must, if successfully executed, bring down the grinding weight of military, financial, and political exhaustion upon an enemy still much too shaky to overcome it without major reforms of its basic, institutional structure. These reforms, in turn, could only be carried out if the French government bought time and peace at the price of failing to conquer Normandy. We are therefore dealing with a document which looks confidently to the future, rather than uselessly recalling past glories or fulminating about some dire vengeance.

Assuming the correctness of this hypothesis, certain major questions remain to be answered in order to complete the framework of the present

23. *Ibid.*, pp. 579–580.
24. *Ibid.*, p. 580.

study. Did the concepts just discussed emerge on a seemingly hasty and *ad hoc* basis in September, 1435? Were they thus developed only after the unilateral peace agreement between France and Burgundy had become a certainty? Does Fastolf's proposal for a new-type, professional force of permanent cavalry reflect his own, "modern" revolution in military thinking? Or does this plan merely reflect institutional and personnel changes whose outlines were already well understood and whose implementation was already well in hand before September, 1435? Finally, and most important, if the report is primarily a staff summary and a formal restatement of accepted facts, under what circumstances and under whose auspices do these concepts actually develop as English military doctrine?

Any attempt to answer these questions within the context of the total English military and financial preparations before the Treaty of Arras requires a brief, although somewhat detailed, consideration of the English military position in France in the years immediately preceding the Burgundian withdrawal. It is necessary to select a chronological point in time at which one operational phase of the Hundred Years' War had clearly ended and another had just as clearly begun. For the purposes of the present study, this particular moment is the month of July in the year 1433.

By the summer of 1433, the psychological and military disturbances stirred up by the dramatic and controversial appearance of the Maid Joan had quieted down and the situation in northern France had been given enough time to stabilize itself. Having inspired the French army to fight for the rejuvenated and once-again respectable national symbol of the Valois monarchy, if not for France itself, Joan's work around Orléans and in the Loire Valley had had a permanent effect. Followed up by her march into Champagne and the assault on the walls of Paris itself, Joan's initial impact had carried sufficient momentum to cause the soldiers of Charles VII to give up their supine defensive stand and to move offensively into areas which had been under English domination for many years.

More specifically, the spring and summer months of 1433 were marked by a series of swift raiding movements, carried out by strong parties of French horse under veteran free-lance captains. These thrusts penetrated deeply into the above-mentioned frontier buffer zones. In the north of the Norman perimeter, French cavalry struck in the general direction of that Somme frontier which separated the duchy from Burgundian Picardy. There seems to have been a conscious intention on the part of the Valois to deny the English the use of the lower Somme and its vital estuary. The French columns developed their attack by moving down the line of the river through Amiens in the late spring of 1433, basing their attack upon the major French bastion of Beauvais, a stronghold recovered from the English during the campaigns of Joan. The forward movement on the Somme then became a strong probe toward the English fortresses in and near the estuary, specifically Saint-Valéry-en-Caux and Haplincourt, near Bapaume. Both English positions fell in quick succession, and not for the first time, to a combination of French cavalry dash and a timely revolt of the local population.

Significantly, however, the English reaction was both swift and decisive, thus presenting important indications of the recovery from the shock of Joan's campaigns and the emergence of new plans at the strategic and tactical levels. English mobile forces, men-at-arms, and mounted archers already at full alert for swift counteraction under the command of Robert, Lord Willoughby, and Pierre, count of St. Pol, a Burgundian captain of the famous Luxembourg family who served loyally and well at English pay, struck hard during the months of July and August, 1433. Both Saint-Valéry and Haplincourt were quickly retaken and the command of the Somme estuary returned to English hands. In fact, the entire northern frontier of Normandy returned to a state of tranquility, the experimental or probing attack of the French horse having ended in a sharp defeat. The upper perimeter of the duchy was thus secured by a strategy of a mobile defense and the tactics of swift counterattack against a penetration of a vital zone which would later be delineated as such by Sir John Fastolf.[25]

The French probing attacks and the English counteractions were not limited to the Somme frontier. Other Valois thrusts were attempted by reconnaissance or observation forces in widely separated, but uniformly vital, areas all along the English defensive perimeter. All of them were clearly intended to test the English strength at specific points along the lines which were by now emerging as the military frontier between the opposing armies. In every case the importance of the Norman approaches is underscored by the direction of the French attacks and the immediacy of the English reactions. Once again, the English defensive strategy and its necessary tactical implementation can be seen in a series of operations which extended from the marches of Brittany to the Loire Valley, the county of Maine, and the still-English Isle de France and the *pays chartrain*,

25. For these French attacks and the English countermoves, see Sir N. H. Nicolas (ed.), *Proceedings and Ordinances of the Privy Council*, 6 vols. (London, 1834–37), IV, 163, 169, 178 (hereafter cited as Privy Council, *Proceedings*); Jean Le Fèvre, Seigneur de Saint-Rémy, *Chronique*, ed. François Morand, Société de l'histoire de France, 2 vols. (Paris, 1876–81), II, 268, 271.

a series of probes and repulses which extended throughout the summer months of 1433.[26]

Fortunately, the confirmation of the English defensive strategy and the demarcation of the selected frontier zones for its primary execution do not depend upon this operational evidence alone. The defensive plan and its geographical pattern may also be deduced from a significant piece of documentary evidence of this particular period. This is a very detailed and most valuable strength-and-location report for the English garrisons in northern France during the months of 1433 presently under discussion. This memorandum is a response sent by the English council of Normandy and France to Philip of Burgundy in 1434. The statements and military situation therein date from the council's most recent, complete tabulations, beginning with the musters of late September, 1433. In this rather stiff and hostile document, Bedford's council set out to prove the full commitment of Henry VI's government to the war effort against the common Valois enemy and thus to justify its refusal to reinforce Burgundy's own forces with English troops.[27]

By accounting for the English garrisons located in "France, Normandy, Anjou and Maine" for the period September 20, 1433, to September 29, 1434, the memorandum indirectly sets forth the precise lines of strategic domination to be retained by the English army. Once again, the significant weight of the English power and the core of their emerging defensive perimeter lay along the line of the Somme, within the closest possible reach of the lost valley of the Loire and the pivotal territories of the house of Anjou. In addition, heavy English forces were echeloned in depth along the Seine itself, from above and beyond Paris (Meaux, Montereau) to far below Rouen. It seems almost unnecessary to point out the evident strategic importance of the great river valleys in these pre-Fastolf military dispositions, which surely bear the stamp of conscious military planning. This logical geographical coverage, and the evidence of strategic and tactical conceptualization it presents, was also reinforced by a specific enumeration of the disposition of the English *mobile* forces, again as given by the document now under discussion.[28] Their task, as shown by their strength and calculated location on the map of English France, was to

26. A description of these somewhat confusing and obscure operations is to be found in: *Journal d'un Bourgeois de Paris, 1405–1449*, ed. A. Tuetey (Paris, 1881), pp. 294, 295 (hereafter cited as *Bourgeois de Paris*); Enguerrand de Monstrelet, *Chronique*, ed. L. Douet-D'Arcq, Société de l'histoire de France, 6 vols. (Paris, 1857–62), V, 68; Ramsay, *Lancaster and York*, I, 449 and n. 3.

27. The council's response to Burgundy is located in Stevenson, *Letters and Papers*, Vol. II, Part II, pp. 540–546, 551, *passim*.

28. *Ibid.*

command and dominate those zones not so easily or fully protected by the fixed garrisons.

In addition to these strategic and tactical arrangements for the summer of 1433, the document under consideration here provides confirmatory evidence of planning and foresighted preparation from an organizational and financial viewpoint. The English Exchequer was now paying the troops serving in France directly, instead of filtering monies through the Norman or French financial structures at Rouen and Paris.[29] As will soon become apparent, this direct payment was the first example of a major change in the financial structure of the war effort which was to become a permanent arrangement in 1434. These financial arrangements, however, still were founded upon the traditional four-month or quarter-year, short-term indenture system. This was the long-approved and accepted contractual basis used between the English government and its captains, a system now in the process of basic and necessary change under the force of new circumstances and whose final discard would be formally suggested by Fastolf.

The significance of the frontier defenses emerges immediately from even the most cursory study of the troop dispositions given in the council's response to Burgundy. There were 1,600 professional English troopers, lances, and mounted archers in a balanced and significant ratio, serving under Robert, Lord Willoughby, in the valley of the Somme, along with 500 less reliable Burgundian mercenaries under Pierre, count of St. Pol (this was the same force, in fact, which had carried out the counterattack operations against Saint-Valéry and Haplincourt mentioned earlier). The sensitive and vital marches of Brittany were being protected by 1,200 English troops under the command of John Holland, earl of Huntingdon, a very skillful soldier and veteran captain whose service at the tactical command level both on land and at sea went back to the days of Henry V. The third, or Loire, sector of the strategic zones was being covered by a smaller, but highly picked and extremely mobile force of 900 troopers who ranged down from Maine into Anjou and to the banks of the great central river under the control of John FitzAlan, earl of Arundel, a master of the timed counterstroke tactic whose reputation among the French enemy was only surpassed by that of the fierce John, Lord Talbot, himself.[30]

29. *Ibid.*

30. The field forces commanded by the earls of Arundel and Huntingdon, Lord Willoughby, and the count of St. Pol are all documented by Stevenson, *Letters and Papers*, Vol. II, Part I, pp. 257–258. The *Bourgeois de Paris*, p. 305 note, confirms the back-dating of the mobile force disposition to the summer of 1433, stating, for example, that Arundel contracted to serve, from June 1, 1433, with "200 lances and 600 archers."

According to the calculations made possible by the document, the English mobile field forces thus totaled 3,700 English veterans and 500 Burgundian mercenaries. This force, carefully distributed with regard for strategic and tactical requirements, did not include the static, or purely defensive, garrisons in the English fortress positions, many of whom could, of course, be counted upon for counterattack operations in their own immediate areas. Nor did this field force include the mobile troops available in the Seine Valley itself, a series of large companies under various commanders, all of whom are enumerated in the council's memorandum and whose primary mission was to thicken the already formidable defensive shield in this, the most vital of all the defensive zones. As for the fixed, or garrison, strengths in all the frontier zones, taken as a total, the English had "more than 6000 men" echeloned in fortress locations stretching back from Paris and its protective outposts as far as the Cotentin and the Channel coast of Normandy at such towns as Coutances and Bayeux.[31]

The document discussed above permits certain important and positive conclusions concerning the development of a full-scale English plan as early as 1433. Beginning in the spring of 1434, the English army in France emerged as a force recruited and deployed on a full-time, professional basis. This was a force, furthermore, whose organizational, command and payment arrangements were all clearly based on the successful experience of 1433 described above. Even more importantly, the army of 1434 functioned, from both the strategic and tactical viewpoints, according to the doctrines which have also been discussed in these pages and which were to be formally stated by Fastolf in the report of September, 1435.

From the very outset of the 1434 recruitment and the military operations of that year, the English mobile columns limited their activities to the defensive zones which had now been clearly marked out for retention and domination. The formalized organizational and operational structures of the English army in 1434 confirm, in fact, the existence and pragmatic adoption of every basic concept later included in Fastolf's proposals at the time of Arras. The army of 1434 was, for example, an almost purely English force of picked, regular soldiers and its commanders were the cream of the war-hardened English baronial captains available for such assignments. At least one of these forces, and it was almost certainly the

31. The figures on the garrisons and the evidence for the mobile force protecting the Seine are derived from an analysis of Stevenson, *Letters and Papers*, Vol. II, Part II, pp. 540–546, 551, *passim*. A very useful discussion of the English military situation in 1433 is given by Ramsay, *Lancaster and York*, I, 448 and n. 4, 5, continued on p. 449.

most important of the 1434 columns, operated in the field in a manner which was so precisely similar to Fastolf's later tactical schemes as to lay the originality of Sir John's proposals in this regard open to the most serious doubt. A study of the new forces for 1434, from the recruitment of its baronial-level professional generals, down through the organizational arrangements for its gentry subcommanders and their retinues, as well as the financing and tactical operations of this same army, will confirm the adoption and employment of the doctrines stated earlier on a basis of hard, practical prior experience in the field. We are, furthermore, given evidence that these organizational and operational precepts had been accepted at the highest, official level by early 1434, many months before the crisis of Arras brought forth Fastolf's formal position paper on these matters.

The success or failure of the new, professionalized English army and that of the new doctrines now coming into formal acceptance both depended, in the final analysis, upon the personalities and qualities of the veteran battle-captains who were to be employed in the strategic and tactical missions assigned by John of Bedford. The organization, recruitment, and deployment of the 1434 army may therefore be expounded from their most directly relevant viewpoint, that of leadership and its institutional or governmental background. This leadership and background may in turn be approached through the convenient, yet viable model of a chief captain in the army of 1434. Most fortunately, it is at this particular point, beginning with the early months of 1434, that the precisely focused military career and institutional involvements of John, Lord Talbot of Goodrich, directly coincided with the much larger changes and permanent politico-military arrangements necessary to restructure the English army in France.[32]

Some portions of Talbot's career and examples of his involvement in the broader changes of this period are therefore pertinent to the context of the present study. The objective of this discussion is the examination of a convenient example for the command apparatus of 1434 and the consequent framing of a complex historical problem within viable limits. From both the institutional and operational viewpoints, Talbot and his powerful mounted retinue serve as extremely useful models for changes and developments of a major nature. At the same time, Talbot and his

---

32. No detailed study on Lord Talbot exists at the present writing with the exception of my own unpublished Ph.D. dissertation, "An English Captain of the Later Hundred Years War: John, Lord Talbot, c. 1388–1444" (Princeton University, 1966). This study will be corrected, amplified, and brought up to Talbot's death at Castillon (July 17, 1453) in a book now under preparation.

combat column fully demonstrate the depth of the English preparations to carry out a strategic defensive in northern France.

John Talbot's direct connection with the new army being formed in 1434 dates from his return to England for the preceding winter season. Captured at Patay by the army inspired by the presence of Joan of Arc (June 16, 1429), Talbot had remained a French prisoner until the late summer of 1433. His freedom had been regained only after a very complex series of ransom negotiations and at a high, if imprecisely stated, price in gold.[33] Returning to action immediately, Talbot received an assignment in the campaign of 1433 now just completed. He had commanded a small cavalry group in token support of a Burgundian operation around Pacy-sur-Yonne,[34] and had thus gained renewed experience and an enhanced reputation in the type of swift, mobile warfare which was now about to become the basic English strategy. For the remainder of 1433, Talbot had occupied himself with various garrison commands in the primary areas of the English frontier zone[35] and as a result was now familiar with the defensive side of the rapidly emerging master plan for the retention of Normandy and northern France.

For reasons which were connected with a crisis in his own personal finances, as well as those relating directly to projected military operations, Talbot returned to England at some time during the winter of 1433–1434. The first direct documentation certifying his presence in London is a Minute of the Royal Council, dated February 4, 1434, which also establishes Talbot's direct connection with the army now being formed.[36] As a matter of fact, the minute under discussion is the first and most direct confirmation of the statements made above concerning the new mobile force and it is therefore valuable evidence from the larger, strategic and

33. Talbot's ransom is discussed in Brill, "An English Captain," chap. vi, pp. 197 ff. *passim.*

34. The duke of Burgundy's campaigns of 1433 in his own duchy and the county of Tonnerre as well as Talbot's involvement as a cavalry commander, are discussed by Monstrelet, *Chronique,* V, 62–69, and Le Fèvre, *Chronique,* II, 268–277. For modern interpretations, see André Bossuat, *Perrinet Gressart et François de Surienne: Agents de l'Angleterre* (Paris, 1936), pp. 208–209, and notes citing MS material (Archives du Nord); Ulysse Plancher, *Histoire générale et particulière de Bourgogne,* Vol. IV of 4 vols. (Dijon, 1781), p. 171; Ramsay, *Lancaster and York,* I, 449–450; Beaucourt, *Histoire de Charles VII,* II, 47 and notes.

35. Talbot had commanded garrisons successively at Coutances, Bayeux, and Pont de l'Arche, alternating several times in these commands with Robert, Lord Willoughby. See the document cited above in Stevenson, *Letters and Papers,* Vol. II, Part II, pp. 541, 545.

36. Privy Council, *Proceedings,* IV, 197.

organizational viewpoints, as well as from that of Talbot himself. Through Talbot, as a captain of the mobile force, we are given insights into the legal arrangements and institutional framework needed to put this new and professional array into the field on a basis of permanent service to the crown of England.

For one thing, the choice of language in the document is highly significant. The wording repeatedly emphasizes the "long-time" or "continuous" nature of the service upon which Talbot and his company are about to embark. The same expressions are used to specify the extended nature of his forthcoming "absence in the king's service in the wars of France."[37] Another interesting point made by the same document also bears upon Talbot's forthcoming service and absence from England. Here the minute concerns itself with future homages and feudal dues which might become due from Talbot or from any of his "retinue" (a technical expression which was here intended to include the subcaptains who would soon sign indentures with him as the directly recruited royal captain and prime military contractor). These homages and dues covered any of his lands in Wales, England, or Ireland which might descend to Talbot or his subordinates during their French service. No homage, or the required and concomitant payment *pro relevio suo*, was to be exacted until that French service was completed.[38]

Talbot and his personal following were being permitted, in effect, to prepare themselves legally and financially for long careers in France, casting off any concern for the serious difficulties which might arise over their personal affairs during their absence. In Talbot's own case, this legal release was destined to free him for duty as a first-rank field commander for the approximately ten years between May, 1434, and the Truce of Tours. Unless the English command was indeed acting upon the strategic precepts of a careful plan, intended to produce a long-service, professional army for continuous French service, it seems highly doubtful that the council would have risked setting a legal and fiscal precedent of such importance. That they did so, as early as February 4, 1434, shows both the depth of the military reform necessary to place columns such as Talbot's in the field and also places that reform in proper chronological sequence with Fastolf's report of September, 1435.

The legal and financial arrangements just discussed released Talbot and his retinue for almost purely military preparations for the balance of the spring of 1434, an additional confirmation of the council's purpose in

37. *Ibid.*
38. *Ibid.*

issuing this document. By April of that year, Talbot was definitely forming the retinue which would accompany him to France early in the following summer. This is confirmed by a protection, or immunity from legal prosecution, which was made out for a man "about to go to France with Talbot in his company."[39] But the definitive date for the assembly of Talbot's personal retinue, and therefore that of the larger professional force of which his company was a part, is May 16, 1434, on which date Talbot's formal indentures with the crown were sealed.[40]

This contract applied only to Talbot's personal company and to the men who followed him directly. Talbot's direct indenture therefore created a force amounting only to 800 men, divided in the by-now customary manner between lances and mounted archers.[41] The array was nothing more than a personal nucleus for a much larger force. The other units of this column would be commanded by professional captains on subcontract to Talbot, as well as crown indentures of their own, making up a large, mobile force which would rally for tactical purposes behind Talbot's banner of the Red Lion. This nucleus theory is, in fact, confirmed by a vital document of June 18, 1434, evidence which also fixes Talbot's time of arrival back in France and within the English fortress-bridgehead of Calais.

The document consists of letters patent, ordering Talbot, as commander and chief captain of the force, to take the royal muster of his army as it arrived in Calais, Talbot being "already on the scene there."[42] These letters confirm the nucleus theory by giving a most useful and precise accounting of the forces to be mustered under Talbot's command. But their greatest value for the present study is to confirm the new organization of the English mobile forces and its specific leadership at the subcaptain level. What emerges here is the type of striking column which was later to be described in Sir John Fastolf's report, an almost modern divisional organization of cavalry and mounted infantry, as viewed within the reduced framework of medieval warfare and the relatively small number of troops involved. These divisions would, from the summer

39. T. Rymer, *Foedera, conventiones, literae et cuiusque generis acta publica* . . ., original ed., Vol. X of 20 vols. (London, 1721), p. 577.

40. Ramsay, *Lancaster and York*, I, 463 and n. 4, citing R. Pauli, *Geschichte von England* (London, 1853), whose authority rested upon manuscript sources.

41. Jean de Wavrin, *Recueil des Chroniques et Anchiennes Istoires de la Grant Bretaigne, à present nommé Engleterre*, ed. W. and E. L. C. P. Hardy, Rolls Series, 5 vols. (London, 1864–91), IV, 43; Monstrelet, *Chronique*, V, 91.

42. Great Britain, Public Record Office, *Calendar of Patent Rolls*, Henry VI (1429–36), 359.

of 1434, be formed under hardened commanders of noble, but secondary rank, of whom John Talbot is but one typical example. The direct, small-unit leadership of the individual companies in these columns would in turn be provided by the gentry-level captains of retinues.

These statements are directly supported by the letters patent presently under consideration. The only subcaptain of the old Anglo-Norman nobility listed is John, Lord de Clinton, a veteran captain. Clinton, who was to serve in conspicuous military positions from 1434 onwards, brought over a retinue of 20 men-at-arms and 60 horse-archers. After listing Clinton and his company, however, the document becomes a muster of the gentry captains and their retinues. Four of these professional soldiers, namely Sir William Chamberlain, Sir William Bucton, Sir Thomas Hoo, and Sir Richard Woodville (later Earl Rivers and the father-in-law of Edward IV), each mustered a force of 20 men-at-arms and 60 archers. Sir John Lampet provided 12 lances and 36 archers. Sir Philip Chetwynd, representing a family who had provided combat-level leadership since the days of Crécy and Poitiers, commanded a very sizeable array of 50 lances and 150 mounted archers, a force almost large enough to merit an independent command for its captain. Finally, there was a group of smaller, but nonetheless significant retinues, each of them commanded by gentlemen of experience and ability. Two brothers, Sir John and Sir William Damport, held the joint leadership of 10 lances and 90 archers. Sir James Standish led 5 men-at-arms and 45 archers, while a composite group, under the joint command of Sir William Hanley, Sir John Tailboys, and Sir Robert Soutyll, brought into the field a force which consisted of themselves (mustered as 3 men-at-arms) and 39 archers. All told, the army mustered for service in Bedford's new army by John Talbot totaled 180 men-at-arms and 660 archers, for a grand aggregate of 840 combat troops of all ranks, not counting pages, servants, and other noncombatants. This total, moreover, did not include the 800 fighting men Talbot had himself brought from England. With his personal retinue, his combat force was almost exactly doubled in strength and striking power.[43]

Talbot now had mustered into the royal pay a first-class, completely mounted and mobile force with an aggregate strength of almost 1,700 seasoned, professional soldiers and veteran captains. From its very inception, this was a new force for a new and specific mission, rather than a gathering of reinforcements for the troops already deployed in France. The tactical operations of Talbot's cavalry command for the remainder of 1434 confirm the fact that its recruitment, muster, and employment were

43. *Ibid.*

all integral parts of a now fully developed plan to put such a column in the field. These same operations also make it clear that the purposes of this plan are those outlined earlier in this essay.

Furthermore, it must be emphasized once again that Talbot and his command are only a single model. Other examples could easily be drawn for similar organizations in the spring of 1434 and some of these, along with their leadership, will be discussed in the portion of this study devoted to the tactical implementation of the theories advanced above. But the formation and composition of Talbot's division serve as useful microcosms of the broader plan and the wide-ranging structural changes now involved. As such, they are evidence of serious and conscious reorganization on the part of the English high command to meet a new situation in France. From this organizational and institutional viewpoint at least, the English army was preparing to fight Sir John Fastolf's "new war" more than a year before the writing of his report.

But these military preparations, and the resultant reorganization of the English army in France, would have been impossible without changes of a far less visible, but equally important nature in the areas of financial planning and fiscal support for the war effort. A parallel development of the military reorganization for 1433–1434 was John of Bedford's stringent restructuring of the financial base which kept the English armies in the field. This new planning was carried out from both the short-range and long-term points of view, for grave problems had now surfaced which required immediate as well as extended treatment. In the immediate future lay the pressing problem of paying the existing garrisons in France, not to mention the new and expensive mobile forces described above. The long-range problem was concerned with the entire financial basis, and fiscal feasibility, of the war, with particular reference to the strategy now being projected for the future.

The questionable financial basis of the English war effort before the reorganization of 1433–1434 arose from a far-reaching decision made by Henry V in the last year of his life. After the Treaty of Troyes and the creation of his "dual monarchy," Henry had wished to avoid pressing an obviously reluctant English Parliament into paying the heavy charges for securing or continuing his French conquests. His solution had been to make each one of his kingdoms self-supporting and responsible only for the expenses incurred within its own boundaries. All the military operations in France were to be supported by French taxes and by grants of the various estates in the territories under English control. The English Parliament, on the other hand, would be called upon only to pay the crown's English expenses and those incurred for possessions which had been held before Henry V reopened the Hundred Years' War in 1415. The latter category included the fortified enclave of Calais, which thus was funded and administered as a military district separate from Bedford's lieutenancy of France and Normandy.

This division of financial responsibility, with all of its evident political and institutional shortcomings, had never worked out in actual practice before 1433 and the strategic reorganization which dated from that year made a candid re-examination of King Henry's financial structure a necessity. There had to be a full acceptance of immediate fiscal responsibility for the war effort by the English council and Parliament, and an official recognition that this obligation would continue for the foreseeable future and that this responsibility extended to all military operations in France. It was now essential for John of Bedford and his French council to insist upon the permanent funding of the military structure on such a basis. The financial restructuring could only be accomplished in this manner if Bedford could legally combine the French resources, primarily supplied by the *états normands*, with those derived from the English government. Another legal and fiscal problem of utmost urgency was to bring the Pale of Calais into the larger French picture. An outdated arrangement dating from the time of Edward III restricted Calais funds, including the royal proceeds of the wool staple located there, to use for the defense of that bastion alone. Bedford sought a full military commitment of all available monies on an unrestricted and unhampered basis.

The financial crisis facing Bedford in 1433 was one of immediacy as well as a matter requiring long-range adjustment. This urgency was signaled by a dramatic and dangerous incident which took place in the spring of 1433. In April of that year, the garrison of Calais mutinied when their demands for long-standing arrears of pay were ignored by the English government. Although details of the rising and the precise reasons for the causative financial stoppage still remain obscure, the situation was sufficiently serious to arouse angry and official reaction from the ruling council in London. The revolt itself was extinguished only with very great difficulty and only after extended and complicated negotiations. The incident resulted in the execution of four ringleaders, the dismissal of another two hundred fifty participants from the English service without their arrears in pay, and in general anger in all quarters.[44]

44. Sir N. H. Nicolas and E. Tyrrell (eds.), *The Chronicle of London, 1089–1483* (London, 1827), pp. 119, 120; Privy Council, *Proceedings*, IV, 139; Great Britain, Parliament, *Rotuli Parliamentorum*, 7 vols. with index (London, 1767–1832), IV, 173; Ramsay, *Lancaster and York*, I, 449 and n. 1.

A dangerous precedent had now been set since the English armies were made up of paid, professional volunteers. Troops would not be anxious to serve a government which treated their legitimate demands in such a fashion. The fact that the mutiny took place in what was certainly the most famous and undoubtedly one of the most important garrisons in France is equally important, for nothing could have pointed to the need for reform in a more urgent fashion. At the same time, other incidents, involving valuable captains and commanders, as well as troops and garrisons, confirm the existence of a generalized financial crisis close to the intensity which had sparked the Calais mutiny. By 1433, these endemic outbreaks and an over-all dissatisfaction registered by the English forces all over northern France had pointed out the unsound nature of the existing financial arrangements and the need for remedial action to the degree Bedford required for approaching the council in London.[45]

In addressing himself to these problems, Bedford's solution was necessarily drastic, but at the same time simple enough to have a chance of lasting success. On June 14, 1434, Duke John submitted a lengthy memorandum to the council in London, a document consisting of a series of articles which were speedily approved by that often-dilatory ruling body. The first portion of the memorandum described the current situation in France in great detail, with particular and repeated emphasis upon the dangerously low state of morale in the English garrisons and upon the increasingly desperate methods he was being forced to employ in avoiding mutinies and the plundering of the countryside by unpaid troops. The dissatisfaction of the army over its pay, when combined with the large area of his command responsibility, presented a crisis in available manpower. This crisis, which Bedford felt was threatening his future success as lieutenant and governor of France and Normandy, could in turn be blamed almost completely upon an inefficient and unreliable supply of funds.

The solution of the problem, Bedford continued, could only be a major and permanent diversion of a sizeable portion of the English crown's revenues to military purposes. At the same time, there must now be an important and long-overdue reorganization and regularization of the administrative structure in France, so that military and financial efficiency could both be greatly improved. The funds, Bedford suggested, should

45. The preceding statements are based upon a careful study of the primary sources for 1433, both government records and chronicles. The most important evidence is supplied by Bedford's own memorandum to the Privy Council, in which he recommended solutions after discussing the nature of the problem. See the following footnote and below pp. 235–237.

come from the royal patrimony, the revenues of the duchy of Lancaster which were the personal holdings of the royal house. According to Bedford's plan, these monies, now entrusted to Cardinal Beaufort and other feoffees for the carrying out of Henry V's pious bequests, should be diverted to paying for the war which was quite clearly another legacy of the same king. The reorganization, Bedford said, must come in the consolidation of Calais with the other English domains in northern France. The garrisons of the town and its marches, a large body of troops requiring and often not receiving major financial backing, should be brought under the control and payment of the governor at Rouen and Paris—Bedford's own control at present.

His tone increasing in sharpness, Bedford openly blamed the home government for the poor management of the clumsy and unnecessary separate administration at Calais, as well as for the general crisis in funds and manpower he was now facing in France. There had to be an immediate increase in the economy and regularization of recruitment, payment, and all other matters concerning the army in France if the present situation was to be improved. Not only were the domains of the king in danger at present, Bedford warned, but future defensive and offensive operations would require even more funds and an even more efficient use of manpower if his own lieutenancy were to have a chance of success. With this suggestive reference to new strategic plans, Bedford completed his presentation with a generous personal offer. He would do his own part in solving the financial and manpower crisis by diverting his own private revenues, granted to him from Norman tax income by Henry V, to the prosecution of the war for the next two years, or until new and permanent funds could be raised and committed.

In response, the council recorded in its minutes a motion of deep and heartfelt thanks for Bedford's generous offer, as well as a very favorable reaction to the duke's common-sense suggestions for reform of the war's financial foundations. The cardinal and the other executors of Henry V's legacies from the Lancastrian funds immediately agreed to the prompt diversion of the revenues for which they were responsible, stipulating only that they be freed of legal liability for such a breach of the late king's will. Bedford's suggestions for the consolidation of Calais with "France and Normandy" also were accepted in full. All contracting of captains and troops, as well as their payment, for Calais and the larger theater of French operations, were brought under Bedford's control as lieutenant. The hitherto untouchable revenues of Calais were consolidated for general use with the other French income. Bedford could therefore look forward to a large increase in his permanent military funds, with the additional monies to be provided by the staple and the other royal establishments in the Calais *entrepôt*. Not only was this a great improvement in financial efficiency, but the council's action eliminated an archaicism which had, until 1434, actually placed Bedford in competition with his own government for the limited supply of English troops and commanders.

To alleviate the present crisis, Bedford's personal offer was accepted with deep thanks and the formal appreciation of the council. They prayed that he might put this offer into immediate effect, in order to provide emergency funds while the rest of the reform took shape. But other funds were also to be made available at once. In order to strengthen the weak financial position of the high command in France without undue delay, five thousand marcs from the revenues of the duchy of Lancaster were to be disbursed immediately and dispatched at the earliest possible moment to Louis of Luxembourg, bishop of Thérouanne and chancellor of France for Henry VI and his lieutenant, the duke of Bedford. These funds were to be used for the payment of archers and men-at-arms in the fortresses of France for the Easter term just past, an official attempt to make up at least some of the dangerous arrears which were beginning to accumulate in the overseas army. The council also assumed the responsibility of paying the new troops now being raised at home for French service. The council thus put its belated, but legally and politically essential, seal of approval on the changes required by John of Bedford through a large-scale shuffle of revenues and a major change in the organization of the English administrative commands in France. In this way, they were helping to implement the military reform the duke had already put into effect. They were also sponsoring, at the highest, institutional level of the English government, those adjustments in the financial base of the war effort which Bedford felt were necessary for the long-term strategy now being made operational in the war zone.[46]

Even while he was still in London and busy securing conciliar approval for his new financial and administrative scheme, Bedford already was implementing a fuller military use of his own financial resources in his

46. The preceding discussion of Bedford's memorandum, of the council's agreement to his proposals, and of the means taken to implement them are based upon a detailed reconstruction and analysis of Privy Council, *Proceedings*, IV, 222–236, *passim*. Ramsay, *Lancaster and York*, and other modern works consulted support the conclusions herein, but without documentation. Other than the minutes of the council, no other primary source material is known to exist for these financial reforms and administrative arrangements. This lacuna is, of course, an example of the well-known fifteenth-century gap in detailed information of the kind required here.

capacity as royal lieutenant of France and Normandy. Any plan for financial reform or the improvement of the fiscal base for military operations must of necessity include the fullest possible cooperation of the one local French assembly still in English control by 1434, namely the estates of Normandy.

Duke John returned to Normandy in the early summer of 1434.[47] A meeting of the Norman estates took place promptly at Rouen. The only business set before the *états* was that of finance. Bedford wanted, and received, immediate and concrete support for the campaign of 1434, parts of which were already under way. It is noteworthy that the Norman grant was directly and specifically tied to the forthcoming operations of Bedford's mobile columns. There is, in fact, particular and stated reference to the functions of John Talbot's division, the formation of which was described earlier in this study. Even more significant is the amount of the grant passed by the estates. They agreed upon the enormous sum of £344,000 *tournois* as a contribution to Bedford's military and financial plan. This was the largest amount voted for the war effort by the estates since the time of Henry V and the somewhat euphoric days just after the Treaty of Troyes.[48]

When combined with the large grants of money and the basic, English administrative-financial restructuring already proposed by Bedford and approved by the council in London, this Norman grant provides essential confirmation of a major financial reorganization. It is almost inconceivable that financial and administrative changes on such a scale, affecting as they did the basic institutional bodies of both England and Normandy at this time, could have been carried out without direct and conscious reference to a higher strategic and tactical plan of the English command. This financial reorganization therefore places additional credibility upon the existence of the English preparations to fight an entirely new war by mid-1434. These same adjustments simultaneously deny the interpretations of newness and originality attached to Sir John Fastolf's proposals of 1435.

While these organizational and financial preparations were being completed, the English had already begun the tactical implementation of Bedford's new strategy. Carried out in the face of increasingly severe French pressure, the campaign of 1434 is of particular interest to the

47. Bedford landed in France on July 1 or 2, 1434. Ramsay, *Lancaster and York*, I, 460.

48. Charles de Beaurepaire, *Les états de Normandie sous la domination anglaise* (Évreux, 1859), p. 46. The references to the functions of Talbot's division in the campaign of 1434 are located in *ibid.*, pp. 45–46.

present study for two principal reasons. First, its actual operations are models for the defensive-offensive concepts discussed earlier. Second, the narrative of the campaign proves that the ideas later advanced by Fastolf at the time of Arras were already in operation a full year before the composition of his report. The entire campaign is therefore the synthesis of and the definitive response to the hypothetical questions raised following the analysis of Fastolf's report. Viewed within the larger context of the financial, organizational, and strategic preparations discussed above, the actual maneuvers of Bedford's columns contain the final evidence for this essay. Although the campaign of 1434 is itself a fine example of tactical execution in mobile warfare, its chief interest here lies along broader lines. The entire sequence of events may be seen as the successful field test of a new kind of warfare; its end result would eventually mean the blunting of the Treaty of Arras from the military viewpoint, for this campaign was to be the model for the highly efficient attrition warfare waged against the Valois during the years 1435–1444.

From its very outset, the campaign of 1434 demonstrated the strategic and tactical patterns which have been argued in this study. Military operations for the year had already commenced before the formation of the new mobile columns and well before Bedford completed his new financial arrangements. Predictably, the campaign opened with a series of heavy probing attacks, carried into English territory by strong detachments of French cavalry. Each one of the areas endangered by these thrusts was one of those three clearly defined zones designated earlier as the primary English frontier zones. From January, 1434, onwards, groups of raiding parties, operating completely independently of each other in the uncoordinated fashion which was one of the chief premises of the countering English strategy, stabbed toward the Somme, toward the Vexin jugular of the Isle de France and the Seine Valley, and against Maine and the southern border of Normandy. In dealing with each of these enemy moves, the English response conformed to the stated strategy of zone defense and to the tactics of immediate counterattack by picked mobile columns.

The French attacks commenced in January, 1434, with a heavy strike in the Somme area. Strong parties of Valois horse, operating from Burgundian Picardy, crossed the river and once again seized the often-exchanged town and fortress of Saint-Valéry-en-Caux, cutting off English communications and commerce in the lower part of the river basin as they had in 1433. In February, some of Charles VII's loosely controlled free lances attacked a vital area of the eastern, or Vexin, sector.

Under the command of Amadeo de Vignolles, brother of the famous captain called La Hire, this force occupied and refortified the dismantled strong-point at Beaumont-sur-Oise. De Vignolles thus positioned himself to dominate the lower reaches of the Oise, an important feeder which flowed into the Seine only a few miles below Paris itself. By doing so, he disturbed the already tenuous flow of foodstuffs which came into Paris from the north and west, while at the same time he placed himself astride the lines of communication between Normandy and Bedford's political capital. Other French partisan cavalry groups were driving raids deep into the county of Maine and menacing the heavy line of frontier castles which protected southern Normandy. These movements of French light horse in the south not only endangered the important fortresses at Argentan, Falaise, and Domfront, but threatened the security of the Maine buffer zone itself.[49]

The English strategy of an offensive defense, with its tactical corollary of prompt, swift-moving local counterattacks, went into operation without delay. In southern Normandy and the zones of Maine and Anjou, the counterstrike and area-domination functions came under the local command of John FitzAlan, earl of Arundel. A most capable and experienced professional commander who had long occupied positions of trust under Bedford, Arundel now struck a decisive counterblow against the southern French inroads and set back their offensive plans in such a fashion as to confirm Duke John's confidence in his abilities.

In January, 1434, Arundel began his counterattack with the capture of Saint-Celérin, a stronghold in Maine which had been acting as a base and rallying point for French raiding parties. Although this move necessitated a brief investment and siege operation, the results were more than justified in this particular case. They are, in fact, an example of what Bedford expected as the end product of the tactical discretion given his mobile force commanders. The captured French advance base turned out to be a key geographical and military holding. Its fall upset the French power structure throughout the county of Maine and permitted Arundel to sweep the disorganized bands of Valois troopers from that territory and

49. The French recapture of Saint-Valéry is described by Monstrelet, *Chronique*, V, 85. For De Vignolles's operations in the Vexin, see the *Bourgeois de Paris*, p. 298. The French operations in Maine and against southern Normandy are given by Jean Chartier, *Chronique de Charles VII, roi de France*, ed. A. Vallet de Viriville, 3 vols. (Paris, 1858), I, 162–63; Guillaume Gruel, *Chronique d'Arthur de Richemont, Connétable de France, Duc de Bretagne (1393–1458)*, ed. Achille Le Vavasseur, Société de l'histoire de France (Paris, 1890), pp. 79–81; E. Cosneau, *Le Connétable de Richemont (Artur de Bretagne), 1393–1458* (Paris, 1886), pp. 200–206.

most of Anjou as well. His forward movement, a model of directed mobility and purposeful employment of professional cavalry, did not lose momentum until it reached the banks of the Loire River itself. Arundel's actions after the capture of Saint-Celérin not only put an end to the French threat against Maine and southern Normandy, but also reversed the forward flow of the Valois military domination in the Loire area which had begun with the English defeats around Orléans in 1429. A tactical maneuver thus resulted in a strategic victory, since Arundel's sweep reduced an entire French offensive sector to the much less effective posture of a quiescent defensive. From Saint-Celérin, Arundel moved swiftly into the hinterland of Maine, overwhelming the strongpoints of Sillé-le-Guillaume and Beaumont-le-Vicomte in quick succession and driving large bands of French horse before him into Anjou. Arundel's clearing of Upper Maine thus deprived the French of their line of departure and assembly area for any future offensive into southern Normandy.

Arundel's clearing of Maine and his sweep to the Loire were now to be raised to an unmistakably strategic victory by a brilliant combination of tactical skill and psychological superiority applied at a key moment in the total campaign. After his local victories and after driving the French raiders out of his protective zone, Arundel clearly possessed the offensive initiative. He now used it to drive the main French army back from the frontier they must control in order to mount any future offensives in this area. When the primary Valois force, commanded in this case by the constable Arthur of Richemont, the duke of Alençon, and Count Charles of Maine, attempted to intervene at Sillé-le-Guillaume, Arundel accepted the challenge and offered battle with his far inferior numbers.

The earl's gamble was well considered and its results highly rewarding. Richemont and his colleagues simply did not dare subject their shaky troops to the test of a general action. Instead, they beat a hasty retreat to the Loire and took their forces completely out of the campaign, an occurrence which surely proves the overly delicate balance and faulty timing of the French army in this period. Arundel promptly drove home the strategic significance of the Valois ineffectiveness with his march on the Loire and by reducing the French threat in the southern sector to a state of almost complete impotence for the next several years. The principle of tactical counterattack, turned into a major and almost bloodless victory over an entire sector of the Norman border zone by the use of the military initiative and well-timed moral superiority, had thus enabled Arundel to present Bedford with a strategic triumph which fitted well into the duke's over-all plans and objectives for 1434.[50]

The Somme frontier was even more easily stabilized than the southern sector, undoubtedly because the French strength in this northern area was not very great in 1434 and because the strong Burgundian possessions north of the river and the still-significant English power above Paris limited the northern Valois operations to hit-and-run raids. The Somme was still simply too far distant from the main centers of Charles VII's power, e.g., Berry, the Orléanais, Poitou, the Bourbonnais, etc., for a major effort on the part of the French army in this direction. Nonetheless, the great river which divided Normandy from Picardy and Artois was as important to Duke Philip of Burgundy as it was to Bedford and the English. Not even a limited Valois danger was tolerable here, for the French capture of Saint-Valéry and the closing of the lower Somme posed as great a threat to Burgundy's western possessions as it did to Normandy. As a result, Bedford was able to employ reliable troops in the Somme sector who rode under Duke Philip's colors, but who were paid by the English crown and therefore completely dependable for Bedford's purposes. At the same time, Bedford had also deployed a solidly established mobile column of native English troopers in the Somme sector.

In the spring of 1434, therefore, a highly competent Anglo-Burgundian force was ready to deal with the French threat in the north. The Burgundian mercenaries were commanded by the renowned and skillful head of the Anglophile house of Luxembourg, John, count of Ligny. The tactical command of the English column was shared by the veteran Robert, Lord Willoughby, and Ligny's younger brother, Bishop Louis of Thérouanne, Bedford's chancellor of France. Operating as a unified force, the two columns overwhelmed and recaptured Saint-Valéry in a single rush and then followed up their tactical success by seizing an irritating French raiding base at Monchaux, also located in the *pays de Caux*. From a strategic viewpoint, these victories by English and Burgundian columns cleared the northern Norman frontier of enemy raiders and secured the free navigation of the Somme from Amiens to the sea for some time to come.[51] The lack of Valois positions and strength in this area was to play

50. Arundel's campaign is fortunately quite well documented. The above discussion is based upon an analysis of the following sources: Chartier, *Chronique de Charles VII*, I, 164–169; Cosneau, *Richemont*, pp. 206–209, and document printed in Appendix, p. 545; Beaucourt, *Histoire de Charles VII*, II, 49 and n. 1; Ramsay, *Lancaster and York*, I, 462–463; Gruel, *Chronique d'Arthur de Richemont*, pp. 82–86.

51. The operations in the Somme and the *pays de Caux* areas are given by Le Fèvre, *Chronique*, II, 298; Monstrelet, *Chronique*, V, 87–88; Beaucourt, *Histoire de Charles VII*, II, 51 and n. 5.

an important role in lessening the military impact of the Treaty of Arras when Burgundy left the war in September, 1435. Burgundian neutrality, combined with an active French offensive threat in the sensitive northern sector, could well have posed serious future problems from the English viewpoint, not only for the security of the Somme Valley, but for that of the Caux and perhaps even the Seine itself. That this potential military threat was eliminated before such a political situation arose in 1435 was owed to the successful operation of Bedford's frontier-defense plan in 1434.

Having thus reduced the French threats in the northern and southern zones to an insignificant level for the foreseeable future, Bedford could now concentrate his attention on the chief danger facing his defensive perimeter in 1434. This peril was, of course, posed by the Valois operations and incursions into the eastern sector and astride Bedford's primary, Rouen-Paris communication route in the Vexin. For the primary task of destroying this threat and thus of carrying out the main English operations in 1434, Duke John selected the division commanded by John, Lord Talbot.

Soon after the Calais muster of June 18, 1434,[52] Talbot moved his mobile column down through Artois, Picardy, and Upper Normandy to the English capital at Rouen. Turning east, he hurled his swift-moving force of veterans into the disputed borderlands of the Vexin and began his clearing operation with a lightning strike at the French raiding base of Joigny. The Valois force stationed here, midway between English Gisors and French Beauvais, had recently been terrorizing the countryside for miles around. Talbot marked his first victory of 1434 and struck a telling and ruthless psychological blow at French morale by hanging every prisoner captured at Joigny, regardless of their rank. Talbot was therefore practicing war *à l'outrance* on the tactical level long before it was recommended as strategic policy in Fastolf's report. Small French bands, most of them semibrigands at the very least, would henceforth hesitate before entering any area protected by Talbot and his column, an objective for which the English captain and his immediate superior, the duke of Bedford, were undoubtedly striving.[53]

After moving on to Paris and acquiring additional troops for his division from Bedford himself,[54] Talbot now proceeded cross-country and struck the vital and dangerously threatened Oise Valley with full force and

52. See above pp. 231–233.

53. The Joigny operation and its punitive aftermath are described by Monstrelet, *Chronique*, V, 91.

54. Wavrin, *Recueil des Chroniques*, IV, 43; *Bourgeois de Paris*, p. 299 n. 2; Monstrelet, *Chronique*, V, 91.

a large measure of tactical surprise. After driving Amadeo de Vignolles from his advanced post at Beaumont-sur-Oise,[55] Talbot swiftly followed that French captain up the river valley, pinned him into the important, permanent French outpost at Creil and took the castle and town there after a brief, but severe siege. This deviation from mobile warfare proved to be highly worthwhile and a proper exercise of Talbot's tactical discretion, as had been the case with Arundel's move against Saint-Celérin. Talbot not only eliminated a dangerous French position at Creil, but also doubled the significance of his victory through the chance death of Amadeo de Vignolles in a sortie and the utter destruction of de Vignolles's strong column of horse. By capturing and fortifying Creil to the extent of leaving a large permanent garrison when he moved on up the Oise, Talbot was advancing the English frontier and deepening the buffer zone between the major French stronghold at Beauvais and the essential artery of the Seine Valley.[56]

The capture of Creil was the final objective of Talbot's main effort, which had been the clearing and deepening of the frontier zone facing the Beauvaisis and the re-establishment of security in the Vexins. But Talbot's campaign did not end there. At this point, his operations became a broad-sweeping cavalry raid with a higher purpose and objective than mere fighting or destruction. After Creil, Talbot was maneuvering, at all times deep in French territory, with the objective of pacifying and terrorizing the neighboring enemy districts into a shocked state unlikely to support a major offensive in the near future. Talbot's continued campaign therefore serves as the model of the pre-emptive attack, a thrust designed to give the English army a superior balance of functioning forces in a given area. Once again, Bedford's pragmatic strategy and tactics of 1434 reflect the theoretical precepts later recommended by Fastolf.

Beginning with the capture of the fortified bridgehead over the Oise at Pont-Saint-Maxence, Talbot continued his sweep by turning sharply

55. For the recapture of Beaumont-sur-Oise, see the *Bourgeois de Paris*, p. 299 and n. 2; Gruel, *Chronique d'Arthur de Richemont*, p. 87 and n. 4; Cosneau, *Richemont*, p. 212 and n. 3; Wavrin, *Recueil des Chroniques*, IV, 43–44; Monstrelet, *Chronique*, V, 91; Beaucourt, *Histoire de Charles VII*, II, 49 and n. 1; Ramsay, *Lancaster and York*, I, 463 and n. 5. Talbot again neutralized the position at Beaumont by destroying the fortifications of the castle.

56. The instrument of surrender for Creil is given in *Bourgeois de Paris*, p. 299 n. 3. See also Gruel, *Chronique d'Arthur de Richemont*, p. 87 and n. 4; Cosneau, *Richemont*, p. 212 and nn. 3, 4; Wavrin, *Recueil des Chroniques*, IV, 45; Monstrelet, *Chronique*, V, 91–92; Ramsay, *Lancaster and York*, I, 463. For the captures of both Beaumont and Creil, see also P. LeCacheux, *Actes de la Chancellerie d'Henri VI concernant la Normandie sous la domination anglaise (1422–1435)*, Société de l'histoire de Normandie, Vol. II of 2 vols. (Rouen, 1908), p. 296 n. 1.

to the east and invading the old Capetian royal domain, the Valesin being marked out for his particular attention. Several small fortresses surrendered upon seeing Talbot's personal banner, but Crépy-en-Valois put up a desperate resistance until it was overwhelmed and the entire garrison put to the sword. War *à l'outrance* was again being employed as a salutary lesson in applied psychology. From Crépy, Talbot swept back to the north and west, receiving the surrender of Clermont-en-Beauvaisis at discretion, and then finished his daring and completely successful raid with a typically flamboyant gesture.

A quick slash into an area which had been a French stronghold since the time of Joan served to flaunt Talbot's banner before the walls of Beauvais itself, although it was perfectly obvious that nothing of a serious nature could be attempted here without a major offensive of the type the English could no longer afford. But even this seemingly useless gambade of Talbot's can be seen as a part of Bedford's higher plan. The Beauvais raid placed the French forces all over that area in a state of strategic and tactical defense for many months to come; any attacks which may have been planned were promptly cancelled. Even the free lance companies were recalled from raiding operations and placed upon a costly and fruitless alert against further sweeps by the English cavalry. The measure of Talbot's total success, and that of the higher plan which had launched his operation, may in fact be seen through the lack of any serious French action in the area triangulated by Rouen, Paris, and Beauvais until the late months of 1435. Once again, Bedford and his captain John Talbot had bought England time and preserved her domination over a frontier zone vital to the security of Normandy.[57]

The success of the campaigns of 1434 guaranteed, in fact, English control over all the frontier areas designated above until long after the Treaty of Arras. Even after the loss of Paris in 1436, Bedford's defense plan was maintained in all essential points in the Vexin and the Oise Valley until a major French offensive captured Creil and Pontoise in 1441. Even then, the frontier of Normandy in the east was held by the English until the fall of the entire duchy in 1449–1450. The Somme became the border between English territory and a Burgundy which was at first an unfriendly neutral immediately after Arras and then became an active enemy. But the northern frontier of Normandy was never seriously

57. The preceding narrative of Talbot's campaign after Creil is based upon Wavrin, *Recueil des Chroniques*, IV, 45–47; Monstrelet, *Chronique*, V, 92–93; Beaucourt, *Histoire de Charles VII*, II, 49 and n. 1; Ramsay, *Lancaster and York*, I, 463; Cosneau, *Richemont*, pp. 213–214. See also Lt. Col. A. H. Burne, *The Agincourt War* (Fairlawn, N.J., 1956), p. 274.

breached after 1434, despite Burgundy's not very effective efforts in that direction. It remained English until the loss of all the English holdings in the north. The same statement applies to the southern frontier with Maine and the marches of Brittany; these were not breached until Richemont's final campaign of 1450 and the disastrous battle of Formigny.

It may be said, therefore, that the control of the frontier zones was essential to and marked the success of the entire strategic and political plan whose implementation lay at the root of Bedford's painstaking preparations. With numerically inferior, but highly organized and controlled forces of qualitatively superior professional troops, plus a carefully conceived plan of strategic defense and tactical counterattack, the English high command had therefore accomplished three primary objectives. First, they had blunted a series of potentially dangerous French thrusts into vital areas of the Norman frontier system. Second, they had maintained the strategic and geographical integrity of Normandy and its protective buffer districts. Third, and perhaps most important of all for the future of English France, they had severely demoralized the main offensive forces of the Valois army at a moment when the political reversal of the Anglo-Burgundian alliance was already being signaled by a series of official and personal actions on the part of Duke Philip the Good, King Charles of France, and several of their immediate advisors.

As the events and accomplishments of the 1434 campaign apply to confirming the existence of a conscious and predetermined English plan for the unassisted defense of northern France more than a year before the Treaty of Arras, so too must they be studied with a view toward reinterpreting Sir John Fastolf's report itself. The basic concepts of the memorandum—mobile warfare, a strategic defensive, tactical superiority through prompt counterattacks, and the maintenance of the local balance of forces—had therefore really emerged through a combination of previous experience and the necessities of the military situation in 1433–1434. It seems logical to assume that Fastolf, as Bedford's chief of staff and primary military advisor throughout this period, was not only aware of everything which had taken place in the period preceding the writing of his report, but was also reflecting that previous experience in his "theoretical" memorandum. A modern reinterpretation of the document must, therefore, take this probable and quite understandable eclecticism into account. We must re-evaluate the report as a very able, but unoriginal staff summary or position paper, reflecting the situation not only as it stood at the time of the treaty, but as it had existed for the previous two years. Fastolf's concepts could not have been developed as a result of the actual

Congress of Arras and its political-diplomatic impact on the English military position because these same concepts had been fundamental to the English preparations dating back to 1433. The English command, including Fastolf himself, had long known they must soon be prepared to fight alone and had long prepared to do so. For these reasons, the military impact of the Treaty of Arras was discounted long before that treaty was drawn up.

Finally, it seems proper to proceed one more step in this analysis and to give long-overdue credit to the man who was responsible, in a much deeper and truer sense than Fastolf, for the successful English preparations described in this study. The reference is, of course, one which directs proper attention to John of Lancaster, duke of Bedford, that loyal and able preserver of his brother's somewhat terrible French legacy. Especially when they are viewed in the light of Bedford's increasing weariness and of the mortal illness which carried him off just before the Treaty of Arras became final,[58] his wisdom, patience, and amazing qualities of foresight must be given the highest possible evaluation. Whether or not his brother's original campaigns and conquests can be castigated as piratical aggression against a neighbor then rent by internal strife, Bedford carried out the last part of his own lifework in the highest sense of a sacred fraternal trust.

From the broader framework of later medieval and early modern European history, Bedford's preparations to meet the exigencies of a situation in which England would have to withstand the full power of the Valois state were to have decisive results. For England, the result of his work was the retention of Normandy until 1450 and Guienne until 1453. For France and the rest of western Europe, the reforms of the Valois army, state institutions, and finance made necessary by this successful English defense contributed heavily to the emergence of the modern national French state. The dominant French power of the Italian adventures pursued by Charles VIII and Louis XII and the resultant, decisive quarrel between Valois and Hapsburg can be traced, in the final analysis, to the preparations carried out before the Treaty of Arras by Bedford and his very able corps of English coadjutors.

58. As noted earlier, Bedford died on September 14, 1435, just one week before the final signing of the Treaty of Arras. Ramsay, *Lancaster and York*, I, 474.